THE RUSSIAN DILEMMA:
A Political and Geopolitical View

THE RUSSIAN

ROBERT G. WESSON

A Political

DILEMMA and

Geopolitical

View

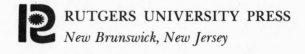

RUTGERS UNIVERSITY PRESS
New Brunswick, New Jersey

Library of Congress Cataloging in Publication Data

Wesson, Robert G
    The Russian dilemma; a political and geopolitical view

    Includes bibliographical references.
        1. Russia–History. 2. Geopolitics–Russia.
3. Eurasianism. I. Title.
DK43.W4   327'.1'0110947   74-1412
ISBN 0-8135-0774-X Cloth
        0-8135-0787-I Paper

The ornament on the title page is from the work of the Russian designer Y. Chernikhov, whose *Ornament* was first published in Leningrad in 1930. It is here reproduced from *Russian Geometric Design and Ornament*, selected by Edmund V. Gillon, Jr. (New York: Dover Publications, 1969).

Contents

Preface   vii

Chapter 1 EMPIRE

Expansion   3
The Russian Idea   12
Autocracy   17
Autocratic Society   23
Imperial Patterns   29

Chapter 2 RUSSIA: EUROPEAN STATE AND ORIENTAL EMPIRE

Dependent Empire   35
Duality: Foreign Policy   41
Duality: The State   43
Duality: Society   48

Chapter 3 A CENTURY OF STRAINS

Confused Intelligentsia   54
Nationalism   59
The Last Years   63

Chapter 4 THE LENINIST RESYNTHESIS

Failure of the Liberals 68
Autocracy Restored 73
New Faith 78
New Universalism 82
Inverted Westernization 87

Chapter 5 SOVIET AMBIVALENCE

Universalism in One Country 94
National Sovietism 99
Western Alliance to Cold War 105
Peaceful Struggle 110
The New Style 116
Nonnational State 120
Dual State 124
Dichotomy of Policy 133

Chapter 6 LENINISM DECADENT

Renewal by Revolution 141
Fading Ideology 147
Subsidence of Leadership 152
Conservatism and Élitism 155
Weakening Control 161
Disintegration of Leninism 165

Chapter 7 RUSSIA AND THE NEW WORLD ORDER

Western Influences 171
Nationalism 177
Changing World Environment 181
The Russian Situation 189

Notes 201

Index 213

Preface

The purpose of this book is to relate Russia's development more closely to the geographic situation in which its people found themselves at the end of medieval times.

The drama of history is shaped by the natural setting, which cannot of itself determine but which facilitates certain lines of development and impedes others. A featureless plain does not compel but facilitates broad conquests and large states, much as an insular realm invites to commerce and perhaps overseas expansion. The development of classical Greece is incomprehensible without consideration of its setting, the islands and peninsulas in and around the Aegean; and much of the course of British history is clearly related to a situation adjacent to Europe. For various other peoples, from the ancient Egyptians to the modern Americans, historical development has been more or less obviously related to the peculiarities of the natural environment; and this is not least the case of the Russians.*

The geopolitical basis of Russian history is, however, more subtle

* It is in this sense that this book attempts a "geopolitical" interpretation. Conventional geopolitics has amounted mostly to strategic geography, usually with a strong bent for theorizing, as in Mackinder's doctrines of the special significance of the Eurasian "heartland." It has focused on borders and potentialities for expansion; in the Nazi Haushofer school it became a pseudoscience of German imperialism. A good treatment is Robert Strausz-Hupé, *Geopolitics: The Struggle for Space and Power* (New York: Putnam, 1942). Despite this perversion of the word, there is no better one for the relatedness of geography and political development.

and complex than the obvious facts that Russia has a Eurasian heritage and that the lack of clear-cut or defensible boundaries was a major factor in the formation of the vast Russian empire. The interpretation of the Russian psyche as impregnated with the featureless and infinite horizons of the steppe is suggestive but analytically unhelpful. The crucial fact of Russian history is that Russia grew up in the transition zone between Europe and Asia, the area between the Baltic and Black Seas. Occupation of this zone meant that an indefinite space for expansion was opened to the Russians, although they did not cease to be Europeans on the edge of progressive European civilization.

By continual expansion, Russia became a political entity fundamentally different from the nation-states of Western Europe, and much of Russian politics becomes more comprehensible by comparison with such empires as the Roman or Chinese.* Yet, unlike most traditional universal empires, Russia has had powerful and progressive independent states as neighbors and has been partly shaped by intercourse with them. Otherwise stated, Russian politics has been and remains burdened by the overwhelming task of managing large numbers of alien peoples within its imperial body and at the same time competing and getting along with the Western state system. In light of this interplay of opposites, the peculiarities of the Russian career, political and psychological, and the profound ambivalences often noted by historians become more understandable. Russia has been a mixture of East and West not merely in the trite sense suggested by its straddling Eurasia but in the sense of mixing "Eastern" empire with "Western" state, with all the consequent strains and ambiguities.

In this broad view, conventional modes of interpreting the Soviet Union fall into place. Its own version, that it represents a new historical force propelled by the victory of the revolutionary working class, or by a new governing élite acting for the proletariat, is here seen as merely part of the ideology of renewal of Russia, a restatement and reinforcement of the messianism of the empire. The analysis of the Soviet experiment as essentially a vehicle of modernization similarly fits into the long-term pattern of interaction of imperial and Western-progressive motifs, the alternation between periods of catching up and of falling behind the

* The paradigm of the universal (continental) empire was much used by Arnold Toynbee in his *Study of History;* political aspects are developed by Robert G. Wesson, *The Imperial Order* (Berkeley: University of California Press, 1967).

West, the ruthlessness of its methods as well as the intensity of its purposes corresponding less to needs for speed than for combining economic and political imperatives. The approach of this work likewise encompasses the totalitarian approach to Soviet politics. It is undeniable that the all-embracing modernized despotism called totalitarianism was largely begun by the Leninists; but it was an understandable, in a sense suitable response to Russian needs; and its limitations as well as its strengths are inherent in the Russian situation. The conventional interpretation nearest that of this book is to regard Soviet Russia as basically a continuation of the tsarist state; but it may be remembered that the continuity rests not simply on tradition and inherited political culture but on the fact that Russians have faced the same major political problems since 1917 as before: namely, to hold together and rule the huge multinational realm in the face of solvent forces of modernity and to modernize economically (and militarily) without modernizing politically. Leonid Brezhnev, like Ivan IV, invites possessors of superior technology to his realm while shutting them off from his people and warning against subversive ideas from the West, not because it has been done but because it has to be done.

In this view, many peculiarities of Russia, tsarist and Soviet, which might seem quirks assume aspects of inevitability. For example, in the seventeenth as in the twentieth century Russia had a peculiar nonfunctioning pseudo-parliamentary body. The rigor of cause and effect in history is, of course, vitiated by many more or less accidental factors. It is highly doubtful, for example, if there could have been anything like the Russian Revolution if there had not been a Lenin, whose personality was neither inevitable nor repeatable. It is doubtful whether the Revolution would have occurred without a Rasputin, or for that matter a Gavrilo Princip to shoot Archduke Ferdinand in 1914. But the interest of an historical analysis is that it puts many events into a broader framework and makes them clearer as parts of a single picture.

It is also to be hoped that this analysis may have predictive value. The probability with which given outcomes may be scientifically predicted varies with the complexity of the system and the extent to which its variables are known, from virtual certainties of physics to estimates of meteorology and approximations of psychology; and political affairs are at the extreme end of this gamut. Yet the analysis of the Soviet situation as here presented permits a number of broad conclusions as to the prospects of the Leninist state, the validity of which rests with events of the next decade or two.

Robert G. Wesson

Santa Barbara, California
October, 1973

Acknowledgments

I wish to express deep appreciation to Professors Richard Pipes, Leonard Schapiro, and John S. Reshetar, Jr., for reading the manuscript. The latter two made detailed and helpful suggestions, without which the book would be much weaker, although they do not necessarily agree with all its interpretations.

My wife, Deborah, has been of invaluable assistance at all stages in the preparation of the manuscript, and she must share any credit that may come from this book.

R. G. W.

THE RUSSIAN DILEMMA:
A Political and Geopolitical View

1

Empire

EXPANSION

The Soviet Union is generically different from most states at a similar economic level of development. By most indicators of production it ranks among the advanced industrial countries, in steel production, for example, not far from the top; but it does not belong to the political and economic breed of Western Europe, Japan, the United States, its friends and detractors agree. It is less obvious that some, at least, of the specialness of Russia is of long standing. If Lenin gave some outwardly new answers, they were to old questions. The tsarist empire of the nineteenth century, which Karl Marx saw as the gendarme of reaction, was alien to Western Europe in political and philosophical outlook even though it was attempting to modernize and to bring itself technologically abreast of the advanced world of the day. Earlier, in the eighteenth and seventeenth centuries, the land of the Russians was a strange world from which travelers brought tales of extravagant despotism, splendor, and degradation. The West, ever since it came in contact with the Muscovite state emerging from the wreckage of the empire of the Mongols (or Tatars, as they are usually called in the Russian context), has found Russia special and strange.

Broadly speaking, Russia was special and strange in politics and outlook because it was a different type of state from those of Western Europe, a semi-Asiatic empire as opposed to the nation-states. But the Russians' success in forging one of the greatest empires of history and the kind of empire they forged are understandable in terms of the geography seconding and shaping cultural factors. Over many centuries, it had been rather a misfortune to live in the western part of the Eurasian steppes, for nomadic and warrior peoples, mostly from Central Asia, swept through these lands in recurrent waves. The last such conquest was the worst. The Tatars in the thirteenth century ravaged and subjugated the ill-defined aggregation of several score loosely joined or independently sovereign states and cities which constituted Kievan Rus. Yet the Tatar yoke was the beginning of imperial greatness for the Russians, because under it there took shape a strong state able to profit from Tatar decay in the fifteenth and sixteenth centuries and eventually to appropriate all the immense Tatar domain and more.

This was possible because the Russians were strategically located between Europe and Asia. In the fifteenth century, while Tatar power subsided in political divisions, the lands of peninsular and maritime Western Europe embarked upon what was to become the scientific-technological-industrial revolution of modern times. Printing and firearms quickly came into widespread use, along with a multitude of less spectacular improvements in the arts of peace and war. In that century also began the era of overseas discovery and colonization, wherein the men of the West rather suddenly found themselves much stronger than the peoples they met in Africa, Asia, and the Americas and able easily to subject them.

The Russians were close enough to Europe to take over much of the new technology and to use it both to defend themselves and to overcome their more backward neighbors. They could make themselves beneficiaries instead of victims of the upsurge of Europe because they shared, at one remove, the technological and consequent political upsurge of Europe. Their culture was basically European, with roots in Greece and Byzantium, and they were physically similar to their neighbors to the West. No racial mistrust inhibited borrowing whatever they usefully might. Previous to the Mongol invasions, contacts with Western Europe, especially along the waterways, had been close and frequent. The tenth-century awakening of European commerce spilled over to the Russians, whose trade at that time centered on Kiev and the Baltic–Black Sea route. Their towns shared some of the prosperity of European towns in the eleventh and twelfth centuries and were as advanced as most centers of northern Europe. Most important, the inhabitants were Christians, having officially received the Orthodox faith in the year 988, long before the Baltic peoples and the Lithuanians. The Russians were partly torn away from Europe by the Tatar hegemony, and their lands were impoverished and for a time severely set back. But the nomads were not at home in the forested country west of the Volga; parts of western Russia, especially Novgorod, were not conquered at all because of surrounding marshes. The Tatars did not rule their Russian domains closely or very harshly and were soon satisfied with a moderate tribute. The Russian Church was permitted much freedom, even exemption from taxes. Contacts with the West were never quite cut off.

Consequently the Russians benefited from the technological knowledge filtering in or purposefully brought from the West and were excellently situated to push outward across Asia as the overextended Tatar empire disintegrated. Concurrently the maritime powers of Western Europe were acquiring dominions overseas. Like the Portuguese in the Indies or the Spanish in Mexico and Peru at the same time, the Russians were Europeans fighting against technologically less progressive peoples. If their relative advantage in the arts of war was less than that of West Europeans over the Indians of America or India, the Russians did not need as great a margin of superiority against contiguous non-European peoples as Western nations operating at the end of a very long thin line of ships. It was also the fortune of Russia to face no competition in its field of expansion until very late, not until Japan became a power on the eastern margins.

The Russians were more compelled to expansion than the Spanish or Dutch because they had no natural or historically fixed boundaries. Long before the Tatars, the Eurasian plain had been the home of wanderers. Waves of invasion came and ebbed, and "Russia" was only vaguely delimited. Novgorod reached the Urals by 1200. The Tatar invasion forced a large part of the Russian people into the northeast, where they absorbed earlier pagan Finnish settlers. There Moscow became the new center, although much of the Muscovite population was unstable, moving at times away from troubles, at times toward available lands, until tied down by serfdom in the sixteenth century. Since Russian borderlands have always held mixed populations, they have caused a perpetual anxiety and required a special effort to secure them. It was never taken for granted that boundaries should be fixed and the state limited; growth of the realm always seemed normal and elemental.

The imperial power of Moscow began very humbly in the service of the Tatar khans. At first, the Tatars killed Russian leaders who were potential agents of rebellion. Having thus made themselves respected, they put submissive aristocrats to use as agents of indirect rule. The princes of Vladimir were the first to be favored as tribute collectors, then those of Tver. One of the latter, however, rose against Tatar overlordship; and his failure was an opportunity for Ivan I, surnamed Kalita ("Moneybag"), of Moscow to show his loyalty to the Golden Horde. He acquired the title of Grand Prince in 1431 and managed to secure nomination as tax gatherer for all Russia, thus becoming superior to all other Russian princes.

Moscow owed something to its advantageous location for trade with the East by river routes to the Caspian, Black Sea, and Baltic. It was also assisted by the Orthodox Church, whose metropolitan established residence in Moscow in 1328 and attached his fortunes to those of that city's prince. The Church helped to keep alive Russian feeling through the centuries of foreign domination, and its support strengthened the hegemony of the princes of Moscow over their fellows. But the rise of Moscow and its successful engulfment of all Russia were primarily political. The Muscovite rulers craftily used their Tatar overlords; by intrigue and bribery and by showing themselves the most faithful servants, they gained Tatar support against all rivals. Through patient diplomacy, marriages, purchase, and warfare, they increased their domain thirtyfold in a hundred and fifty years, each taking pride in ruling over more than had his father. Their consolidation of Russia was carried out by some of the same methods used at about the same time in the integration of large nation-states such as France and Spain.

The concurrent strengthening of Muscovy and the loss of will of the divided Tatars enabled the grand princes to solidify their position, until in 1476 Ivan III practically declared his independence. Although the Tatars still raided from time to time and Moscow found it judicious to pay occasional tribute, the Russians had the upper hand. Liberation merged insensibly into conquest. There was no sharp separation of Russian and non-Russian territories to the east, and defense against the Tatars (who burned Moscow in 1571 and threatened it as late as 1591) implied taking the offensive against them.

Ivan III (1462 to 1505) earned the epithet of "Great" by increasing the Muscovite state fourfold to an area larger than England. By marriage to the niece of the last Byzantine emperor he acquired a symbolic claim to the succession of that empire. His son, Basil III (1505 to 1533), largely completed the incorporation of ethnic Russian lands. Ivan IV (1533 to 1584), surnamed "the Terrible," went on to the conquest of Kazan and Astrakhan and the annexation of the Volga khanates, thereby making himself successor of the Tatar rulers. As such, tsars saw themselves entitled to expand indefinitely towards the East, to which they were lured by dreams of trade with the Orient and by the real possibilities of exacting tribute in furs from native peoples. The Urals, gently sloping and of moderate height, were never a real barrier. In 1598 the last Siberian khan was defeated, and only scattered resistance was encountered on the rest of the long way to the Pacific.

Often people moved ahead of the state, mostly peasants seeking new land and freedom from serfdom and military service; and the state kept pushing its authority outward over them. Sometimes, on the other hand, settlement was organized by the government to secure the land. The treeless steppe to the south and southeast invited colonization but had to be guarded against nomads. Maraudings across ill-defined frontiers were good reason or excuse for pressing the frontiers farther away. Occasionally there was a purposeful drive for strategic territory. Ivan IV fought many years for an outlet to the Baltic to get a better route for acquiring Western arms and goods than via Archangel in the far North; he even wanted to incorporate Sweden into his domains.[1] Peter the Great succeeded in opening the desired window to the West. Much has been written of the undying urge, more romantic than economic, to obtain warm-water ports; and a perennial objective for sentimental and strategic reasons was control of Byzantium, ancient seat of Orthodoxy. Peter had dreams of glory in India and Constantinople and attacked Persia, but he was unable to hold his gains there. Paul, at the end of the eighteenth century, started a campaign toward India.

From the conquest of Kazan with the help of a Tatar faction, the Russians used dissension among their opponents, dividing, subverting, and bringing weaker peoples into alliances, which, like the alliances formed by expanding Rome, it was held treason to break. It was a regular practice to set upper against lower classes. Themselves upholders of autocracy for strength, Russian rulers would support particularistic rights in neighboring countries to weaken them, as, for example, the rights of nobles against the crown in Poland and Sweden. They sought legal excuses, often accusing neighbors of harassment or of conspiring against Russia. They extended protection at the real or pretended request of peoples, saving them from supposedly worse subjection by incorporating them in the Russian empire. The Orthodox Ukraine, fearful of both Catholic Poland and Muslim Turkey, pledged allegiance to the tsar in the middle of the seventeenth century in return for military assistance and a promise of autonomy. Later, Christian Georgia and part of Armenia accepted Russian suzerainty to escape pressure from Persia and Turkey. In the latter part of the eighteenth century, Catherine II claimed the right to intervene in Poland-Lithuania on behalf of the Orthodox peasantry, although or perhaps partly because many peasants were fleeing from Russia to the relative freedom of Poland. For decades, the Russian ambassador practically ruled Poland, and he engineered the partitions that gave Russia the lion's share of that once huge country.

The price of expansion has often been war, and the Russian state has usually been preoccupied with things military. In the time of Peter, Russia was much poorer than France and had only two-thirds of the population, but its forces were nearly equal. The advance to the West has usually been blocked by strong states, and the march south against the Turks cost a dozen armed conflicts. But never in modern times have the Russians attacked a major power; always expanding into areas of weakness, they have halted on encountering strong opposition. They have fought much better on the defensive than on the offensive; and when they have been attacked (by the Swedes, the French, and the Germans in successive centuries), they have usually been victorious and have thereby gained additional lands. Always claiming to be defending themselves, they fairly well convinced historians that their empire was acquired as a result of self-defense or for security.

The growth of the empire continued into modern times. The Napoleonic wars brought Finland and most of ethnic Poland into the fold. To the south, Russia crossed the best natural frontier, the Caucasus chain, by the annexation of Georgia (1801). The pacification of the Caucasian region cost a great deal of fighting up to the middle of the century. A push towards the ancient goal of Constantinople and the Straits was thwarted by the Crimean War (1854 to 1856). A generation later another effort to place much of the Balkans under Russian protection was successful in that the Turks were roundly defeated; but again the Russian purpose was largely frustrated by pressures from the Western powers. In compensation, Russia turned (as Dostoevsky urged) to Central Asia and the Far East. The penetration of Turkic Central Asia, in part by the initiative of local governors and generals, was easy and quick once undertaken, but it meant acquisition of a large bloc of dark-skinned Muslims. For the most part, they were ruled indirectly as long as the tsarist empire lasted; not until the 1920's were they fully incorporated, by the Bolsheviks. Advancing in the Far East, Nicholas II ventured war with Japan in 1904; but that nation had Westernized more rapidly and successfully than Russia and was able to force one of the few contractions of the Russian sphere.

At the beginning of this century Russia was severely strained by the need to keep up with the progressive Western powers, and its government was becoming ever more anachronistic. Yet it vaguely aspired to the rulership of such areas as Manchuria, Mongolia, Korea, Tibet, Persia (where it held a recognized sphere of influence), and the region of the Straits. A onetime Russian diplomat, Constantine Leontiev, in 1890 foresaw the tsar organizing world socialism from Constantinople under the banner of the Orthodox Church. "To the Russian mind, China is to be Russian, Persia is to be Russian, India is to be Russian. It is Russian power which is to restore the cross to Jerusalem. . . ." [2] At the beginning of World War I, Russian goals included East Prussia, the Polish provinces of Germany and Austria, Galicia, Bukovina, Bohemia, Slovakia, and part of Hungary, as well as the traditionally coveted Straits. As a leading Russian paper wrote in 1912, "After a thousand years [Russia] is still on the march toward its natural political boundaries." [3] But the Russians could congratulate themselves on a tremendous achievement, the dominion of a sixth of the earth's land surface, an area nearly equal to all of North America; and the tsarist empire took pride, as does the Soviet Union, in its hundred or more diverse peoples, supposedly happily joined into one political family.

The British, too, and other successful imperialists have taken pride in the extent of their possessions and the multitude of peoples under their sway. There are parallels between the imperialism of Muscovy and the expansion of other European nations that built great empires in modern times: Portugal and Spain, the Netherlands, France and Great Britain. All these developments were expressions of the exuberant rise of the West, which by virtue of burgeoning technology and better-organized states after the Middle Ages found itself more and more superior to the heathens before whom it had often trembled. Russian expansion coincided in time with that of the Western European powers. Voyages to India and then to the Americas began as the Russians were pressing back Tatar power, and Spanish penetration of most of the Americas was contemporaneous with the Russian sweep across Siberia. The resurgence of colonialism in the latter nineteenth century and the carving up of the remaining independent areas of Africa and Asia coincided with the Russian colonization of Central Asia. Moreover, the Russians, like the Spaniards, Dutch, and English, considered themselves bearers of civilization, spreading a faith, a way of life, and a higher culture among the benighted of the earth.

Yet there were decisive differences. The Western nations mostly proceeded from rather straightforward commercial motives. Russian expansion had an economic purpose in some cases, as in the quest for furs (mostly under official aegis); but the interests of the feeble mercantile classes were secondary. The aggrandizement of noncommercial Russia was usually undertaken for the greater power and glory of the state. Religion provided a more important reason, weapon, or excuse than was usual with the maritime powers. Russian empire building was akin to that of the Spanish, who continued the reconquest of the Peninsula from the Moors into a crusade to spread Roman Catholicism in the New World. The tsars expelled and pressed back heathen Tatars and then infidel Turks. The enemy was always non-Orthodox, and there were often fellow Orthodox on the other side of the border to protect.

The distinctive characteristic of Russian expansion was that the Russians annexed contiguous areas, whereas Western powers took possession of territories across great oceans. To this day, in the Russian concept, "imperialism" is only overseas expansion. The overseas holdings of England or France were like estates, held by and for the state but not a part of it; for Russia there was no firm and unerasable boundary between new and old acquisitions. Being contiguous, new Russian possessions were always to be assimilated. They were almost automatically brought under the Russian social and administrative order and became not colonies but parts of an expanding whole. Protectorates were by fits and starts molded to the common administrative pattern and subjected to the centralized imperial authority.

At first, even Russian areas brought under the wing of Moscow, for example, Novgorod, Pskov, and Riazan, were granted autonomy; but this favor lasted only a generation or two. The promised autonomy of the Ukraine was infringed almost from the beginning of the protectorate in 1654. Muscovite officials were sent in, and the Ukraine was prevented from conducting its own foreign relations. An attempt by Hetman Ivan Mazepa to break away was severely punished, and within a few years the Ukraine was almost fully incorporated into the empire. Under Catherine II it became simply a part of Russia; eventually the Ukrainian language was decreed nonexistent. Having conquered the Baltic region, Peter confirmed local rights in order to facilitate recruitment for his bureaucracy and army. But this was anomalous; a complaint was logically raised in the Great Commission of Catherine II: "Livonia and Estonia are not another state, they are not distinguished from the Russians by climate, agriculture, and other occupations; therefore they can and should be under the same law as we." [4] By 1783, Baltic autonomy was largely removed. Poland, although incorporated as a separate kingdom, was deprived of special status as a result of rebellions in 1830 and 1863; Russian was made the language of instruction in all schools.

The practice of expanding into contiguous territories meant that the annexed populations were usually not very different from their neighbors inside the empire; Russians settled on the new lands and went into the cities of Central Asia. There was racial mixture, and local aristocracies regularly mixed with the Russian, making something of a multinational élite. In the nineteenth century, two-thirds of Russian noble families were of non-Russian origin.[5] Russification was successful in swallowing up many small and backward peoples, although less so with the more advanced, especially Muslim peoples.

The empire merged with the Russian state and so became much more important for Russian than for Western powers. Security always seemed to be served by pressing the borders farther away, both to overcome enemies on the frontiers and to occupy territories from which an attack might be launched. Size was a prime strength and a compensation for the fact that the Russians, though technically superior to the Asiatics, continued ever to lag somewhat behind the West. Space saved Russia from the Poles in the seventeenth century, the Swedes in the eighteenth, the French in the nineteenth, and the Germans in the twentieth. Russia has always been extremely reluctant to surrender any lands once firmly occupied. It has given up some noncontiguous holdings, such as Alaska, but to yield any part of the borderlands would be regarded as a calamity of the first order. Similarly, France could give up West Indian islands or Canada, or recently an African empire, with no tremendous sense of loss; but the tearing away of Alsace-Lorraine in 1871 was felt as an unbearable national disaster. The world at large has practically acknowledged this difference; it tends to regard all Russian holdings as legitimately forming a single state, as do the provinces of Spain; a call for the breakup of the Russian empire or the Soviet Union has not been seen as equivalent to a call for the liberation of British or Portuguese colonies. Anticolonialists demanded that the French withdraw from Algeria, not that the Russians evacuate Turkestan or Georgia.

Imperialism meant for Russia not the acquisition of possessions but the swelling of the state; and the state became accustomed to enlargement, developing a sense of mission and traditions of ecumenical rule. Expansion was the overwhelming fact of Russian history. For over six hundred years, almost every generation saw a substantial growth of the lands under the sway of Moscow. The few setbacks, as in the Crimean War and the defeat administered by the Japanese in 1904, were in due course overcome. Hugeness legitimated the political order, and the political élite acquired a material interest, as the people acquired a psychological stake, in the empire and its growth. Russians became accustomed to the idea that border states should bow to them and that the frontiers were movable. Aggrandizement fed on itself. The poet Fedor Tiutchev expressed the fuzzy ideas of the extension of the Russian realm as follows: "Seven inland seas and seven mighty rivers/From the Nile to the Neva, from the Elbe to China/From the Volga to the Euphrates, from the Ganges to the Danube. . . ./This is the Russian empire." [6] The empire seemed a polity of a different and higher order from those around it. Protection by such a land could only be a blessing. The feeling for its rightness was so strong that in the nineteenth century even liberal Russian intellectuals regarded the sympathy of the West for Polish independence as proof of malevolence. Confidence and self-righteousness facilitated further expansion, and the greatness of Russia in its mission overawed Russians and subject peoples alike.

THE RUSSIAN IDEA

The Tatars recognized no independent powers and claimed to rule the world, "the face of the earth from sunrise to sunset"; for a time, in fact, they established a "Pax Mongolica" from Poland across Cathay. The Russians were not less impressed with the greatness of their dominions. "The mind grows numb," wrote Nicholas Karamzin, the first important Russian historian, as it contemplates the greatness of the empire built, civilized, and enlightened "without violence, without crimes, but only by the example of her own superiority." [7] As the publicist Nicholas Nadezhdin wrote in 1831, "You have only to look at the map of the world to be filled with awe at Russia's future destinies." [8]

Then a year or two was needed to journey from the Baltic to the Pacific, but the sheer extent of the Russian land still serves as inspiration in the jet age.* A Soviet poet writes of

> . . . villages and cities
> Of the fabled land unconfined
> Stretching for thousands of versts
> From the Baltic to Sakhalin
> In all its giant size. . . .[9]

Pravda urges Russians, " 'Look at the map of the RSFSR'—this phrase of Lenin's has become proverbial. It is an invitation to sweep your eyes over our native land, its immeasurable spaces . . . to think, to dream." [10] Russia had and has to be something special in the world, not a mere nation like the European nations which are dwarfed by its immensity, but a world, as Dostoevsky and many others saw it, capable of subsuming nations. The Russian landscape itself adds to the sense of boundlessness as men are swallowed up by plains that extend as though forever into space. Russian culture became impregnated with this sense of the empire.[11] It was not decisive that most of the territory was of little economic importance, being either too cold or too dry for agriculture. Siberia had only a few hundred thousand people before the Russians arrived and only eight million at the beginning of this century; thinly settled and backward Central Asia was more of an economic burden than an asset. But even empty space bespoke greatness.

The map was as convincing for Russians as for Brazilians, who have long taken the endless Amazon jungles as proof that theirs is "the land of the future" and so acquired a national spirit different from that of most countries of Latin America. The self-evident greatness of Brazil became the major premise of political thinking. In the words of the

* Closely related is the propagandistic use of Siberia, with its endless forests, gargantuan rivers, and inexhaustible resources, to inspire Russians and foreigners with visions of infinite progress and power.

Brazilian national anthem, "Gigantic by decree of nature, thou art fair and brave, dauntless colossus, and the future mirrors thy greatness." *

If the United States was suffused with "Manifest Destiny" by crossing North America and acquiring the Great Plains and the western lands of vast expanses and natural grandeur, Russia spread across nearly three times as much when it embraced the Eurasian steppe; and it was endowed with corresponding self-confidence. The idea of Russia dominating if not ruling the earth seemed by no means fantastic; the idea was as consoling for its oppressed as it was seductive for its leaders.

In the Russian mind the territorial evidence of a special role in the world combined with a sense of religious mission. From the fall of Byzantium, the Russians saw themselves as the custodians and champions of the true faith; and Russia, in successful struggle against infidels and heretics, became Holy Russia. As the monk Philotheus wrote near the end of the fifteenth century, "And may thy dominion realize, O pious tsar, that all the empires of the Orthodox faith have come together in thy sole empire: thou alone in all the earth art tsar to the Christians . . . all Christian empires came together into thine alone, that two Romes fell, but the third stands, and there will be no fourth. . . ." [14] Russians have always been inclined to credit their successful empire building to moral superiority, as in the passage cited from Karamzin. The restoration of the empire in the period 1919 to 1922 was ascribed primarily to the rightness of Marxism-Leninism, not to the Red Army.

It has been nearly impossible for Russians to apply to their country the same standards they applied to others. According to the poet Tiutchev, "One cannot understand/Russia by reason/And measure her by a common yardstick,/She has a peculiar nature/One has just to believe in Russia." [15] It was not a mere country but an abstraction, an ideal, a value in itself. Russia could not be really wrong; even the nineteenth-century intellectuals, though fiercely critical of their society and gov-

---

* To the Brazilian mind, the vast interior always guarantees the future, and the size of the land is a consolation for any trouble. [12] The geography of Brazil has inspired thoughts strikingly like those of nineteenth-century Russian intellectuals, who also were impressed by the grandeur of their country but troubled by its backwardness. For example:

"Being a young people, uncontaminated by the spiritual diseases of declining countries, we are already pointing out to the world the way to social progress, and in various areas we have already been an example for old peoples.

"The new world arises now in all its healthy virility to serve as a new model for the world. Stand up proudly in it, our Brazil!" [13]

ernment, saw Russia as morally superior, the potential savior of humanity—the grandeur of the state and its mission compensating for personal
humiliation.[16] As builder of a great unity, Russia should restore faith
to a disputatious world and bring order when nations sank into anarchy,[17] saving the bourgeois West from its iniquities. Somewhat immod-
estly, Dostoevsky claimed for his beloved land extraordinary spiritual
virtues and humility; as one of his characters put it, evidently speaking
for the author, "But there is only one truth, and therefore only a single
one out of the nations can have the true God. That's the Russian
people." [18] Even as individuals, the Russians should be special beings.
Catherine II proclaimed the intent of raising up "a new race of people," [19] much as Stalin evoked "the new Soviet man" and Khrushchev's
Party Program promised that people under communism would approach
moral and physical perfection.

Self-confidence merged into self-righteousness; morality and purpose were self-given. Under the tsars as under the Bolsheviks, the good
of the state was for many almost a religious value; and Russia was
always seen as right and generous. As Dostoevsky said in his speech
on Pushkin in 1880, which was received with indescribable enthusiasm,
"For what has Russian policy been doing for these two centuries if not
serving Europe, perhaps, far more than she has served herself?" [20] Russians saw subordination to their empire as liberation; Russia was not a
conqueror but brother, protector, and teacher. Russian soldiers averred,
near the end of tsardom, that "Russia has never waged war except for
an ideal." [21] For Nicholas Danilevsky, deep political insight on the part
of lesser peoples consisted in "voluntarily recognizing the hegemony
of Russia after having gained their independence. . . ." [22] Some of this
superiority is generously shared with minority peoples in the Soviet
view of history; such peoples as the Georgians and Armenians have
always been pacific and freedom-loving, even in Roman times, whereas
their non-Soviet neighbors, the Persians, Arabs, and Turks, were exploiters.

Since Russians seldom doubted their mission of saving mankind,
the question has been not whether but how it was to be fulfilled. The
principles of peace, order, and harmonious union in the empire were
the highest desideratum and *summum bonum*, a blessing that rightly
must be spread as widely as possible. In Russia, chauvinism was no
narrow, selfish feeling but a holy cause and the height of virtue. Danilevsky saw Russia duty-bound to spread civilization in the East and re-

sented Europe's disapproval of concomitant territorial expansion.[23] As a priest proclaimed to Alexander III, when Russia's mission was wearing thin, "Your Tsar is necessary to Russia, to Europe and to the world. He is the peacemaker of the human race." [24]

Dostoevsky was an eloquent but not atypical exponent of such themes, which became almost an obsession with him in his latter years: Russia, land of freedom under the fraternal tsar, should save Europe from its imminent collapse and usher in a new era of history. Its greatness was universality of soul, and it should bring unity by brotherly love if possible:

To become a true Russian, to become a Russian fully means only to become the brother of all men (in the end of all, I repeat), to become, if you will, a universal man. . . . And in the course of time I believe that we—not we, of course, but our children to come—will all without exception understand that to be a true Russian does indeed mean to aspire finally to reconcile the contradictions of Europe, to show the end of European yearning in our Russian soul, omni-human and all-uniting, to include within our soul by brotherly love all our brethren, and at last, it may be, to pronounce the final Word of the great general harmony, of the final brotherly communism of all nations in accordance with the gospel of Christ.[25]

Freedom, on the contrary, seemed to him a burden and a bar to happiness.[26]

The radicals and rebels seemed nearly as convinced of the special right of Russia as the religious conservatives. Decembrists plotting against the monarchy were indignant about mooted plans to transfer some border territories to Russian Poland, of which the tsar was king.[27] Peter Chaadaev, the Westernizer declared insane because of his criticisms, nonetheless stated: "It is for us to introduce the saving principle of order into a world that has fallen prey to anarchy. Russia ought not to abandon that mission which has been entrusted to her by the heavenly and by the earthly Tsar." [28] The anarchist Michael Bakunin prophesied in 1848, "From a sea of flames and blood the Revolution's star will rise in Moscow, high and wondrous, becoming the lodestar for all mankind." [29] Alexander Herzen went abroad and stayed there permanently to escape tsarist tyranny, but his personality remained so steeped in Russianism that he soon began pleading for the supernal role of the country he had abandoned.

If the present was at times defective, glory lay in the future; and Russian thought became infused with nebulous apocalyptic expectations, as of a new coming of Christ ushering in a golden age, or of the building of the Third Rome, proclaimed in the days of Ivan III.[30] The claim to the right of succession to the Byzantine empire meant taking over its mission of defending and spreading the true faith. Peter's assumption of the title of Imperator implied renewal of the claim to the heritage of Augustus, lawful ruler of the universe. The contest between Russia and the unenlightened was a battle between the forces of light and darkness, as it had been ever since the Tatars were expelled in the name of the true faith; and the right must one day emerge to victory.

The sense of mission was the Russians' strongest armor in the secular struggle. Force is the more respected, the more it is self-righteous. Russia's confidence in its justice was a major asset in overcoming the resistance of smaller and feebler nations and in persuading them of the inevitability of their condition after their incorporation in the empire. For the Russians it gave reason to bear patiently the burdens laid upon them by autocracy and to serve the unworthiest and cruelest autocrats as long as they were successful rulers of the empire. It was the motivation of subordination of the individual, the *sobornost* ("togetherness") of tsarism and the collectivism exalted by the Soviet Union.

It was not necessary that the Russian ideal should inspire all, only that a guiding minority should be infused with its spirit while the many accepted it passively. Signifying status, dignity, and purpose in life, it supported the continual forward drive, and held the land together in times of troubles, as at the beginning of the seventeenth century and in the years 1918 to 1920. It sustained the national dignity in the face of the cultural assault of the West in the nineteenth century, and it made possible a mission of world renewal under the leadership of Lenin.

AUTOCRACY

Despite a cultural heritage from Byzantium, with its late-Roman emphasis on absolutism, hierarchy, obedience, and a caesaro-papist faith, pre-Tatar Russia was a loosely knit society. Princes, nobles, and people had their place and rights in a semifeudal order, as in medieval Europe. The ruler was usually less a sacred power than a manager engaged to stand at the head of the city. There were popular assemblies, veches, which held great authority in cities such as Novgorod and Pskov, which were centers of a lively intellectual life. But the expanding Muscovite state crushed the rights of all but the autocrat; and for five hundred years, except for slight intermissions, Russia has known only strong government, varying from despotic to monarchic-authoritarian, or oligarchic when the monarch happened to be weak.

The Tatars, for whose circumstances absolutism was inevitable, brought it to Russia. Their strength was unqualified discipline in an atmosphere of insecurity conditioned by their rootless life.[31] Their right was force and conquest, solidified by terror; and their government was patterned after the refined despotism of imperial China. Their ideology, "As there is but one God in heaven, so there should be one ruler on earth," made rebellion against the ruler's command sin and crime together. Their society was authoritarian down to the tyranny of men over wives and children.

As the Tatars settled down to exploitation of their empire, they imposed their ways of rule.[32] Russian princes who kowtowed to the khan expected their subjects to kowtow to them. Sanctioning the authority of princes as their agents, the Tatars delegated power over the fractious and independent aristocracy, helped suppress rebellions and annul the old popular assemblies; princes became practically proprietors of their cities. The Tatars introduced administrative forms, the census, judicial torture, conscription, and a standing army. They brought the idea that all were obliged to serve the state, in contravention of the earlier principle that boyars were free to leave a prince; land tenure was made conditional upon service. Previously there had been only light feudal dues; under the new masters, who were above all interested in taxation, peasants became subject to a head tax and were more bound to the land in order to assure payment. The best way for a prince to secure the favor of the khan was to extract as much as possible from the people. The Tatar influence in this area left its mark in the Russian language, such words as "money" (*dengi*), "treasury" (*kazna*), and "customshouse" (*tamozhnia*) being of Tatar origin. Tatar military contingents were attached to Russian princes, while Russians were recruited into Tatar armies and served as far away as China. Although not many Tatars settled in Russia, their officials traveled over the land, and Tatar residents guided the princes somewhat as Russian residents long afterward stood beside nominal rulers of Central Asian protectorates.

The rulers of Moscow rose, not by rebellion against the Tatar hegemony, but by adopting its heritage [33] and methods, dealing with craft and cruelty beyond Russian tradition. Association continued close long after Moscovy had achieved substantial independence. Although European by race and Christian by religion, fifteenth-century Muscovy joined indifferently with some remnants of the Golden Horde against others.[34] The Tatars helped Ivan III round out his domains, especially in the campaigns against the free cities of Novgorod and Pskov; and numerous Tatars served Moscow as administrators or officers in the fifteenth and sixteenth centuries. Ivan IV used many Tatar troops, not least in the capture of the khanates of the Volga. The Tatar ruler had been called Tsar by the Russians,[35] and Ivan, in claiming the succession of the Great Khan as his own, called himself Tsar of Kazan and Astrakhan. Tatars were prominent at Ivan's court; he made a descendant of Genghis Khan nominal tsar of the greater part of his domain to bolster his legitimacy.[36] A Tatar had only to accept Orthodoxy to become Russian, and a substantial portion of the Russian nobility was of Tatar origin.

Under other circumstances, the Tatar legacy could have been left behind; but expansion over and rulership of less advanced peoples promoted authoritarianism,* and autocracy corresponded to the Russian political reality. Not only were there profound psychological effects; as a practical matter, strong government was essential to maintain imperial unity. Even in uniting Russian lands, Muscovy had to overcome the self-will of many free cities and principalities, from Vladimir and Suzdal to Novgorod; and it was something of a cultural and racial mélange even before it shook off Tatar hegemony and started its career of Asiatic conquest. Unity, which could only mean subjection to a single will, was seen as essential to strength; defeat by the Tatars was attributed to the previous disunity of Russia. If the nations that came to constitute the Russian empire were to be held forcibly together, they could not be permitted to participate in the government. No one could be permitted to threaten unity by sharing the ultimate power. As the Russians saw it through the centuries, the autocratic power created the empire, animated it, and made possible its continuation.

---

* The eastward expansion of Germany in the Middle Ages had effects somewhat similar to but less striking than those of the much more successful eastward expansion of Russia. Colonized eastern Germany offered a stronger basis for territorial power untrammeled by traditional limitations. Princes there established uniform administrations with a military basis, through which they could dispose more freely of subjects' lives and property.[37]

Any concession to constitutionalism, republicanism, or particular rights was a threat to Russian greatness. ·

As Alexander I said, "The least weakening of autocracy would lead to the separation of many provinces." [38] In his Memoir to Alexander I, Karamzin declared, "Any change in her constitution has led in the past and must lead in the future to her perdition, for she consists of very many and different parts: what save unlimited monarchy can produce in such a machine the required unity of action?" [39] Or, in the words of the enlightened finance minister under Nicholas II who presided over a successful industrialization program, Sergei Witte:

The world should be surprised that we have any government in Russia, not that we have an imperfect government. With many nationalities, many languages, and a nation largely illiterate, the marvel is that the country can be held together even by autocracy. Remember one thing: if the tsar's government falls, you will see absolute chaos in Russia, and it will be many a long year before you will see another government able to control the mixture that makes up the Russian nation. [40]

These sentiments hardly lost force as tsardom neared its end. In 1915 a conservative bureaucrat, Alexander Krivoshein, declared,

Tsarism is the mighty bond of the different elements which the work of centuries has brought together in the Muscovite empire. Throw away this mighty basis and you will immediately see how Russia is split and falls apart. [41]

After the abdication of Nicholas II, the leader of the liberal party, Paul Miliukov, frantically begged the ex-tsar's brother to accept the crown:

If you decline . . . it will be the end. Because Russia . . . is losing . . . its helmsman . . . the only pilot of the ship of state . . . there will be chaos . . . anarchy . . . rivers of blood . . . there will be no government . . . no Russia . . . there will be nothing. [42]

The need was real. According to the Marquis de Custine, Nicholas I conceded that in the diversity of races, cultures, and religion, "The differences are basic, the uniformity superficial, and unity is only apparent." [43] When the state was weakened by accidents of personality in the first years of the seventeenth century, the Time of Troubles, not only did the aristocracy reassert itself but so also did the Cossacks and other minorities; nearly half of Russia fell temporarily away from the rule of Moscow. Peter the Great had to contend with rebellions of Bashkirs, Finno-Ugrians, and Cossacks; and such elements supported the recurrent peasant uprisings, such as those led by Stenka Razin and Emelyan Pugachev, terrifying the élite into unconditional adherence to the crown. When Ivan the Terrible in 1564 withdrew to a monastery, the folk of Moscow entreated him "not to forsake his people, but to rule as best pleased him, and mete out such treatment as he deemed fit to those of whom he had reason to complain." [44] With the downfall of the Romanovs in 1917, the empire fell apart, to be reconstituted under a refreshed and stronger absolutism.

Empire not only required, facilitated, and excused, but sanctified autocracy, which became a principle of national life, part of the moral order, flourishing even when the autocrat was personally a nonentity. The tsars saw their power as holy, standing for the holy empire, with one faith and one ruler giving justice and peace to the nations. The tsar became a half abstraction, like heaven; and Russians took pride in what foreigners saw as a fault, submissiveness to despotism. Absolutist government was lauded as part of the Russian superiority by writers from the time of Ivan the Terrible to the end of tsardom.

Ivan the Terrible, a religious man who blessed each morsel of meat before eating it, supposedly committed his atrocities as part of his duty as God's vicar, resistance to whom was rebellion against God; and he held it shameful of neighboring states that they were not equally autocratic. At a later day, autocracy was equated with the welfare of all. Outwardly or in changed terms, it was the ideal of most radicals and of the intelligentsia in the nineteenth century, down to Lenin and his apotheosis of the dictatorship nominally of the proletariat. The rationalist critic Vissarion Belinsky wrote, "In the tsar is our *freedom*, because from him will emerge our new civilization. . . . Unconditional submission to tsarist authority is not only useful and necessary for us but it is the highest poetry of our lives—our nationality." [45] Russian intellectuals perceived political struggle in Europe as weakness and disorder, while congratulating themselves on order and harmony. From the Western point of view, one could oppose the government while remaining completely loyal to the nation; this was impossible in Russia, because the absolutist regime was the bond of the state. For the West, pluralism meant freedom and absolutism was suffocation; for Russia, pluralism meant anarchy and single rule was order.

The Fundamental Law of the empire until 1906 was, "To the

Emperor of All the Russias belongs the supreme and unlimited autocratic power." Catherine stated in her Instruction, after noting the
extent of her dominions,

9. The sovereign is absolute; for there is no other Authority but that which
centers in his single Person, that can act with a Vigour proportionate to
such a vast dominion. . . .
11. Every other Form of Government whatsoever would not only have
been prejudicial to Russia, but would even have proved its entire ruin. . . .[46]

Toward the end of the regime, a British observer found that "in Russia
the Tsar is everything, literally everything; that not only is his will law
but that it is also heaven-inspired right; that his land and his subjects are
his to dispose of wholly as he will. . . ." [47] He was so exalted that he
had to crown himself. There was a vague feeling that authority came
from the people, but they had transferred it to the tsar to exercise as
he saw fit.

From Muscovite times, the tsar was theoretical owner of all the
land, although he was pleased to allow individual usufruct; and this
theory was never entirely set aside. He lived in Oriental splendor which
was the grander by contrast with the poverty of the land. He alone
had rights; his subjects had only duties. Likewise the theory was maintained, although practice was moderated, that it was the duty of everyone to serve the state. A man was important exactly in the degree to
which, and no longer than, he was favored by the ruler; those who fell
from favor became unmentionable nonpersons.[48]

Depending on personality, various tsars acted the part of the despot, not only such notorious tyrants as Ivan IV, who well deserved his
common English sobriquet by reason of the individual or wholesale
slaughter he decreed for all whom he conceived capable of opposing
his will, and Peter, who became "the Great" by turning arbitrariness
to useful ends, but also Paul, who flailed and executed as freely as a child
might tear wings from flies. The empire seemed to excuse all, for the
people endured capricious sadism and monstrous abuses with the greatest passivity; Ivan IV was genuinely popular. The people were not to
think; Nicholas I did not even want praise—his subjects were not entitled to an opinion. They were to be faithful soldiers. When the artillery once had to cross a deep ditch in a training exercise, the infantry
(it was said) filled it with their living bodies to make a bridge for the
horses and guns.[49]

Tsardom was more like Oriental despotism than traditional European monarchy in sundry ways, especially before Western influences tempered it in the nineteenth century. Early tsars chose brides, not from royal houses and with an eye to diplomacy, but by a sort of competition among virgins of the realm. Ivan IV had a harem of some fifty concubines in addition to his series of wives, and most tsars and tsarinas before the nineteenth century were licentious. Catherine II, many of whose guards worked in her bedroom, was not exceptional. Various Russian autocrats, such as Ivan IV, Peter I, Anna, Peter II, Elizabeth, Catherine II, Paul, and Alexander I, turned into sadists, paranoids, lechers, or eccentrics, indulging in excesses hardly known in Western monarchy.[50] Not the person and family of the autocrat but the office was important. Before the nineteenth century, succession was irregular, and reigning tsars were frequently set aside if not murdered in palace coups. Catherine, a German princess with no blood relation to the royal lineage, was perfectly acceptable as autocrat. She was first turned to irregular relations by the empress-mother, who, indifferent to royal legitimacy, urged her to take a lover to provide an heir.

AUTOCRATIC SOCIETY

The institutions and mentality of the Russian state were shaped by the overwhelming political power and became much like those of other strongly ruled continental empires. A political police without legal or moral restraints protected the ruler against real or supposed opposition and enabled him to indulge his caprices. Although not so well organized and efficient as in Soviet days, the tsarist police apparatus was at times a dreadful scourge (as, for example, Ivan the Terrible's *Oprichnina*); at other times it became lax and decadent, and it was frequently reorganized, as its Soviet counterpart has been. Censorship, though variable in drive and effectiveness, was a standby of the regime from the time that printing became significant. Through the eighteenth century, most printed works were religious and hence useful or innocuous for the state; in the nineteenth century, there was usually precensorship; in times of relaxation, the government relied on warnings, closures of newspapers, prohibitions of certain subjects. Permission was required to possess printing machinery, and the importation of books was severely restricted. In the sixteenth century, as under Nicholas I in the nineteenth and under Stalin, death was the penalty for attempting to leave Russia without license. It was difficult likewise to enter, and travelers were much distrusted; foreign ambassadors before Peter's reign were often treated like prisoners.

Since everything depended on the tsar, there could be no such divisions as legislative or judicial branches separate from the executive; at best, there was a separation of functions. There was no room for local autonomy except as incorporation in the empire was completed by degrees. Catherine the Great, in order to neaten the empire, re-divided it, with little regard for historical boundaries, into fifty "govern-ments"; the governors, agents of the autocrat, had full powers over their districts. Centralization was such that the only important city was Moscow, with St. Petersburg after Peter the Great. They were the centers of light and life for the huge empire, as London has been for England; provincial towns were much duller and more uniform than those in the small countries of Europe. Catherine, seeing herself as enlightened despot, set up agencies of local self-administration; but they withered for lack of authority. Unlike towns in medieval Europe, those in Russia were never oases of freedom.

Religious authority was subjected to political control. From the beginnings of the Russian state, the Byzantine idea of the union of church and state was favorable to autocracy. The Tatars allowed the Russian Church material privileges in return for its blessing their ruler-ship; and the Church came to favor, not a popular movement against the heathen, but princely power. As early as the fourteenth century the Orthodox Church centered in Moscow became closely associated with the state, serving at times as an arm of the grand prince against his opponents. Ivan the Terrible treated church dignitaries, as he did everyone else, in a very cavalier fashion and confiscated church lands. The Church recovered stature in the Time of Troubles. Patriarch Nikon wished to regard himself as a pope, practically coruler with Tsar Alexis; but the latter disabused him by bringing about his deposi-tion in 1666. Peter replaced the patriarchate with a Holy Synod of bishops named by himself and presided over by a lay official, thus mak-ing the Church a branch of the state. Catherine II in 1764 made the dependence more complete and direct by expropriating the lands of the Church and putting the clergy on the state payroll.

Equating Russia with the true faith, recognizing that land as the sole stronghold of Orthodoxy after the falling away of Byzantium, the Church made obedience to the tsar a religious duty. It expressed the imperative spiritual unity of all; belonging to it was equivalent to being

Russian and accepting the regime. Like Marxism-Leninism, the Orthodox Church was at once Russian and ecumenical. Heresy was equated with treason, and the state power supported the Church. No great efforts were usually made to convert heretics, but membership in the Orthodox fold could not be renounced, and apostates were subject to persecution. To the end, the Church remained a pillar of tsardom, offering prayers for the autocrat well after his abdication in 1917. As creature of the state, the Orthodox Church inevitably decayed to intellectual stagnation and spiritual vacuity. But it was able to fill the empire and Russian minds with a religiosity that was remarked by visitors from more easygoing lands, although piety seems often to have been more formal than moral; it is said that robbers would ask saints to bless their enterprises.

Although sundry individuals were as influential as the monarch permitted, there was no room for a powerful nobility; claims to independent authority by reason of birth were irrelevant. Ivan III, real founder of the state, ended the old custom of sharing the prince's holdings with his relatives and began the practice of granting landholdings conditionally on service, mostly to men of lower class or foreign origin. The unification that he carried out severely reduced the status of the prince's liegemen, the boyars, as they no longer could switch loyalties when dissatisfied. Ivan IV made service obligatory for all ranks and dispossessed and ennobled with equal abandon; thousands of the top ranks were slain and replaced by those whom he thought more faithful. By his veritable revolution, the traditional rights of the boyars, descendants of independent princes, were practically effaced. Like the Church, the nobility recovered some standing in the subsequent disorders and weakness of the autocracy, but it was subdued with little resistance as the Romanovs restabilized the throne. Peter completed the reduction of the nobility as he degraded or slaughtered those who displeased him, rewarded with landholdings his servitors of humble birth, bootblacks or servant girls, and made status dependent in theory solely on his will. He set up a table of fourteen ranks. All were to be equally entitled to enter at the bottom and supposedly to advance according to merit and effort; a commoner of talent and dedication could thus raise himself (as Lenin's father did) to hereditary nobility. The table of ranks was the general yardstick of status, not only for administrators and military men but for everyone with official connection; even singers in the imperial theater had a rank or *chin*.

After Peter, the career open to talents was more theoretical than real, but birth continued to count for little compared to favor at court. Even when, late in the eighteenth century, the nobles were formally released from state service and received unconditional titles to estates (in imitation of Western practice), they had little of the corporate sense of a Western feudal class. In the ordinary imperial pattern, estates and titles, meaning little in terms of power, were shared by heirs under Russian as earlier under Tatar law As in the France of the Ancien Régime, nobles became very numerous, holdings were splintered, and titles were debased by multiplication until there were approximately a million nobles at the end of the nineteenth century. "Nobility" implied few privileges (chiefly that of owning serfs before the Emancipation) and little prestige.

If lineage was no great advantage and the tsar advanced those whom he preferred regardless of class background—sometimes with preference for those most completely dependent upon his favor—there was considerable feeling for equalitarianism. Strong tsars, such as Peter and Alexander I, endeavored to make equality of opportunity a reality. Alexander wanted equal access to education for all, and the reforms he projected would have made all positions dependent solely on merit. Tsars to some extent, especially in the Muscovite period, relied on popular support against the aristocracy (and they are so credited by Soviet historians, who see nobles but not tsars as exploiters). Peter, who mingled with common folk, was called a "democratic" tsar, as was Ivan the Terrible; and the Romanovs claimed popular election of the dynasty. The autocracy boasted of the close unity of tsar and people as one of its major strengths; however unreal the "intimacy" of these opposites, it was widely touted, even by foreigners. In the nineteenth century, it was argued that Russia was more democratic than Western countries because poor boys could become ministers and generals, that the people had social equality which was better than legal, that there were no independent classes, and that the autocracy obviated capitalist exploitation.[51]

Some poor boys were lucky enough to find a sponsor, enter a military school or otherwise get onto the ladder which rose to the heights beside the throne. The mass of the population, however, were serfs, practically chattel slaves until 1861 and not much better off thereafter, with no more rights or hopes than slaves elsewhere. Bondage was instituted by the Tatars as a tax-gathering device [52] and was

successively strengthened by tsarist absolutism: just as the nobles were
bound to serve the tsar, the peasants were obliged to serve their masters, working the land and so enabling the nobles to fulfill their duties.
At first, peasants were permitted to depart after the harvest was gathered; their leaving was banned in certain years (beginning in 1580);
soon it was prohibited altogether. Rights of landholders over their
serfs, to punish or to use them as desired, were gradually increased
until serfdom became slavery. The emancipation of 1861 was a concession to needs of modernization; but it left the ex-serfs deprived of
much of the land they had been cultivating, burdened with redemption payments to their former owners for the land assigned to them,
and tied to the commune through which they were taxed and controlled. A corollary was a semicommunal economy of families within
the village and of individuals within the family.

If autocracy subjected the landholders to the state and the peasants to the landholders, there was little room for independent or middle classes like those which grew strong in the pluralistic international
society of the West. Rights of ownership in general were equivocal,
little esteemed, and insecure. Private property was widely held to be
sinful, and important private interests were regarded as a blemish on
the state. Merchants and commercial values were generally despised.
The chief purpose of industry was and has remained to serve the
state. This was the chief consumer, mainly for military needs; and
most industry was established by official initiative or under official protection. Private enterprise gained importance in the nineteenth century,
but down to the end of tsardom the state owned many industries,
regulated others, granted concessions, provided credit, and took the
largest share of production. Of private capital, much was foreign; and
a disproportionate number of managers and merchants were non-
Russians.

As a result, Russia suffered economic and cultural retardation. The
country emerged from Tatar domination far behind the West, but this
was not so much the result of physical devastation or lack of means
of communication as of political alienation and the autocratic system.
Whereas Western Europe suffered many wars, Russia lay in relative
peace for the two centuries of Tatar hegemony, and contacts with the
West were never broken.[53] From the sixteenth century tsars were
aware of the need to modernize for strength, and at times, as under
Peter, the gap was reduced. But the government would again become

complacent or lethargic and fail to carry forward the work of modernization with sufficient energy. The basic difficulty was that progress
depended primarily on the state, the orientation of which was inevitably political rather than economic. The autocratic regime stifled
initiative, discouraged enterprise, and suffocated original thought. Practically unchecked by countervailing powers, the government taxed
mercilessly; particularly under ambitious tsars, such as Ivan and Peter,
the country was exhausted.

Advancement was attainable not through production but by political connections; the great question was who protected whom. Power
and prestige belonged to whoever chanced to enjoy the autocrat's favor
and to the vast arrogant bureaucracy which used power for its own
purposes. Despotism was a school of corruption in which all manner
of people learned to extort from those at their mercy. Private enterprise could never really prosper; it was only making a good beginning
as the tsarist system decayed in the last part of the nineteenth century.
Russia, despite size and amplitude of resources, remained basically poor,
much behind neighboring European countries not only in industry but
in agriculture. Grain yields at the end of the nineteenth century were
typically one-half to one-third of those of other grain-producing countries. Travelers crossing from East Prussia to Russia were struck by the
contrast between neat and prosperous farmsteads on one side of the
border and near desolation on the other, under identical natural but
different political conditions.

Impoverishment was not only material but psychological. Western
travelers to the early Muscovite realm saw character compressed by
despotism and fear: "Vile subservience to superiors and unbounded
arrogance to dependent persons." [54] There was little encouragement for
creativity and none for originality. Appearances took the place of
realities; the Potemkin village was not a Russian invention but a Russian specialty. Like the Soviet Union, tsarist Russia gloried in all manner of formal distinctions, honors, and orders. Intellectual life remained
anemic and highly imitative until well into the nineteenth century.
Then the Western-influenced upsurge of thought and writing was
almost entirely anti-state. Even so, the tenor of thought was tinged
with absolutism, moral-political themes overshadowed the factual-
empirical that were more at home in the West, and the idea of compromise, inherent in representative government, was rejected in principle.

IMPERIAL PATTERNS

Men of Western nations have often been amazed by the vagaries of Russian government, from the playful cruelties of its rulers to the magnificence of its constructions. But states of the West have shown, at some time and in some degree, traits like those of Russian autocracy. There were parallels between Henry VIII of England and Ivan IV, and not only in the number of wives; under mercantilist guidance France endeavored in the eighteenth century to promote trade and production; Stuart England had censorship and its official church. But the differences between the Russian polity of the past six centuries and those of countries of maritime Europe have been deep. Even when monarchs of the West, following the example of the Sun King, Louis XIV, were prating of absolutism and Divine Right, travelers to Russia were struck by the arbitrariness of the power of the tsar and the abasement of his servitors. Rulership in Russia, like the winter, has been untempered, as it were, by proximity to the ocean.

In this respect, Russia has not been exceptional. Broadly speaking, the political climate turns harsher as one moves from the region of the North Sea toward Asia—ways of government become, so to speak, more continental. From the strongly libertarian traditions of England and the Netherlands one passes to more authoritarian Germany, and western Germany has been more liberal than the eastern Germany of the Prussian junkers. Poland, with its highly developed constitutional rights, was somewhat exceptional; and in the conditions of Eastern Europe Poland proved unviable. Russian autocracy in turn was transitional to what has been commonly and somewhat unfairly termed Oriental despotism, of which imperial China provided the world's best model.

In part, this political gradient can be laid directly to the influence, or the utility, of the sea, principal carrier of commerce prior to the building of railroads. The greater difficulty of overland trade contributed to making society in the interior of Eurasia less commercial and hence more political. Probably more important, however, was the effect of the natural divisions of Western Europe. Mountain ranges and arms of the ocean dissected it into fairly well defined units where nations were able to solidify after the Middle Ages and, thanks to the balance of power, to maintain themselves indefinitely. In Central and Eastern Europe, on the other hand, natural boundaries are fewer and less definite. Political borders were less permanent, defense was more difficult, soldiering was more important, and states grew bigger. The impulse to nationhood has usually been not autochthonous but Western-derived. Prior to World War I, Western Europe was composed of national, constitutional states, Eastern Europe mostly of multinational, authoritarian empires, the Austro-Hungarian, Turkish, and Russian.

That these empires were autocratic was to be taken for granted; they could not have existed otherwise. Catherine II was pleased to agree with Montesquieu, "A large empire presupposes a despotic authority in him who governs"; [55] and it was appropriate that the first rulers of an enlarged Russian state should call themselves Caesars (Czars, or Tsars) and adopt the double eagle and other symbols of the Byzantine rulers who had claimed dominion of the world in the succession of Julius and Augustus Caesar.

Russia followed in the fundamental lines of great continental empires like the Roman and Chinese. These, along with other grand historical empires, such as Moghul India, Achaemenid Persia, the Ottoman empire in its times of glory, the Inca empire of the Andes on a more primitive level, the Egyptian and other early empires of the Near East, form a fairly well-defined political genus. They are so large as to seem a world apart to their subjects, and their primary task is to maintain unity of authority over their vast dominions. The political has hence swamped other aspects of life, and the state has become overwhelming. The despot could always claim, probably rightly, that he was indispensable for the integrity of the realm and consequently for the multitudes of officials whose authority rested on his. Preservation of the status of the ruling class required unity, all the more because its position was artificial; and unity meant submission to a single will. There has seemed to be no way, at least no regular or formal way, for the governing élite to check the despot without endangering itself. The empire needs and excuses unequivocal rulership; it also makes despotism easier to maintain, in accordance with the principle that the advantages of the center increase with the size of the organization.

From these basic realities, the main characteristics of the imperial pattern follow with the regularity of human nature.[56] Rulership has been legally unrestricted, and the rulers have held more or less title to all property or all land. They have often abused their power; and often they have used it for grand purposes, from the erection of awe-inspiring palaces to the making of public works such as canals and roads. The ruler has been exalted, ordinarily wrapped in a religious mystique and treated as a god on earth, probably both to satisfy his vanity and to make him a more effective symbol of authority.

This does not mean that the exalted emperor is necessarily the effective ruler of the realm. Aside from the fact that there is far too much for him to keep aware of and that he is probably bored, in the loftiness of supreme power, with mere administration, his character is likely to be unsuited to it. Empires have never found a way to select as despots persons best prepared to govern; to the contrary, the atmosphere of the palace tends to produce devious if not weak characters. Consequently government is likely to be exercised mostly by an obscure group of insiders, who rule in the name of the sacred monarch. More broadly, the administrators who execute the decrees form the ruling class; great empires make oversize and oppressive bureaucracies.

Unrestricted power has unrestricted means of defending itself. Some sort of political police has been omnipresent; and terrorism, sometimes mild as under Augustus, sometimes monstrous as under Caracalla, has been recurrent. Satisfaction in the wielding of boundless power and overestimation by rulers of their own beneficence and wisdom join with convictions of the need for ruthless action for supreme goals. Censorship is likewise inevitable, and rulers have always been ready to suspect thoughts of treason behind any lack of respect. Conversely, they have felt entitled, if not duty-bound, to educate and indoctrinate their subjects. Taking the view that people are born more or less perverse and need to be reshaped, empires have been the great patrons of ideologies (such as Confucianism) and official religions under state churches.

Since there are no independent rights and rulers do not esteem competition, there are no strong independent classes. Institutions and initiatives are of the government, not of the people. All those between the exalted rulers and the lowly masses are shrunk. The court has no appreciation for an independent aristocracy; status rests upon relation or utility to the highest. Still less does the autocracy care for a commercial or industrial class, whose position has a quite different basis; moreover, the temptation to partake of the wealth created by the labors of others is likely to be irresistible for greedy officials and needy autocrats. Liberalism everywhere has been promoted primarily by middle classes; they have always been the movers of constitutional government and generators of ideas of civil rights and individualistic attitudes.

But without security, no middle class develops to temper the political atmosphere and to bridge the gap between the privileged and the lowly. Freedom is seen as valueless or is simply not conceivable; the concept is absent from Chinese culture, for example. For the Russians, freedom was taken as the organic union of wills in the spiritual community under tsardom; in the Soviet Union true freedom is in Marxist fashion seen as the acceptance of the inevitable. Freedom consists in cooperation with the higher will.

Since the purposes of the empire are overwhelmingly political, it cannot expect to be very successful economically. Rulers at times may use their authority fairly sagely to promote trade and industry, as did Caesars like Trajan and Hadrian, turning peace into prosperity. But eventually political vices frustrate economic opportunities. Enterprise is discouraged by ubiquitous overregulation, corruption, and extortion; anticommercial, that is, antiproductive, values prevail. Overtaxation oppresses commerce, industry, and agriculture to impoverishment. The unchecked regime uses its power to draw wealth to itself and so undermines the ability of the people to produce wealth. Economically, the great empires have never been progressive; and their peoples have always been eventually crushed to the margins of existence, while the élite have luxuriated in opulence.

The psychology and intellectual atmosphere of the imperial society differ from those of looser, more commercial states because values differ. In the politically ordered realm, originality and innovation are not encouraged. Gifted men make inventions (and the Russians, like the Chinese, have many to their credit), but the stiff bureaucratic order inhibits their application. Artists produce grand and ornate works, but they are imitative and decorative; the interpretation of life is fixed and given by the governing powers. The philosophies of the empire are not critical and searching but absolutist, concerned more with justice or the order of society than with facts. Roman and Chinese philosophers have been primarily preoccupied by ethics, just as the issues of Russian thought before and after 1917 have been wholly ethical or political, whereas thinkers of Greece and the West have endeavored rather to analyze reality. In the absence of competitive groups, there are few debates to start new currents of thought and generate new ideas. Sincerity and honesty are less esteemed where the means of success is to please the powerful.

Every state has ideals that are taken for granted, but the ideologies

of empires are monopolistic and far more intense than those of pluralistic states. Like Confucianism, or the state cults that have surrounded
various imperial regimes, or Orthodox Christianity or Marxism-Leninism in Russia, they serve the vital functions of legitimating the rulership, cloaking political reality, and making the regime more bearable.
The imperial ideology decrees that the rulers rule by some unassailable
right and that they rule for the welfare of the people; it is an essential
part of the well-conceived structure of empire, whereby people are led
to accept subjection if not contribute to it. The rulers congratulate
themselves on their mission of rule and their supposed or real devotion
to the welfare of the people, while the masses are comforted by the
concern of the masters. Probably, too, the philosophy of the empire
has an outwardly equalitarian cast. As all stand so far below the god-
like Caesar or Son of Heaven, there is a certain sense of equality; no
one can claim special rights except by the favor, which may be at any
moment withdrawn, of the All-Highest, who proclaims his love for all
his children.

Anti-individualism and the sense of collective responsibility combine with disesteem for private property to give the great empires a
communistic tinge. Everybody should serve the common welfare, and
bourgeois attitudes are disdained. Private wealth is far inferior to political influence; it is even suspect, because wealth implies cheating the
state or the people. The idea of sharing is favored by the government;
people are supposed to be glad to yield their possessions to the sacred
cause. Taxation may foster communal attitudes, also. In order to assure
its revenues, the Russian government made peasant communities col-
lectively responsible, and lands were redivided periodically so that
every household should have productive fields to enable it to pay its
share of taxes. It was in this spirit that a Polish writer declared in 1854
that "Russia is a vast communist society ruled by an autocratic and
simultaneously military authority." [57] Alexander I tried to bring order,
efficiency, and happiness to his dominions by organizing military-com-
munistic colonies, where all men drilled and plowed together.[58]

Communistic ideas on the official level, however, usually remain
only vague philosophic inclinations. The empire is in practice a vast
system of material privileges that the beneficiaries have no desire to
share. But for the underprivileged the idea of more equal distribution
is very attractive, and it has figured prominently in the thinking of
dissident movements. For many centuries, Chinese peasant rebellions

regularly demanded sharing of land if not of property in general, and various Russian religious sects believed in sharing more or less of their material goods. Dreams of a society free from the curse of private property, chief cause of division in society, merged into utopian visions of a perfectly ordered and hence (in the mentality of the empire) perfectly happy life.

Utopianism, in a spirit more emotional and chiliastic and less logical than that of Plato and his successors, is characteristic of the empire. Where the regime is overwhelming, men assume that by perfecting it everything can be made perfect. Improvement is not to be made by adjusting interests or permitting men to improve themselves but by imposing the right rule of society. If there should come a fittingly wise emperor, he could and would sweep away all the abuses of his false servants and bring, like a savior or messiah, pure justice, tranquillity, and the satisfaction of all longings. But the old emperor and his train of corrupt officials will not go away of themselves, and salvation comes to mean revolution. This is a concept less appropriate for more loosely structured societies, where the government manages less and, in any case, is subject to change by peaceful processes. Revolution is the counterpart of the imperial idea of authority. Since the government dominates life, the way to improvement is to change the dynasty—the purpose of countless uprisings through Chinese history—or, at a more sophisticated level, to elevate a new faith or ideology to power, as Lenin promised.

2

Russia: European State and Oriental Empire

DEPENDENT EMPIRE

The Tatar (and secondarily Byzantine) inheritance of autocratic ways combined with physical extent and the political mission of broad unification to give Russia, since the days of Ivan III, the political traits usual to great continental empires. So gigantic was Russia, so far away from its centers were independent powers, that to ordinary Russians their domain seemed a universe to itself. What might happen in distant and vaguely known independent lands was seldom of concern. It is true that the Russian population was relatively sparse until modern times, much surpassing leading European states in numbers only in the nineteenth century. But Russia deserved the title of universal empire not only because it possessed several times the land area of all the rest of Europe together but because it united a hundred or more distinct peoples; and it could be held together only in the manner of other universal empires.

Yet the paradigm of empire is incomplete for understanding the Russian development. The typical universal empire has been able to feel itself practically alone in the world. Rome, for example, with semi-barbarian Germanic tribes to the north and desert dwellers to the south, had no neighbors which it had to respect as near equals; the only strong independent state with which the empire was in contact, Parthia, was too far away to be very important. China was a better example still; surrounded by mountains, jungles, and the ocean, it had only small tributaries (such as Korea and Vietnam) or nomadic peoples (such as the Mongols or Tatars) on its borders.

Russia, to the contrary, has never been able to relax in complacent enjoyment of possession, as could the Roman realm; even the traditional Turkish enemies were soundly defeated only late in the eighteenth century. Worse, the states to the west, although smaller and seen as politically inferior, were culturally and sometimes militarily superior. It is embarrassing for a would-be Lord of the Universe, such as Ivan IV, to see neighbor states richer and more technically advanced than his own.

Nor could the Russians prevent unfavorable comparisons by simply closing off their realm, for the most salient superiority of the West derived from the improvement of tools and ways of warfare. Conflict or fear of conflict with Livonia, Poland-Lithuania, or Sweden was chronic; and the lessons of defeat were forceful. Relative size could compensate for some inferiority; but it was absolutely indispensable for Russia, if it was to defend itself, continually to copy the advances of the fluid and more inventive West in everything related to combat or necessary to support military strength.[1] The great problem down to this day has been the overcoming of relative backwardness. Only borrowed technical (and organizational) superiority gave Russia a permanent advantage over Asiatic peoples and made possible the empire, which in turn enabled Russia to face the West with some pride and confidence.

There were no cultural obstacles to borrowing. The Russians felt themselves to be Europeans, defenders of European civilization from the barbarians of the steppes, and (in psychological compensation for their dependence upon the West) bearers of Western culture to the Asiatics. This was their advantage over Asiatic peoples like the Turks. These had ample opportunities to appropriate European knowledge but suffered such impediments to Westernization that they eventually became victims and instead of enlarging their empire lost it. Most of the peoples with whom expanding Europe came into conflict, from the Chinese to the Ethiopians (with the remarkable and not readily explainable exception of the Japanese), showed themselves unable to admit the obvious need of adopting European means to gain strength to resist European encroachments. The Russians have always had an exceptional capacity for taking up useful foreign ideas and treating them as their own, and they have never fallen for long into the conceited smugness to which masters of so grand a dominion might easily succumb.

Unlike the Tatars, the Russians were quick to adopt firearms in the fourteenth century and after. When Russia was still tributary to the khans, Ivan Kalita brought in Italians to build the Kremlin. In 1448, Ivan III asked the king of Hungary to send him artillerists, goldsmiths, and masons. Ivan III and Ivan IV were both sufficiently conscious of the need for learning that they strove to open up a path to the Baltic. Russia's immediate neighbors to the west were correspondingly aware of the dangers to themselves of Russian acquisition of modern technology and tried to shut off the Muscovite state. The Duke of Alba said that it was "inexcusable to provide Russia with cannons and other arms, and to initiate Russia into the way war was carried on in Western Europe, because, in this way, a dangerous neighbor was being educated." [2] Poland long tried to halt the flow of Western knowledge to its Russian foes, and the failure of Ivan IV's war against Livonia resulted in closure of the Baltic to Russia. Gunpowder had to be brought from England via the White Sea. But foreign engineers helped Ivan capture Kazan, the gateway to eastward expansion; their work included blowing up the walls of the city. Ivan also introduced printing to Russia, but for decades it was used only for devotionals.

By the beginning of the seventeenth century there were some 18,000 foreigners (mostly Poles and other East Europeans but including numerous Germans, Dutch, Scots, etc.) in the land; [3] merchants, craftsmen, and soldiers were lured to Moscow in growing numbers. The first Romanovs hired Western experts to drill and lead their armies, to build ironworks for military purposes, and to teach Russian workmen. Interest in the West greatly increased under Alexis (1645 to 1676), who had an English physician. The wealthy took to Western literature, painting, and architecture, and German was spoken at court. Heretic foreigners were so numerous that in 1652 they were ordered to settle in a "German quarter" of Moscow lest they endanger the Russian faith. Sophia, regent for Peter and his sickly half brother, was intrigued with Western ways and wished to reform the state after the Polish model.

The stage was thus well set for the spectacular Westernization of Peter. As a boy, he associated with a corps of foreigners who filled him with the lore of more advanced lands and aroused his determination to raise Russia to their level. Although he was always fascinated by things Western, the need for learning was thrust upon him by his first unsuccessful battles with the Turks and then by the battle of Narva (1700), when his troops were routed by the Swedes despite a more than fourfold numerical superiority. Peter diligently studied his requirements, especially for artillery and a navy; his pilgrimage to the shipbuilding centers of England and Holland, followed by the importation of a thousand Dutch sailors, was a profound expression both of need and of resolution. His construction of a new capital on the marshes at the head of the Gulf of Finland was a typically Russian achievement, a display of political virtuosity and power at the cost of many thousands of lives and suffering that would have been accounted unbearable in a Western land. But it gave a direct sea route to Europe and through succeeding centuries facilitated the importation of Western knowledge and modes, wrenching the capital into modern ways. Peter naïvely believed that requiring his subjects (or those around him) to shave and smoke would help to modernize their thinking. He thereby aroused considerable opposition—there has always been a party hostile to the importation of foreign ways. But Peter acted wholly as a Russian in trampling on Russian traditions.

Peter seems to have felt that he was doing an unpleasant although necessary onetime job. "For a few score years only we shall need Europe. Then we shall be able to turn our backs on her." [4] But the new industries and academies that he created were not self-sustaining, the West continued to advance rapidly, and it was necessary to keep borrowing on a larger and larger scale. After Peter foreign influences, especially German, grew massively. He had annexed, in the Baltic area, a considerable population of West European background and high cultural level, the German Baltic aristocracy. The tsars now had their own subject Westerners, and for generations thereafter they recruited a large proportion of their officials from these descendants of the Teutonic Knights. Royal marriages with German princely families also became customary and remained so to the end of the regime. Consequently, the court was overrun with Germans, and at one time German favorites were the most influential personages at court. In like manner, the Russian Academy of Sciences included hardly any Russians.

After the middle of the eighteenth century, French influence largely displaced German. France was the world's intellectual leader, and Western influence came increasingly through the printed word. The court adopted French manners and language. In the time of Catherine II (1762 to 1796), Westernization was beginning to engender philosophical subversion, but it was as essential and profitable as ever; it enabled Russian armies to defeat vastly superior numbers of Turks. The French Revolution sent a flood of aristocrats and hangers-on to Russia; and in the Napoleonic Wars Russia found itself more than ever involved with the West. Many thousands of Russian soldiers became acquainted with foreign countries, especially France. With the upsurge of industrialization and the burgeoning of modern science in the nineteenth century, technological lag increasingly meant impotence, and borrowing had to be stepped up to keep pace. Russia was only partly successful in this, as shown by defeats in the Crimean War (1854) and at the hands of Japan (1904). And the problems of assimilating Western culture while holding the old political forms of the empire essentially intact were becoming increasingly acute. As a patriotic publication wrote at midcentury, "we stand in need of the fruits of their education and enlightenment, but we reject their corrupt teachings as poison. . . ." [5] But the tsarist government had no way to sort out the nourishing from the poisonous.

Men have often asked whether Russia belonged to East or West. It was seen as Asian (at least politically) in Europe and as European (at least technologically) in Asia. It was an empire of the Oriental style mingling in and dependent upon the European world of nation-states, its political inferiors (in Russian eyes) and cultural superiors. Because of its location, it had special needs, to rule Asian style and to progress in technology Western style. The ability to do this made possible the building of the proud empire; also, stimulation and competition saved Russia from the depth of decadence that has invariably overtaken isolated empires after two or three centuries of splendor.

It was obvious to Russians that if they could only take over thoroughly the ways of the West, the size of their realm should enable them to overcome the world. This they could not come near doing, but they were able to build their greatness on a dual basis. One leg is Oriental-imperial-political; the other is Western-technological. An imperial political structure made possible not only the governance of the huge empire but also the mobilization of its people and resources; on the other hand, the power-centered structure was always detrimental to trade, innovation, and industry (except sometimes when defense-oriented), and it was necessary for Russia to take over and apply the achievements of a liberal, pluralistic civilization well enough to defend

itself and overpower Asian peoples. The Russians could regard themselves as saviors of the world, bearers of the light, thanks to borrowed
knowledge and imported machines.

But the two bases of Russian greatness were and are profoundly
contradictory. The anomalous and uncertain role they imply has caused
the Russians endless political and psychological difficulty. It has resulted
in a deep ambivalence, or a series of ambivalences or dualities, that
writers have noted in various terms: the Asiatic substance and the
European veneer; the mystical and the rational; the state (nowadays,
the party) and the people; the "black" masses and the modernized élite;
the submissiveness of the people and their individualism or rebellious-
ness. Russian foreign policy, political institutions, and culture have likewise been permeated with this duality, the basic uncertainty whether
Russia should be considered an indefinite empire (in Leninist terms, a
world revolutionary movement) with a special destiny or a state among
states, following in the stream of Western civilization.

Just as the geographical position of Russia is peculiar, its anomalous
character is without close historical parallel. An analogy might be
drawn with the Roman empire in its early days. In contact with Greek
colonies in the south of Italy as well as with metropolitan Greece by
commerce, Rome drew from the city-states techniques of civilization
and warfare that facilitated wide-ranging conquests. Roman art and
literature were highly imitative, and Roman science was little more
than an uncritical compilation of Greek works; yet the Romans looked
down upon the Greeks as decadent, somewhat as Russians scorned the
"bourgeois" West as decadent in the nineteenth and twentieth centuries. The experience of the semibarbarian Chinese state of Ch'in in the
third century B.C. was somewhat similar. For the sake of strength and
in order to organize Ch'in for conquest, the Ch'in court imported
scholar-advisers from the more advanced and less autocratic states
which formed the core of Chinese civilization. More broadly, there is
a parallel between Russia and various relatively crude, authoritarian,
and power-driven peoples who, living on the fringes of a great civilization, have borrowed civilized arts and organization and adapted them
to their own purposes to embark upon a career of conquest. Such were
not only Rome and the state of Ch'in but many others, including
Assyrians, Persians, Macedonians, Incas, and Tatars.[6]

Such peoples, however, have been able eventually to vindicate
themselves by conquering the respective center of civilization and ex-

propriating its wealth for the empire and thereby to solve their dilemmas. This the Russians have been unable to do, at first because the nation-states of Europe progressed technologically too rapidly, far more successfully than any predecessors, and recently because new powers, the United States, Japan, and China, have come forward to block Russian expansion. But Russians have naturally felt that they should solve their problems by universalization of their authority, and this is the essence of the Russian destiny as seen and desired by the Slavophiles and the Bolsheviks.

DUALITY: FOREIGN POLICY

The Russian state claimed to be unique, an ideal polity pursuing ideal and universal goals, standing above the petty strife of nations; yet it had to respect independent nations, sometimes fear them. The Russian rulership dealt with non-Russians mostly as subjects to be ruled by psychological and coercive means; yet it had to deal with other states as equals to secure advantages of trade, culture, and diplomacy. It was advantageous for Russia to participate in the balance of power for security; but Russia, for which foreign policy was in large part an extension of internal policy, could not well follow balance of power rules, making or changing alliances for purely foreign policy considerations. On the one hand, foreign polities were useful partners in peaceful intercourse; on the other, they represented heathen and alien powers, to be shut out if not reduced to obedience. In dealing with backward and weak countries, there was no severe problem; Russian influence was extended over them as feasible or desired, in the name of the Russian mission. But Western powers, heretical in faith as well as alien in political philosophy, could hardly be treated as inferiors or recognized as equals; Russia needed their cooperation, yet they could not be trusted or embraced as real friends. Western ambassadors were invited to Moscow, there to be treated as spies; travelers were generally unwelcome, yet it was necessary to bring in many experts.

Contacts with neighbors to the west were continuous from the beginnings of Russia, and relations with more distant powers became significant in the sixteenth century. Commerce with England, via the White Sea, began in 1553. Ivan IV developed this trade and wanted not only military supplies but an alliance and the hand of Queen Elizabeth. James I of England negotiated for trading rights along the Volga route to the Orient. In 1613–1614 the tsar solicited aid from

England against Sweden and Poland, and envoys were sent to France for similar purposes in 1625. In the second half of the seventeenth century Russia maintained regular diplomatic relations with England, Holland, Denmark, and Sweden. From the end of the seventeenth century, the empire was definitely a member of the European state system, regularly making war in alliance with Western states.

Some of the boyars of Ivan IV longed for liberties like those of the unruly Polish nobles, and difference of political philosophy joined with difference of religion to accentuate the antagonism of the two powers. Ideology was sometimes permitted to interfere with diplomacy. In the English Civil War, tsarist envoys insisted in dealing only with the overthrown King Charles I, and Alexis tried to help him against the parliamentarians. Prior to the French Revolution, however, ideology figured less prominently in Russian foreign relations because the accepted theory of government nearly everywhere was absolute monarchy. The French Revolution, which raised banners of freedom, and the ensuing wars made political creed an overt issue of diplomacy. Catherine, shocked by the fate of French royalty, recoiled from the rationalism with which she had been toying. Russia took the lead in the fight against Jacobinism despite distance from France and lack of direct material interest in the outcome of the struggle. Ideology also was used, as before and after, as a cover for aggrandizement; the rump of Poland after the first two partitions had to be occupied to save it from the revolutionary disease.

In the euphoria of victory over Napoleon, Russia saw itself bearer of an ecumenical mission of world order. Saying that God wished him to secure the peace of the universe, Alexander I sponsored the Holy Alliance, a league of sovereigns based on Christian and autocratic principles. Through the first half of the century the leading principle of Russian foreign policy was the maintenance of restored status quo and monarchic legitimacy in Europe; Alexander was passionately concerned with liberalism in lands of no direct concern for Russia: Spain and Italy. Russian actions, however, were rather realistically influenced by ordinary diplomatic interests. Thus, after some hesitation, Russia came to the help (in 1825) of the Greeks rebelling against the traditional enemy, the Turkish empire. At the beginning of the Crimean War, Russia insisted on the right to protect the Orthodox subjects of the Turks, but ideology was again much more a justification than a cause of the expansionist urge.

As the century wore on, Russia participated more fully as an equal in the European system and seemed to surrender much of its universalist pretension, accepting the role of state among states. A long step toward the liberation of foreign policy from ideology was the turning away from alignment with ideologically sympathetic Germany and Austria-Hungary toward alliance with bourgeois-republican France in the 1890's. But Russian foreign policy, despite basic realism, was exceptionally concerned with general questions of order and political ideals and given to moralizing; Russia was most fervent in protesting that it acted for ideals, not interests. Its themes were support for autocracy and Orthodoxy, mixed at times with Pan-Slavism; it was regarded as the gendarme of Europe, ready to help suppress liberal or revolutionary movements, as in Hungary in 1848. The messianic vision was fading, but there were still undercurrents of feeling that it was the Russian destiny to free the world from capitalism and materialism—that is, to overcome the Western state system or those aspects of it uncongenial to the empire.

DUALITY: THE STATE

Occasional confusion because of conflicting purposes in Russian foreign policy was unimportant compared to ambiguities caused by the urge or need to follow Western patterns while ruling in an Oriental fashion. Western political ideas and social concepts could never be excluded, and they influenced the privileged and educated, persons of real or potential political weight, including the sovereigns themselves. One could not feel modern and completely reject dominant modern political ways. As contacts with the West grew closer in the nineteenth century, educated Russians became critical in principle of the Oriental quality of their regime and eager to see it, like the economy, modernized. In addition, part of the superiority of Russia over Asiatic peoples, an important advantage in incorporating them into the empire and governing them, was superior government, an asset inseparable from military organization and nearly as important as weaponry. It was essential to have an efficient apparatus of state, which was to be copied from the best-arranged Western states; and good administration was inseparable from reform of basic political institutions.

But probably most important in the secular Russian urge to give a Western cast to its basically non-Western, even anti-Western, state was the conviction that the strength or weakness of a country must be a resultant primarily of its political order. In Russian eyes, Western states were not only embarrassingly rich and inventive but amazingly strong for their modest size. If tiny England was comparable in power to gigantic Russia, even able to check the latter's advance in Central Asia, the cause must be some superiority of British political institutions. The deduction was that the Russian state needed to be shaped more like successful Western countries in order to give Russia proportionate strength. Consequently, Russian rulers have again and again tried to make their government look more Western in the most progressive model, while quite undesirous, perhaps incapable, of altering its autocratic essence. This has introduced some falsity, since reforms have usually proved more cosmetic than genuine and have never touched the heart of the system. There is inherent in imperial government a gap between pretended purpose and less edifying reality; this was compounded in the Russian case by a foreign veneer. But it was no failure; cosmetics can substitute for natural beauty, and the Russian state has been well served by superficial reforms and proclaimed popular purposes.

Such adaptation is very old. Ivan the Terrible instituted an assembly, the Zemsky Sobor, outwardly like the parliaments of medieval Europe. But he was not pressured into convoking it by powerful independent classes demanding to be heard and to have a voice in the expenditure of the monies they contributed. Rather, he desired a simulacrum of general support for despotism, a little like the Supreme Soviet. In the subsequent period of disorder after the old dynasty ran out, there was a revival of feudal powers and the Zemsky Sobor took on some importance. Twice it selected or confirmed the selection of a new ruler. But it represented officialdom rather than the country at large, it never acquired fixed shape, and it was always docile. It had no right of initiative, and no official was ever changed at its instance.[7] The first Romanov, Michael (1613 to 1645), used it to help reestablish central authority; thereafter it withered until it was last summoned by Peter in 1698 to sanction punishment of the former regent, Sophia.

By this time, parliaments had declined in most of Europe, and Peter's Westernization took other directions. He commanded his nobles to bring their women to festivities, required Western garb, and shifted to a Western (Julian) calendar. He changed his own title from "Tsar" to the Latin "Imperator," or "Emperor," which remained the official designation of the ruler. He inaugurated a "Senate," but it was purely advisory and composed of the tsar's nominees, comparable not to the august Senate of the Roman republic but to its weak descendant under the empire. In imitation of Western practice he decreed entail of estates, although without primogeniture (it was soon revoked as impractical in Russian conditions). He remodeled his whole administration in imitation of that of his chief enemies, the Swedes. He inundated the Russian language with foreign terms, especially for his new governmental institutions.

Thereafter the Russian state was ostensibly Western. But in compensation, Peter strengthened the autocracy. He reduced the nobles, burdened commerce with endless controls while trying to foster it, and further enslaved the peasantry, while permitting himself to be deified as perhaps no other tsar. Coarse and ruthless, he was the model Russian ruler, Europeanizing by Asiatic methods, using arbitrary power to make Russia outwardly more like the freer lands of Europe and hence better able to take advantage of their achievements and to cope with them.

Not long after Peter, Russia had a constitution for ten days, at a time when constitutions were a daring concept in the West. A few nobles used a succession crisis to force on Anna a charter granting to an oligarchy rights somewhat like those enjoyed by their Polish and Swedish counterparts; it also contained guarantees of life and property against arbitrary actions.[8] But she had no difficulty in tearing up the document with the enthusiastic support of most of the nobility. The German-flavored autocracy continued as absolute as ever, although the dynasty had become almost entirely foreign, thanks to the custom of marrying foreign, chiefly German princesses.

Catherine II, a very intelligent woman, not only held practically an imported court, with French cooks and Italian dancing masters, but was enamored of modish French political thought and the *philosophes* who carried on a war of words with their own decadent monarchic regime. She wished her rule to be, or at least to seem, among the most enlightened of Europe; as she said, "Freedom is the soul of everything in the world. Without it everything is dead. I should like obedience to the laws, but I do not want slaves." [9] To improve the laws she called a large Legislative Commission and issued for its guidance an Instruction based on the ideas of Montesquieu so liberal that it was banned in France. But the Legislative Commission, like other pseudoparliamentary bodies the tsars sometimes called, was allowed to do nothing; and the Instruction, which had been hailed by liberal thinkers across Europe, remained idle phrases. Seeing local self-rule as a source of initiative and progress in the West, Catherine set up appropriate institutions; but she left all power in the provinces with her governors. Likewise in imitation of Western practice she tried to invigorate the nobility as a corporate body and abolished the old obligation of service to the state, which the nobles had come to regard as an indignity. But the empress surrendered no part of her powers, and the nobles were demoralized by loss of much of their function. Catherine also increased rights of owners over serfs, extended serfdom to areas where it had not existed, and gave away huge tracts of land to favorites, turning hundreds of thousands of state serfs into private chattels. Toward the end of her reign she closed all private presses and set up strict controls over the importation of books.

The grandiloquent proclamations of Catherine won her much acclaim and, along with expansion at the expense of Poland and Turkey, the title of "Great." Although they had little substance, they cannot be dismissed as mere façade, like the false fronts of wood and canvas villages set up by her minister, Potemkin, to cheer her journey across the Crimea. The copying of Western institutions was not merely hypocritical front, but represented a real felt need and one side of the Russian character. It was taken for granted that it was desirable to do things in the proper, modern way, always with the understanding that the needs of the empire had absolute priority. There was no more sense of contradiction in Catherine's liberal despotism than in a nobleman's speaking feelingly of the rights of man while gambling serfs away at cards; the two spheres, the theoretical and the practical, hardly impinged upon each other. Catherine showed the reality of her belief in progressive political ideas by naming a fervent republican, Frédéric de La Harpe, as tutor for the future Alexander I.

Like his grandmother, Alexander I (1801 to 1825) was devoted to French philosophy and military drill, was very fond of noble phrases, to the benefit of his reputation, and was also capable of much brutality. He wanted to improve the regime and repeatedly spoke of turning it into a constitutional monarchy; but he was no more willing or able in practice to restrict his own power than his predecessors. As one of his confidants put it, "In a word, he would willingly have agreed that every man should be free, on the condition that he should do only what the Emperor wished." [10] He would square the circle by admitting the people to share in the government without infringing the autocratic power; after much playing with the idea of a consultative assembly he rejected it. As he applied the theory of separation of powers to government in Russia, it became merely administrative separation of functions. He abolished the political police, only to reestablish it under new auspices. In the latter part of his reign Alexander became increasingly obscurantist and tyrannical. The France of the restored Bourbons seemed to Russian officers serving there a land of freedom; troops coming home were segregated lest they infect the population.

In reaction to the disintegrative tendencies and the Decembrist revolt at the beginning of his reign, Nicholas I tried to tighten the autocracy and exclude foreign contagion. Even Nicholas was aware of the need to import knowledge and to reform outworn institutions; he tried to help the peasants without abolishing serfdom. He also tried to give Russia for the first time an explicit ideology beyond the old Orthodox faith, summarized as Autocracy, Orthodoxy, and Nationality, the last being a concession to Western modes of thought. The triad was a counter to "Liberty, Equality, Fraternity" of French revolutionary glory, and was something of a fake from the outset; its inventor, Count Sergei Uvarov, was an authentic liberal who wrote only in French or German. Russia was converted into a military training camp insofar as Nicholas could arrange it; he drew most of his ministers from the military and drilled incessantly.

The death of Nicholas and the Crimean defeat, resulting from the great technical superiority of Britain and France, opened the way to change. There was a wave of revulsion against the arbitrary ways of the past, and it suddenly became possible to criticize the administration.[11] An unprecedented series of reforms was enacted in 1861 and after: the freeing of the serfs, a necessity not only for economic reasons but also because the nobility had lost morale; the inauguration of autonomous although weak and class-bound local organs, the zemstvos and city dumas, or councils; an independent court system with independent judges and jury trials on the most advanced, mostly French model; relaxation of censorship; reforms of financial administration; and educational reforms granting to the universities autonomy in the choice of courses and faculty. From 1856 to 1880 the number of schools was tripled.

But the monarchic power was not touched, and each reform was vitiated or cut back, partly because conservative forces recovered ground, partly because the Polish uprising of 1863 showed a real danger to the empire. The peasants were tied down in the communal organization after they had been freed from the personal powers of the gentry, and obligatory payments and taxes meant that their condition was little improved. The zemstvos, which became centers of Westernization through their efforts to improve living conditions,[12] were hamstrung and deprived of funds. The police were allowed to bypass the courts and punish administratively in political cases. Education was restricted, with required emphasis on classical studies, Greek and Latin; and an effort was made to exclude children of the poor from secondary schools.

In the following reigns, there was more talk of a constitution, and Alexander II was about to approve a project when assassinated in 1881. But until defeat in war with Japan forced Nicholas II in 1905 to admit some restriction of his power, the Fundamental Law stated, in the first article, the unlimited authority of the autocrat. It was claimed that the empire was not an Oriental despotism but a *Rechtsstaat*, because the monarch was supposed to limit himself by law. But the tsarist regime was essentially chaotic, with no effective demarcation of authority. There was no cabinet and no prime minister; the tsar chose ministers and conferred authority upon them. Perhaps for this reason there were very few outstanding ministers. The whole system was admittedly unsatisfactory, but there was no evident alternative.

DUALITY: SOCIETY

In Russian society, the division between élite and masses was compounded and complicated by the division between the ignorant peasants and the half-Westernized aristocrats for whom home was usually the city even though wealth was drawn from a country estate. This separation, which became marked under Peter, deepened through the eighteenth and into the nineteenth century. The élite dressed like West Europeans (although some, such as clergy and merchants, kept the traditional robes for many generations), built Western-style houses, and decorated them with French furniture and Italian statuettes. They sported titles such as "baron" or "count," or designations borrowed from the German by Peter for his ranks, such as "Staatsrath" and "Geheimrath." In the eighteenth century, proper people spoke French, the distinctive mark setting off people of consequence; and the aristocracy remained predominantly French-speaking until

Russian nationalism began rising in the latter nineteenth century. When they reverted to the Russian language, they flooded it with foreign words; Russian was and is exceptionally receptive to borrowings. In the eighteenth century—to some extent through the nineteenth—Russian journals ran mostly translated material. Russian novelists, with few exceptions, imitated or even plagiarized Western, especially French, literature.

There developed a gap of several centuries between the serf-owner and the serfs whom he misused; and the gap only grew with passing generations, since the élite was drawn into the stream of rapidly evolving civilization faster than the peasants could follow. Education was prerequisite for status in state service—a university degree automatically conferred the lowest rank—but education, despite the best intentions of the government, had to alienate Russians from native traditions in order to be useful. As the educated took on more (imported) humanitarian values, they were struck by the injustice of their position and their separation from the large majority of the people, whom they in compensation idealized. But when young idealists tried to reach out to bridge the gap, they met only distrust. The novelist Turgenev sketched the difference of mentality as follows: a man with white hands claims to be one of the people on the ground that he was chained for six years because "I worked for your good; tried to set free the oppressed and ignorant; stirred folks up against your oppressors, resisted the authorities. . . . So they locked me up." *Workman:* "Locked you up did they? Serves you right for resisting." [13]

But the Westernization of the élite and the educated was superficial. The Orthodox Church and much of the bureaucracy were xenophobic in mentality, and the most Westernized of the intelligentsia remained impregnated with Russian mentality. They could not cease to be loyal to basic Russian values without renouncing their own personalities. Yet Western culture was an essential part of the Russian being. Russia stood uncertainly somewhere between those countries for which Western civilization was entirely extraneous and those which shared in its secular development, and Russian thinking was thereby partly stimulated but the more tormented and confused.

3

A Century of Strains

From the days when rulers of Moscow first gained the special favor of the khans until after the defeat of Napoleon, Russia's career was an almost uninterrupted victory march. Even the losses of the Time of Troubles, when the Muscovite state seemed in mortal danger, were quickly made up. It was a success story almost without historical parallel, the more remarkable as Russia never had a great conqueror, or even many outstanding military leaders; the victories were primarily political. The Russian synthesis of opposites was phenomenally successful.

But after the great victories and huge territorial acquisitions of Catherine II, signs of decay became perceptible. There appeared the first twinges of the ideological indigestion that was to develop into cramps in the nineteenth century. The problem was evident as early as the time of Ivan the Terrible: "Innovations in the world of ideas and belief were feared, even as the material aspects of life were borrowed willingly"; [1] and some of the young men whom Peter sent abroad came back with improper ideas. But the problem was not yet serious, and Peter could import Western ways indiscriminately with few qualms. By the latter part of the eighteenth century this had changed. Russia was more urbanized; the population of the cities quadrupled in the century. Compulsory education for the children of gentry having been introduced in 1736, there had grown up a small educated class interested in ideas and literature and aware of its importance to the autocrat, who was no longer so fully an autonomous personal despot. The control of opinion became a problem. Critical political thinking was coming to life in discussions of such writers as Voltaire, Diderot, and Rousseau. A "repentant nobleman," Alexander Radishchev, enraged Catherine by writing feelingly of the injustices of serfdom and so became the first intellectual to be repressed for taking Western ideals too seriously. Freemasonry, introduced into Russia in the 1770's, became important, enrolling perhaps as many as a third of the bureaucrats until Catherine partially suppressed it.[2] She felt compelled to check Westernization by the measures of censorship previously mentioned; and her successor, Paul, went further in trying to control printing. He also recalled students from abroad and prohibited French fashions.

In the liberal beginning of his reign, Alexander I withdrew the harsher measures of his predecessors, but as he retreated from liberalism pressures accumulated. The result was the Decembrist revolt of 1825, an overt challenge to the autocracy in the name of Western principles, a movement to change not merely the leadership but the character of the state. A group of younger, French-infected officers tried to use the occasion of the succession of Nicholas instead of his older brother Constantine to demand a constitutional monarchy or possibly a republic. The attempted coup was the work of few rather confused men with different ideas; the ordinary soldiers simply did not understand what a constitution was. The regime did not take it very seriously; only five conspirators were hanged and a hundred-odd otherwise punished. However, Nicholas spent his reign combating dissent, drawing something of an iron curtain around Russia. This was in effect a confession of weakness; the Russian government no longer felt able to cope with large-scale Western contacts.

Nicholas' extreme remedy was effective in checking domestic dissent. But, unhappily for Russia, Europe was modernizing and growing economically at a quickening pace as the industrial revolution spread from England to the Continent; and the price of Russian isolation was stagnation and backwardness. The post-Crimean reforms which sought to patch up the system, somehow to make it viable even while maintaining the autocratic essence, were inevitably corrosive of the old order. Emancipation further weakened and demoralized the gentry, the class upon which the regime ostensibly rested. The old extended family of serfdom began breaking up. Despite lack of funds and autonomy, the zemstvos and municipal governments were able to play a growing role in the making of public opinion because they were the only representative organs trained in political action; and they became the focus of activities of many talented persons. It was not without reason that conservative bureaucrats regarded the local bodies with almost paranoid distrust. The courts, although restricted, continued to educate in the rule of law and to develop a professional class of lawyers and judges.

Industrialization, obviously necessary, was increasingly making the autocratic system anachronistic. Thanks largely to Peter's efforts, Russia built up a very respectable industry in the first part of the eighteenth century. Thereafter, chiefly in the first half of the nineteenth, it lost ground. However, in the liberal atmosphere after the Crimean War there was an upsurge of private capitalism, and the 1880's and 1890's saw a successful industrialization program under the leadership of a gifted minister, Count Sergei Witte. He hoped by industrialization to strengthen the state not only against foreign foes in an age of rapid improvements of weaponry and military accessories but also against domestic opposition; the latter endeavor could succeed only temporarily at best. Both heavy and light industry and trade expanded and became less fully dependent on and controlled by the state than in earlier times. Despite bureaucratic harassment, manufacturing tripled from 1877 to 1897.[3]

Economic growth produced the beginnings of an industrial society in the modern sense, turning peasants into rootless city workers, destroying traditional craft production, and swelling the small but growing "liberal" classes, that is, those not dependent upon official position but more self-reliant, receptive to new ideas, and prone to resist interference by the state and expansion abroad. Foreign investment and foreign trade grew to the detriment of the old image of the imperial state. Foreign capital imports for the years 1851 to 1894 totaled 91,250,000 rubles; after 1897, they ran close to 100,000,000 yearly.[4] Russia became an active member of the world trading system with a share of global exchanges several times larger than that of the Soviet Union in recent years. Alexander III was restrained in his reactionary measures by concern for Russian credit standing. More and more people had reasons and means for foreign travel, which although never entirely unrestricted became rather easy. Demand for consumer goods and luxuries grew; industry could not be limited, as earlier, to filling the requirements of the state, but was called upon to serve a growing market economy.

These and other erosions of the imperial-authoritarian way would doubtless have been manageable if the regime had had more self-confidence to impose its will ruthlessly, to explain and legitimize arbitrary power. But allegiance to the autocrat, never sufficient of itself, was becoming a feeble bond and inspiration in the industrial age, the less effective as the later Romanovs were uninspiring. This was probably not, or not merely, an accident of characters but a result of the fact that their rule no longer evoked charisma. Becoming more subject to public opinion, they behaved more discreetly than tsars of earlier centuries. Alexander III (1881 to 1894) particularly felt it necessary to give an example of sobriety in contrast to the license of his forebears. No later tsar had a potential for reform like that not only of Peter but of Alexander I and Alexander II. No one was tempted to label any one of them great; and they seemed, from Alexander I onward, to become part of the bureaucratic machine, successively making less of an imprint on the land despite the supposed fullness of their powers.

The decay of Orthodoxy was more marked. Close association with the state would not have been fatal if men had believed in church and state. But as belief both in the right of the state and in the sacred faith diminished, the Church appeared to be a mere instrument of self-serving power. Religion came to seem a sterile formality, with priests performing hackneyed services for money. Religious feeling shriveled; in 1890 there were 137 priests per 100,000 population, compared to 781 in 1738, and the numbers of churches, monasteries, and monks shrank proportionately.[5] Most of the educated of the latter half of the century became atheists, not for intellectual but for political reasons. Even the seminaries turned out anticlericals and revolutionaries. The Church was exaggeratedly conservative when new problems demanded new approaches; it was totally unable to respond to the needs of the dawning industrial age.

Consequently, the regime, although willing enough to propagandize, lacked credible doctrines. It could not direct writers in its support, and censorship was largely unsuccessful because the censors had only negative criteria and lacked conviction. The power of an expanding educational system could not be turned to bolster the system (as has been done in the Soviet Union), for lack of ideological content. For the conservatives, the only acceptable schools were the Church schools, and there was a rather desperate effort to overcome the ill effects of secular education by multiplying parish schools, whose numbers increased from 109,000 in 1880 to nearly 2 million in 1905. But they taught little more than reading, hymns, and the catechism, and the movement remained lifeless.[6]

Aside from totally unconvincing emphasis on the outmoded autocracy and the sterile Church, the conservatives could only be negative, damning rationalism, Western "decadence," perhaps industrialization, and anything suggestive of a constitution or limitation of the autocracy. The zemstvos, even when modified to be wholly controlled by the nobility, were anathema as symbols of local strength; the idea of a consultative assembly evoked horror, lest it lead to more change. The inherent weakness of the conservative stance appeared in the fear of any reform, a fear which grew as the need grew because concessions would open the way to new demands. Typical of the conservatives' defensive self-contradiction was the outlook of Constantine Pobedonostsev, chief counselor for two tsars and spokesman of Orthodoxy. A man entirely imbued with Western culture and a passionate admirer of it, he utterly rejected its premises for Russia, damning parliamentary government in Western terms. He saw men as inherently bad and in need of guidance to check inborn impulses, but he could offer little more than blinders. Totally committed to the old regime, he believed that the Russian state must collapse because of its hollowness.[7]

CONFUSED INTELLIGENTSIA

The Russian intelligentsia of the nineteenth century was a phenomenon of cultural sociology which acquired historical importance because of the Bolshevik Revolution. The frequently immature and unevenly educated intellectuals were more given to passion than reason and much more impressed with their unhappiness than with the need for factual analysis. Despite occasional brilliance, they would merit only a footnote if history had taken a different course. Yet their intellectual indigestion was a symptom of the sickness of the empire, and it pointed the way toward the Leninist refashioning of it.

The nineteenth-century Russian intellectual was the product of a situation in which a culturally progressive minority chafed under a backward authoritarian regime. As in prerevolutionary France, demoralized aristocrats dallied with radical philosophy and idealized the supposed purity of common man. The ambivalence of the Russian intelligentsia also has its counterpart in that of the intellectuals of many less developed countries today, torn between the desire to follow the ways of the more advanced civilization and basic loyalty to a state to which they belong but in which they do not participate. An educated class was needed for modernization; but to educate, except in the narrowest technical sense, was to alienate from Russian society. Some failed to find suitable employment; some were forced into extremism because they were politically disqualified for careers; many more simply felt morally lost. As Peter Chaadaev put it, "At home we are as if aliens, in the cities we look like nomads." [8] Spoiled for the traditional Russian values and rewards, they became "superfluous people," isolated between a hostile and backward government and the impenetrable masses.

Frustrated and embittered as they were, the intellectuals kept the basic mentality of the imperial state. They looked not to rights or freedom in a traditional sense but to better use of the absolute power or a sublimated empire. They wanted a good tsar to realize their utopian goals of equality, a dictatorship to construct the perfect state; no other way was conceivable. The revolutionaries, convinced of their own superior knowledge, became élitist after learning from experience that the people would not follow them; the enlightened few must take charge. They could hardly be democrats, however they idealized the people, because the people were uncomprehending. They were collectivist and authoritarian; for example, Paul Pestel, the republican among the Decembrists, wanted to have a secret political police and would prohibit private societies in his new order. The hatred of the intelligentsia was not usually for the autocrat, but for the bureaucrats who misused his power. Only late in the nineteenth century did they turn against tsarism in principle.

The thinking of the intelligentsia was absolutist also in an abstract sense. Demanding freedom for themselves, they were dogmatic and intolerant. Claiming to be modern and scientific in outlook, they remained pseudoscientific or mystical in their concepts. They wanted revolution, not reform. Reformers were regarded as deceitful, and "compromise" was a slur. Unable to achieve anything in practice, they had no sense of practicality. Able to express themselves freely only in clandestine sheets (like Soviet *Samizdat*) and exile journals, they stewed in indignation and indulged in extremist daydreams, although they would have been insulted to be called "idealists." They questioned everything except their own moralistic assumptions. Some advocated free love; Peter Tkachev (himself approaching twenty) proposed the killing of all over age twenty-five because he thought them hindrances for the splendid future. Perhaps older people would be unwilling to surrender all "kindred, intimate, or amorous relations" for the cause, as Tkachev demanded.[9] The supposedly scientific thinkers were anti-empirical, determined to see the world picture in simplistic ideological rather than factual terms; they bickered endlessly over theory, to which all else should be subordinated. They wanted an algorithm to transmute misery into bliss.

The intellectuals fully shared the ambivalence of their state toward the West, hating and fearing its threat to the Russian way while admiring if not loving it.* Suffering the disparity between borrowed culture and political backwardness, they wished Western progress and freedoms within the Russian framework. Eagerly deriving nearly all their ideas from the West, they saw it as perverted. Basically envious of its achievements, they believed it irrationally hostile to Russia. They could not accept that great Russia had no nobler destiny than to follow in the wake of the nations of Europe. If the West happened to be ahead, this was attributed to Russia's having borne the onslaught of the nomads.[10] The empire could only be sublimely grand; it lagged in some ways, but they saw it as incalculably better in a way which cannot be disproved: in moral virtues. As early as the time of Peter, some Russians were stressing their moral superiority in compensation for the better crafts of the West.[11]

If the West was materially better off, it must be more depraved. The urge to compensate obvious Western material superiority led to exaggerations: "bourgeois" society was seen as governed by calculated avarice and self-seeking, Russian society by collectivism; Russia was more democratic because in the West the lower classes were denied the franchise, in Russia they enjoyed the equality of peasant com-

* Those who, like Chaadaev and Turgenev, viewed Russian relations quite realistically, were a small minority. Most seemed practically to suffer psychological trauma induced by the dissonance between self-expectations raised by the ostensible grandeur of the country plus their cultural leadership in it and the obvious backwardness of Russia plus their own impotence, with consequent frustration, rage, and resentment against the West, which they felt compelled to imitate and admire.

munal institutions and were supposedly represented by the omnipotent tsar. Russian publicists saw more poverty and hypocrisy in the West than in impoverished and disingenuous Russia. They despised the "bourgeois" virtues of industry, thrift, honesty, and moderation as a reproach if not a threat to Russia. They saw the divisions and disorders of the West as proof of decadence and elaborated on the decline of Europe at the very time it was progressing technically, politically, and economically as never before, bringing unprecedented freedom and affluence to ever more people. It was the Western states, not Russia, which were allegedly based on force and violence, whereas Russia corresponded to the will of the people; as the Slavophile Ivan Aksakov had it, "Our history does not possess, therefore, that fundamental fact which characterizes the political life of Western Europe, the antagonism between the people and a power imposed by conquest. That antagonism, however, is the very foundation of Western constitutionalism." [12]

Conceding the technical advancement of the West, they saw freedom as disorder and held that Russia was better able to organize society and bring harmony to the world. As Vladimir Odoevsky, an early Slavophile, wrote, "There will be a Russian conquest of Europe, but it will be a spiritual one; for only Russia will be able to unite and give integrity to the chaos of European knowledge. . . ." [13] For Dostoevsky, Russia was to be the motherland of all progressive peoples.[14] Europe, he thought, was afraid not of Russian power but of the Russian moral message. In their own helplessness and in the increasing feebleness of their state, numerous intellectuals, like the exiled rebel Herzen, felt called upon to regenerate mankind. The intellectuals were trying to save the Russian world mission in the latter part of the nineteenth century at the same time that the government was giving it up.

To find a basis for Russian superiority, which was not evident in the generally disliked government, the intellectuals looked to Russia's great shortcomings and idealized them into assets. Poverty became virtuous absence of commercialism (somewhat later, in Marxist eyes, it was seen as the virtuous condition of being exploited by mostly foreign capitalists). Ignorance was freshness and simplicity. Backwardness meant that Russia was young and pure, hence suffused with promise for the future. Russia was a construction only begun and therefore certain to be infinitely improved, or it was happily ripe for millennial revolution, and vaguely defined revolution became the religion of many. It was urged that Russia, maturing late, could bypass the bad, capitalistic road taken by the West and avoid its moral breakdown by leaping to socialism; this was a recurrent theme of such men as Herzen and Nicholas Chernyshevsky, later taken up by Trotsky and Lenin. Communal landholding should facilitate the introduction of mechanized agriculture, much as Russian collectivism in general should make it possible to leap straight into the blessings of socialism.

Socialism was the infatuation of the latter half of the nineteenth century, the common ground of Westernizers and Slavophiles, Populists and Marxists. It accorded with the idealization of the common people, who should rescue Russia from the morass into which the upper classes had led it. It also fitted well with the popular dislike of merchants and the bourgeoisie, many of whom were foreign or non-Russian. The name of a vaguely defined order in which wrongs should be righted, men made equal, and the collectivity exalted, socialism could be equated with a perfected autocracy. Yet it was a Western word bespeaking an ideal of justice held by many thinkers from Saint-Simon and Robert Owen to Marx and beyond.

Hence socialism admirably solved the intellectuals' dilemma. They could use a Western idea to criticize the West in their cherished terms of falsity and materialism and to advance at home a basically authoritarian, anti-Western program. Russia had to follow the Western lead; but the advocacy of socialism might enable it to skip over capitalism, use the advantages of backwardness, and come out politically and socially more advanced than the West. This vision was enthralling, as most intellectuals were repelled not only by industrial civilization in the West but by what they saw of it developing at home; as usual in early stages of industrialization, it was crude, uneven, often exploitative, and disruptive of native ways and values, especially the prized peasant communal organization. It was also foreign-dominated and politically vulnerable. Socialism seemed the best, perhaps the only hope of preserving the true Russian, that is, basically imperial, values.

Among the several usually ill-defined movements, the Slavophiles most cherished the old peasant institutions of commune and cooperative as a Russian claim to superiority and means to unity, harmony, and strength with justice, that is, to socialism. Idealizing Russia and its ancient institutions and looking to salvation through a moralized autocracy and a revitalized Orthodoxy, they detested the West as corruption; St. Petersburg was hated as a symbol of what had gone wrong. They saw autocracy as proof of Russian humility and virtue. They indignantly denied that serfdom was anything like slavery, a vice of inferior lands.[15] Taking their ideas not from a study of national life but from foreign writers, they discovered wondrous virtues in peasants who led an almost animal and largely amoral existence given to violence and vodka; and they exalted as pristine freedom and equality the commune created by the rulers, beginning with the Tatars, to facilitate tax collection. But the idea of modernizing and "socializing" agriculture in peasant collectivism, like that of industrialization by the state, had a great future in a more authoritarian Russia.

In exalting the peculiar virtues of the Slavs, with their superior morality and ways, the Slavophiles also represented a compromise between Russian universalism and Western nationalism. Slavs, including Poles, Ukrainians, Belorussians, and Russians, represented over three quarters of the population of the empire. Borrowing from the romantic nationalism of Johann Gottfried von Herder and others, patriotic Russian intellectuals saw the Slavic peoples as peculiarly gifted, the possessors of Orthodoxy (except for the Poles) and bearers of a glorious destiny as a supernation.

Slavophilism ripened in the latter decades of the nineteenth century into Pan-Slavism, less preoccupied with Orthodoxy and peasantism at home and more dedicated to extending the Russian mantle over Slavs abroad, especially in the Balkans. Never officially espoused (although sometimes encouraged by the government), Pan-Slavism became for some of the intellectuals practically a religion. As Danilevsky put it, "For every Slav . . . the ideal of Slavdom must be the highest ideal, higher than any earthly good. . . ." [16] The category of Slav was happily extensible; at times it included not only speakers of Slavic languages (who are racially rather diverse) but Greeks, Rumanians, or Albanians. Pan-Slavism came to its height in the Russo-Turkish War of 1877 to 1878, when Russian victories promised fulfillment of the fondest hopes, and it subsided as these hopes were thwarted by the Western powers.

NATIONALISM

After this disappointment, Pan-Slavism became more explicitly Pan-Russianism, and the most dangerous of Western poisons began seriously to undermine the health of the empire. Liberal political ideas were troublesome, but civil rights were complicated and democracy was unrealistic and might be pretended. Nationality, on the other hand, was understandable and undeniable; the simplest Georgian or Ukrainian could believe that Georgians and Ukrainians were different from Russians and had different interests. For the West, nationalism was a useful principle of legitimation and integration of the nation-state; for Russia, as for the Austro-Hungarian empire, it meant disintegration and death.[17]

The empire was international in inception, over half of the nobility in the seventeenth century being of foreign origin.[18] To be Russian was of no particular importance at the court of Catherine or Alexander I; to many it must have seemed a handicap, since the ruler surrounded himself with foreigners. There were hardly any Russians among Alexander's generals, and only one in his corps of advisers at Vienna. Nicholas I, although the glorification of Russian national culture took shape in his reign, was pleased to advance Balts, Finns, Poles, Caucasians, in his service. But in the French Revolution and ensuing wars, fires of nationalism were fanned as nations sought to mobilize their populations. The post-Napoleonic settlement dampened but did not extinguish these fires; and especially after the revolutionary wave of 1848 nationalism became not only the solidifier of the old nations of the West but the inspiration and awakener of peoples of Central and Eastern Europe, such as Czechs and Rumanians, who had hardly dreamed of nationhood and an independent destiny. With modernization and the expansion of educated classes, Russia could not escape a growing sense of national awareness. The old ideology was turning stale; it was inescapable that the empire should be felt more and more as a Russian achievement and possession; the tsar was called upon to be more a Russian monarch, less a father of all the peoples. The Slavophiles began looking askance at non-Slavs in the empire. Russian literature burst out of its imitative immaturity with great poets, such as Pushkin and Lermontov, and famous novelists, such as Gogol, Dostoevsky, Turgenev, and Tolstoy. Russians turned from shame in their language to high pride in it; the aristocracy ceased to be French-speaking.

Concurrently Russia was behaving more like a nation among nations on the international stage. The effort to suppress dangerous movements abroad was given up after the Crimean defeat, and in 1878 Russia gave liberated Bulgaria a liberal constitution for diplomatic reasons. Rivalries in the Balkans led to friction with Austria-Hungary and its patron, Germany, although for Russians these were ideologically the most congenial of the powers, and to alignment with France, ideologically the most antipathetic of major European nations. A sign of the new age of nationalism could be read in the rising of Alexander III, in July, 1891, to the playing of the "Marseillaise" for a visiting French squadron, at a time when this revolutionary anthem was forbidden in Russia. Russia was half prepared to regard itself as simply a member of the balance of power—a concept abhorrent to the imperial-absolutist mentality.

To maintain competitive strength in the world and to combat rising domestic unrest, it was probably indispensable to cultivate Russian patriotism. But as Russians came to feel that the empire was theirs they naturally expected to benefit thereby. It became disadvantageous to be a non-Russian, politically, psychologically, socially, to some extent economically. Russians felt better entitled to positions in the apparatus and so to chances of power and influence; the government preferentially advanced them because their loyalty was better assured. It was no longer sufficient to be Orthodox and outwardly loyal.

Yet the empire depended (and depends) upon the minimizing of national consciousness. Russianism stimulated minority nationalism and was in turn stimulated by it. The Polish rebellion of 1863 led to a Russifying and conservative reaction, and this was much intensified after the Russo-Turkish War of 1877 to 1878 and the Congress of Berlin, wherein the powers forced Russia to disgorge much of its gains. It became official policy to make non-Russians into Russians, especially by education. More efforts were also made to spread the official faith. Such traditional local rights as remained were chipped away, and increasing centralization placed minority peoples under closer control. The army became a means of Russification as military service was made uniform for the whole empire. But so trying were the inefficiency and lack of credibility of the regime that efforts to make all alike only irritated the peoples against whom they were directed.

The minorities, who totaled well over half the total population, presented various problems. The most serious was with Poland, a solid nation of exceptionally proud tradition. Although joined to Russia only by the Russian tsar's kingship of Poland and favored with a liberal constitution (which was soon violated), the Poles were never satisfied to stand under the Russian eagle. The rebellions of 1830 and

1863, veritable wars, cost the Poles their special rights and convinced
the Russians that Poland had to be held by force. It was simply incorporated into the empire, to be made Russian by decree. The Polish
language was outlawed in schools in 1892. But zemstvos were kept
out of Poland (as out of other ethnically non-Russian areas); it was
possible to treat it neither as a part of Russia nor as a separate entity.
Industrial development, for which the Russian market was vital, tended
to reconcile some Poles to the connection; and hope for national
independence faded in the last decades of the nineteenth century. But
Poles continued to uphold their national identity and whatever they
could of cultural and political rights. Some Russians stated frankly
that Poland should be made to pay like a colony.[19]

The largest minority, the Ukrainians, were less hostile in principle
to Russian hegemony; Ukrainian nationalism was not visible during the
eighteenth century. But the cultivation of Ukrainianism began as early
as the 1820's, when writers began collecting folklore, recording peasant
culture and developing a literary language from the dialects. In 1846
a group of Ukrainian intellectuals led by the national poet, Taras
Shevchenko, demanded federal status for their country. The government answered with severe repressions, but the call for Ukrainian autonomy was not silenced. After the Polish uprising of 1863, printing
in Ukrainian was practically banned in order to choke the flourishing
Ukrainian literature; the decree was accompanied by the inconsistent
comment that there was no Ukrainian language. Much of the Ukrainian
national movement was transferred to the freer Ukrainian territories
under Austrian sovereignty. In 1900 a revolutionary Ukrainian party
began agitating for independence.

Most other minorities were too backward, too small, or too scattered to trouble the empire much. Little effort was made to Russify
Muslim peoples. But discontent was probably growing everywhere as
the non-Russian peoples saw themselves reduced in their autonomy,
excluded from office, subjected to linguistic Russification, and treated
as second-class subjects; and dissatisfaction brought reassertion of national cultures and feelings.

An immediate consequence dangerous to the empire was the partial
coalescence of minority separatist and Russian antiregime movements.
It was even easier for spokesmen of most of the minorities than for
Russians to be anticapitalist and socialist, because industry was poorly
developed in their territories (Poland being the chief exception); they,

like Russian reformers, were pro-peasant in lands more purely peasant than ethnic Russia. They were eager for popular rights, which should bring justice to them also. Hence opposition parties were especially strong in minority areas. Although fearful of threats to the unity of the empire, even moderate Russian reformers saw an ally for their cause in the minority pressure for autonomy. On the other hand, the radical parties drew strongest support from minority nationals, such as Poles, Balts, and the much discriminated-against Jews. In 1906, the Social Democratic (Marxist) party reportedly had 31,000 Russian members, 30,000 Jewish, 26,000 Polish, and 11,000 Latvian, not to speak of numerous other nationalities.[20]

THE LAST YEARS

Witte sanely concluded that Russia would be better off without alien peoples,[21] but the tsarist regime in 1904 thought to resuscitate the ailing empire by acquiring Korea and Manchuria. The expected victory parade turned into the most inglorious defeats at the hands of the newly Westernized Japanese. The inadequacy of the proud autocracy was all too evident. Opposition to the discredited government rose on all sides; censorship and police controls broke down. Unofficial groups became articulate for the first time in Russian history. All manner of organizations sprang up, from workingmen's unions and intellectual clubs to bankers' leagues; and all demanded change.

The government became so fearful that the tsar was persuaded, against his convictions, to compromise autocracy. By the Manifesto of October, 1905, he gave Russia a semiconstitution, with the promise of an elected legislative assembly or Duma. This sufficed for many moderates, who withdrew their opposition; and the revolutionary movement, deprived of upper-class support, gradually ebbed. The army had not been badly hurt, and the government could count on the soldiers for protection against both urban crowds and rampaging peasants. In a year, the government had restored its authority. When the elected assembly, the Duma, met, it ran head-on into the refusal of the regime to surrender any substantial powers; both sides were intransigent.[22] The Duma was dissolved in July, 1906, without serious protest; the demand for a constitution was a passing fever. The Second Duma met a similar fate. A new electoral law was then illegally promulgated, rigging the already highly unequal franchise so as to practically disenfranchise ordinary people and the minorities and to assure control of the assembly by the gentry and the government. This produced a conservative-dominated Duma which quietly lived out its full five-year term. Repressions were resumed, and the rights, such as freedom of political organization, which had been recognized by the October Manifesto were restricted in practice.

The regime thereby surmounted its crisis, and things seemed much as before except for more Western veneer on the autocratic state. But autocracy was not fully restored. The personal role of the autocrat had been weakened by the establishment of a prime ministership. The Duma, although unrepresentative and lacking substantial powers, provided a forum for public opinion, where even radical parties like Lenin's Bolsheviks had a chance to present their views while trying to discredit it. It gave many persons an education in parliamentary practice and a taste for it; no longer was the Russian notion of constitutional government purely theoretical. The zemstvos had gained importance by sponsoring many improvements neglected by the central government—schools, hospitals, agricultural insurance, banks for peasants, agricultural extension, and the like—all of which were resisted by the bureaucracy, which considered local initiative corrosive of the old order. The idea of law distinct from the will of the sovereign acquired more meaning. The courts acted with genuine independence. Liberties were not entirely withdrawn. Religious toleration was accepted. Despite some censorship, a considerable variety of opinion, much of it critical, was published. Nicholas was not able to check a bitter press campaign against the court favorite, Rasputin, the "Man of God." *Pravda* appeared in St. Petersburg in 1912 with a circulation of 40,000. Difficulties of censorship were compounded by the growth of the press; the number of newspapers swelled from 125 in 1900 to 1,158 in 1913.[23] Universities had much autonomy under the government of their faculties. Despite the laws, workers gained some freedom to organize and strike. The fact that the number of strikes grew sharply up to the world war is better evidence of the increasing freedom of the workers than of the growth of revolutionary sentiments.

The opposition was gaining leadership, self-confidence, and an economic basis. Private capitalism was finally coming of age and growing out from under the government umbrella: Russia surged economically, recording the world's highest industrial growth rate. The professional classes who could not be fitted into the table of ranks—journalists, teachers, doctors, lawyers—increased rapidly with the needs of the maturing society. The country was moving steadily toward general secular education. The literacy rate of army recruits rose from 21 percent in 1875 to 73 percent in 1913.[24] In 1914 half of the school-age children were in school, and according to the Duma's projection there should be schools for all children of school age by 1920. It was taken for granted that traditional patterns in agriculture—communal village landholding with periodic redistribution and holdings scattered among dozens of strips—must go. After peasant disorders in the years 1904 to 1906 showed how unreliable the commune was, the government turned away from it under Prime Minister Peter Stolypin. Peasants were allowed to withdraw from communes and invited to form family farms, in capitalist-competitive rather than collectivist spirit—as Stolypin said, "to place the wager not on the needy or drunken but on the strong and sturdy."

Such changes were rapidly making the autocracy anachronistic, and the opposition was becoming more effective as it broadened and became more realistic. The interest of the intelligentsia in revolution and utopianism had been declining since the 1880's, and extremism faded further as political parties became legitimate vehicles of political activity and opinions could be fairly well ventilated in the press. The radical parties became divided and demoralized, and they lost membership and respectability.

In the same spirit, the feeling grew that Russia was not so much antagonistic to the West as part of it. Foreign trade more than doubled in the period 1900 to 1913. A symptom of changed outlook was the 1907 agreement with England delimiting spheres of influence in Asia. The old expansionism was by no means dead, but there was growing skepticism of its value, and Russia had for the first time set itself definite limits.

The old problems, however, remained and, beneath the surface of normality and prosperity, probably grew worse. Despite its achievements, Russian industry led something of an artificial existence, sheltered by tariffs and propped up by subsidies. It was highly inefficient and tended to lose ground in the technological race. Russia was marching forward, but the West was running still more rapidly, so that Russian per capita income was farther behind that of other major powers in 1910 than in 1860.[25] It was also more and more dependent upon foreign guidance and capital; foreign participation in Russian corporations grew from 13 percent in 1861 to 33 percent in 1913.[26] It was becoming necessary to modernize the entire economy, a difficult task for the autocracy. Foreign trade acquired more importance, as did foreign investment; communications and travel steadily increased between Russia and the West. Westernization evolved from an official program to a self-propelling, often unwelcome process.

As Western influence grew deeper, broader, and ever more uncontrollable [27] the moral basis of the autocracy shrank. Its obsolescence became evident in the age of secularism and democracy, and the government was corrupt and demoralized. The monarchy, pervaded by a sense of doom, seemed to try simply to hold back change, fearing all change as dangerous. Under the weak leadership of Nicholas II, it seems to have retreated into its glittering shell, no longer even trying to justify itself to public opinion, and had recourse to such expedients as anti-Jewish pogroms to deflect discontent.

The insoluble problem of handling the nationalities apparently could only grow. A result of the 1905 revolution was the relaxation of pressures; native languages were restored to schools in many areas, and earlier restrictions, for example, on Finnish autonomy, were removed. But constitutionalism was no solution. The elections and formation of parties brought differences of nationality to the attention of many (including Lenin) who might otherwise have given them little thought. In the Second Duma, the "autonomists" formed a league under the leadership of the Poles, and groups which had been entirely silent, such as the Estonians, raised their voices. The Russians, who had persuaded themselves that the Ukranian nationality did not exist, were shocked by a strong Ukrainian call for autonomy. The idea that the Poles might fall away was conceivable, but Ukrainian separatism was an unthinkable threat to the body of the empire. It was consequently deemed necessary to dissolve the Duma [28] and to revise the electoral law so as practically to eliminate Ukrainian as well as Polish representation. Constitutionalism made it necessary to treat the minorities as frankly second-class. In the Third Duma, although they comprised a substantial majority of the population, they had only 39 of 442 seats.

Despite practical exclusion from the Duma, the minorities used the relative freedom of expression after 1905 to organize and develop their cultures and national awareness. They also used the platform of the Duma to state their case. In 1911, the Ukrainians, Poles, Belorussians, Jews, Latvians, Estonians, Buriats, Kalmucks, and Yakuts called for use of the national language in the schools. But the minister of education added thirty-six more nationalities to the list to ridicule it,[29] and he was supported by the Russian majority in the Duma. The minorities received no more sympathy from the Russian assembly than from the tsarist government.

The government showed its temper by fierce and bloody repressions in minority areas in 1906, and it rejected any concessions as likely to lead to stronger demands for autonomy or independence. Prime Minister Stolypin took a Russian nationalistic position to secure support for his government from the Russians, whose outlook was increasingly chauvinistic. In 1912 Prime Minister Vladimir Kokovtsov made a characteristic declaration: to merit favor, nationalities should "recognize Russia as their fatherland . . . and consider their welfare and even their very being to lie in unity with the great Russian nationality." [30] Vexations grew over the old questions of language policy and local management of administration, and whether Russians or natives were to be named to positions—questions which continue to plague the Soviet Union.

The Russian empire thus faced an unbearable dilemma; it could evidently neither continue as an autocracy nor become a democracy. There was no evident middle way to satisfy the desires of the Russian people and the minorities for more freedom without giving freedom to break up the Russian-dominated system. It is not impossible that the liberals or moderates, those of more Western and modern outlook, could have developed some sort of federal relations that would have saved unity while conceding self-rule. This would have meant solving the dilemma of the empire by ending its imperial character and the advantages accruing to the dominant people. But the liberals foundered on this question; it seemed that they would have to betray their ideals of freedom or propose the dissolution of the empire. Moreover, there was no means for the autocratic system, dedicated to self-preservation, to reform itself; and liberals had no idea how the obscurantist governors could be persuaded to sacrifice their own power. Perhaps the regime was destined to fumble along growing gradually weaker until a shock permitted a new integration, the depth of the resultant reorientation corresponding roughly to the severity of the breakdown of the traditional order.

4

The Leninist Resynthesis

FAILURE OF THE LIBERALS

The experience of 1905 demonstrated the frailty of the tsarist regime and the ease with which loyalty could be withdrawn when it faltered. Some persons appreciated this lesson, for there were numerous warnings in 1914, mostly from conservatives, that war might be disastrous for the dynasty. Yet nationalism made it seem necessary to come to the aid of Serbia against Austria; and the government, having lost face in the crisis over the Austrian annexation of Bosnia-Herzegovina two years earlier, felt it could not bear another humiliation. There was also hope of reinforcing the empire by expansion in the Balkans, particularly by gaining mastery of Constantinople and the Straits; and the irritation of Ukrainian nationalism based in Austrian Galicia made it seem urgent to acquire that territory. The regime hesitated but decided to gamble its existence in a trial of arms for which it was not prepared.

It is usual for defeated governments to be overthrown; it is less to be expected that a country which has suffered setbacks but is far from total defeat and which has powerful allies in the field should reject its rulership, not changing horses in midstream but casting away the old horse. In the beginning of 1917 Germany had inflicted painful losses on the Russian armies, but there was no manpower shortage. The Russian forces had been pushed back along most of the front, but the Germans had not penetrated deep into Russia, indeed had not entered ethnic Russia at all. Yet so shallow had become loyalty to the autocrat of all the Russias that mobs rioted in Petrograd over minor food shortages (immeasurably less severe than the famine to come in Bolshevik times), troops refused to restore order, and the generals called upon the tsar to abdicate, with little thought of who or what should take his place. They were not prepared to take power themselves or to establish any institution to carry on the government and the war; they apparently assumed that the autocrat, once exalted as the source of all good, was the source of all troubles, and that all would be remedied if he were set aside.

If Nicholas had not been weak and subject to the influence of a neurotic and foolish wife, he would not have been removed so lightly; if he had had a capable heir, the monarchy might have been preserved at least for a time. But for many years the court had been showing itself more and more unrealistic and detached from the currents and opinion of the country, extremely fearful of popular forces and desperate to sustain its untenable theory of government. Nicholas was even anxious to do away with the semiconstitution he had been driven to accord in 1905; he lacked the strength to live comfortably with a little façade of modern government. The incompetence and unrealism of the supreme rulership indicated that the chief requirement for regeneration of the country should be its removal.

It was correctly assumed by all that the departure of the Romanovs meant the dawning of a new era of Russian history, but incorrectly that Russia was to become like the free and progressive countries of the West. Constitutional government would have been difficult in Russia under the best of circumstances; under the worst of circumstances,[1] it was impossible. The years of war had effected a profound de-Westernization of Russia. The economy was battered by shortages and inflation, compounded by the extreme inefficiency of the government; the business classes were discredited both by profiteering and the inability of industry to supply the armies. Not only the autocrat but the whole structure of rulership became odious. Russia was at the same time largely isolated from the commerce and influences essential to its modernization. The allies, England and France, were far away and cut off by the Central Powers' blockade of the Baltic and Black Sea. Shipments and travelers, who were few in war, had to go by the submarine-infested Arctic route or across Siberia and the Pacific. Germany had been by far the largest trade partner of Russia (accounting for a third of exchanges) and the most powerful and immediate Western influence. Hatred of the Germans was not far from hatred of foreigners (the peasants called foreigners in general *nemtsy,* or "Germans"), and the sentiment extended to the more or less Russified Germans at court. Combined with disillusionment in the Western Allies, who seemed to offer little help while calling upon the hard-pressed Russians to shed their blood, it made for a reversion to elemental Russianism.

Nonetheless, in the days after the tsar abdicated and his cautious brother declined the shaky throne, it was assumed that Western ways were generally applicable, that Russia could only continue on the road of previous decades toward becoming a state like those of the West. A group of Duma leaders of generally pro-Western and democratic orientation formed a new government of sorts. But the liberals got off to a poor start. They weakly permitted the dissolution of the Duma, which was the only good link of continuity with the old regime. They modestly called themselves a Provisional Government, declining to claim the legitimacy that was desperately needed to rule Russia. In the name of liberty, they proceeded to dismantle much of the tsarist apparatus of control without having anything to replace it; Russia lost not only the capstone of autocracy but the pillars holding up the structure. They remained ostentatiously faithful to the Western alliance and in its name promoted a war effort that was beyond their strength.

The euphoric consensus based on release from tyranny soon began crumbling, for the somewhat idealistic Provisional Government proved no more able than the autocracy to solve the problems of Russia. The armies fought no better for free Russia than they had for the Little Father; and the officers who had derived their authority from his found themselves unable to maintain discipline. The government, torn by dissension, could not act decisively to deal with the agrarian crisis; peasants took advantage of the slackening of authority to seize land they had long considered rightfully theirs. It could not bring itself to summon quickly an elected assembly to give Russia a government that could call itself permanent; there was no agreement, perhaps no possible agreement, as to what the outlines of a new government should be. The deep tension of Russian society, between the privileged educated and the peasants and workers who lived in another century and another world, boiled to the surface. The lower classes perceived that it was no longer necessary to behave respectfully toward their former superiors, who wavered between Western democratic theory and fear of loss of status.

Behind all other problems loomed the unanswerable question of how the empire was to be democratically held together. The Provisional Government immediately abolished legal national discriminations, and it was able to concede the independence of Poland (which was to remain closely allied with Russia) because Poland was then under enemy occupation. But it could not agree with the Finns or any other people on the degree of autonomy they should have. Everywhere minorities began rediscovering themselves and forming or formulating their aspirations. A few days after the abdication of the tsar, a celebration in honor of the Ukrainian poet Shevchenko turned into a grand demonstration for Ukrainian autonomy. Ukrainian feeling snowballed as Ukrainian national military units and a shadow Ukrainian government took shape and demands grew for full independence in the face of a resisting central regime. Large concessions were made to the Estonians and Latvians, but the Lithuanians saw no reason they should not have the same independence as the Poles. One nationality followed another in asking why they had to accept Russian hegemony; and even the Cossacks, whom everyone had regarded as Russians or Ukrainians, discovered that they too were a people.

The Provisional Government, which was purely Russian, could do no better than to make concessions where unavoidable and keep up central control when and where possible, all the while postponing basic decisions. Least of all could it bear the idea of possible separation of the Ukraine. The liberal leader, Paul Miliukov, felt that ethnic-territorial autonomy was impossible because border areas would want to join foreign powers.[2] The Socialist-Revolutionaries proposed a complicated scheme for autonomy for various minorities within respective areas. The Mensheviks would allow only cultural autonomy, rejecting federalism as divisive of the socialist proletariat. The most practical solution was that of the Bolsheviks, which was to deflate and confuse the movement by offering complete formal independence while really centralizing through rule by the strongly unified party.

Unable to answer Russian aspirations, the Provisional Government watched its prestige melt away. After the failure of the July offensive, its support disintegrated and the country became chaotic. The armies were falling apart, and desertions became a torrent. Peasant disturbances and land seizures so grew as to menace what remained of the gentry. The economy was skidding downhill, with a worsening food situation, a breakdown of transportation, the government approaching bankruptcy, and rampant inflation. Liberty seemed to bring anarchy.

In the growing chaos, the front commander, Lavr Kornilov, took it upon himself to restore order by taking charge and throwing out the leftists whom conservatives were by now blaming for the unhappy conditions. He failed, but the moderate socialist prime minister, Alexander Kerensky, maintained himself only with the help of the Bolsheviks. The upper classes, who sympathized with Kornilov, turned against Kerensky; the generals were willing to let him sink to discredit socialistic tendencies. No one was satisfied with the nonachievements and indecisiveness of the government. Nearly everyone was thoroughly sick of the unsuccessful war, although only the Bolsheviks loudly promised quick peace.

From the beginning, the Provisional Government always had to share authority de facto with the Petrograd Soviet, or Council, of Workers' and Soldiers' Deputies. Although this body shrank from assuming power until the Bolsheviks gained a majority in it, the fact that it was elected and had a clear claim to representing someone gave it weight; the soldiers were not likely to follow orders of the government unless sanctioned by their Soviet. Hence it was no radical development when, three days before the date celebrated as the beginning of the Soviet state, the Petrograd garrison, troubled by rumors that it might be sent to the front, decided to accept the orders of the Bolshevik-dominated Military Revolutionary Committee and its commissars. The authority of the Provisional Government was thereby practically at an end. The Congress of Soviets, representing cities all over Russia, could probably have taken power from the failing hands of Kerensky and the "bourgeois" ministers without a fight. But Lenin called for the Red Guards to storm the Winter Palace. He sought thereby to make a clear break with the past, to wipe the slate clean, and to install a new autocracy called Dictatorship of the Proletariat.

Thus ended a confused and half-hearted effort to follow Western national political models without surrendering the multinational empire. It would have been difficult to find a compromise in a process of pacific evolution; the semibackward land afflicted by war called for a stronger order.

AUTOCRACY RESTORED

Lenin's party alone was prepared to take the place of the tsar and to provide a strong government in old Russian style with suitable refurbishing. If the anarchists stood for a modernized peasant rebellion, the Bolsheviks stood for a modernized Muscovite autocracy. A few tens of thousands of Bolshevik activists could take control of the state while tens of millions first looked on passively and then bowed in obedience, because the few were dedicated to monolithic organization and to rulership. They were, of all the Russian parties, the determined centralizers equipped by doctrine and character to govern the empire. They were the only party with a paramilitary corps, the Red Guards. Lenin had more authority over his party, strictly his creation and practically his creature, than the leader of any rival party. Like the imperial bureaucracy, his organization was hierarchic and semimilitary in command structure. Like the ruling clique, it was secretive and mutually protective.

No Russian radical party was notably democratic, but Lenin's was particularly indifferent to democratic norms. Marxism relieved the proletariat, as the virtuous class, of responsibility to the majority of the population; Lenin relieved the party, as the vanguard, of responsibility to the proletariat. He thereby solved the old dilemma of the intellectuals who wanted to be for the people, although they knew the people were against them. But if the nineteenth-century Populists had come to regard the welfare of the people as the highest goal, Lenin gave this place to political power. Well aware of the importance of the masses and determined that his party should build the closest contacts with workers and peasants, he gave much effort to methods of convincing and engaging them. But he talked of their will in order to use them and regarded them rather abstractly as a political factor. Himself of upper middle class origin, he kept personally rather aloof; he may never have stepped inside a factory.[3] The Bolshevik leadership had little contact with the workers for whom they spoke; like Ivan the Terrible, Peter, and Catherine, they treated people as instruments of the state or the cause.

To say that Bolshevism incorporated the essentials of Russian authoritarianism is equivalent to saying that it turned its back on the West, reacting against capitalism, liberalism, democracy, rationalism, freedom, and pluralism. This reaction could be successful because the trials of war, defeat, and economic breakdown brought primitivism to the fore in a partly de-Westernized Russia. The Leninists were little troubled by the inhibitions that restrained more Western-influenced parties, such as the Mensheviks, who refused to take power near their grasp because they doubted the possibility of inaugurating socialism under Russian conditions. Lenin had been politically anti-Western long before 1917, looking to anticolonial uprisings in Asia to give a start to his movement. The anti-Western reaction became popular as Russian isolation grew and revulsion against European spread; and in the civil war, the Bolsheviks affirmed themselves as defenders of true Russia against the onslaught of the capitalist Entente. The shift of the capital from Petrograd to Moscow, although dictated by military considerations, was symbolic of a reversal of two centuries of Europeanization presided over by the Baltic capital.

The political realism of the reversion is shown by the fact that it was not imposed by a single revolutionary act or put into effect as the result of a previously calculated program but developed as though organically over the entire first two decades of Soviet rule. From the date of the Revolution to late 1939, when the land was still bleeding from slaughter without precedent in peacetime, there was a steady evolution toward despotism. Sometimes faster, sometimes slower, but never long halted, the metamorphosis was from a state in which freely operating political parties were taken for granted, there was no censorship or political police, the economy was largely private, the peasants farmed as they pleased, and something of representative government was assumed as an ideal, to the opposite, wherein dissent within the monopolistic party was high treason, writers and the press were not only mercilessly censored but told what to write, the political police was a major power terrorizing nearly everyone, and industry, trade, and agriculture were all strictly controlled by a state totally at the behest of the glorified leader.

Narrowing began with the coup itself, since Lenin wanted the party, not the Congress of Soviets, to assume charge. It continued as the elected Congress of Soviets was adjourned early on November 9; "All power to the Soviets," Lenin's slogan in reaching for power, lasted little more than one day. Even most Bolsheviks, aware that they had the support of only a small minority in the country, assumed that there had to be a coalition government; Lenin successfully insisted on undiluted Bolshevik control. Censorship of the press was restored three days after the Revolution, and in a month nearly all non-Bolshevik papers had been closed; the Leninists reverted to the eighteenth-century suppression of the nonofficial press. The political police was restored and began exercising arbitrary powers, first against "class enemies," soon against all dissent. The dissolution of the Constituent Assembly in January, 1918, meant the overt rejection of democracy. Elections thereafter were a formality.

After the unpopular decision in February, 1918, to accept the peace of Brest-Litovsk, which Lenin swung with some difficulty, the outcome of open debates in the party or state was never again in doubt. In the course of the civil war, non-Bolshevik socialist parties were practically eliminated; it became dangerous to manifest loyalty to any party but the Bolshevik. Authority within the party was further concentrated. The Politburo, set up temporarily as staff for the Revolution in 1917, was brought back as a permanent party headship in 1919; and the Central Committee, where it had been customary to discuss all major decisions, expanded and lost contact with central policy making. Lenin became a new autocrat, whose word was law and whose name caused awe. He gave orders and administered justice as he saw fit, in the way of sultans and emperors. In 1921, in logical sequence to the outlawing of other parties, factions within the ruling party were banned. Purges, or reprisals against party members who somehow opposed the leader, were begun. It was made clear that the trade unions, as representatives of the workers, were to have no share of power. The Kronstadt rebels, who stood for the avowed goals of the Revolution but against the Bolshevik political monopoly, were executed as "agents of reaction."

From the time of Stalin's appointment as General Secretary (April, 1922) the political ripening of the Soviet Union is the story of the consolidation of Stalin's personal power. He slowly built his personal following, or political machine, and step by step eliminated contestants for power. First Trotsky, who had stood highest next to Lenin, then the "leftists," Lev Kamenev and Gregori Zinoviev, then the "rightists," Nikolai Bukharin, Aleksei Rykov, et al., were defeated and disgraced. By 1925, Stalin stood high enough for a major city, Tsarytsin, to be named Stalingrad. In 1927, the opposition staged a last futile public protest. In 1929, Stalin was glorified, on his fiftieth birthday, as the great genius leader, and his "cult of personality" was in full bloom.

Having practically eliminated non-Stalinists from the party, Stalin after 1929 felt strong enough to attack the remaining independent forces in the country. The peasants were driven into collective farms, wherein they were made subject to a party-appointed chairman and required to farm for the state. The old commune was in effect renewed and so strengthened as an agency of taxation that millions starved in the first years of collectivization because their crops were confiscated. Industrial production, which had become partly oriented to the marketplace, was again placed entirely under state orders as the Five-Year Plans mobilized maximum resources for heavy, potentially military industry. The considerable part of the old Church which had survived the battering of the Revolution and civil war years was practically liquidated. Writers and artists were organized officially and told what to produce. For years up to the end of 1938, and on a lesser scale thereafter, there raged a terror the like of which the world had never seen, wherein no one except the humblest and feeblest in society and the few highest immediately around Stalin could feel sure that they would not suddenly be carried away to secret trial and death or probably fatal forced labor. Even during World War II, when it was entirely unnecessary to consolidate power, terrorism continued as an expression of the fullness of authority. The prolonged nightmare burnt fear deep into the Russian psyche.

Thus, in the generation after Lenin's new model party seized power, the new party-state came to its culmination. It was as though the rulership gradually realized the potentials for authoritarianism inherent in the Russian situation. Lenin, on taking hold, could have had no notion of the possibilities of his hard-fisted government, just as Stalin could not have foreseen the extent of his purges when he began repressions and spy trials in the latter 1920's. Since it encountered little resistance and each act of arbitrary power seemed useful, the leadership moved forward step by step.

This affirmation of absolutism was possible by virtue of the ideology justifying arbitrary actions and giving the élite confidence that their exercise of power was ideally right. In the mêlée of the Revolution, the Bolsheviks were the only party eager to assume the responsibilities of leadership and confident of their title to rule; others hesitated and feared the responsibility of leadership in adversity. When the people were near despair and calling for guidance, the Bolsheviks were prepared to claim superior truth and justice; resistance to them was hence infirm, and it crumbled as the Bolsheviks pressed forward.

The self-confident and uninhibited Bolsheviks could carry out all manner of measures the tsars could not effectively execute. To check social agitation, tsarist agents tried to organize unions under police guidance, but the movement backfired and had to be given up. The Leninists turned all unions into servants of the party. The censorship that the Bolsheviks imposed was of another genus from the defensive controls of the old regime; the tsarists were somewhat hesitant in smashing their opponents, whereas the Bolsheviks combated heresy as the cardinal sin. For the same reason, police repressions were stronger and more effective; the Soviet police believed in their work, whereas tsarist authorities were a trifle apologetic to political prisoners. The relatively few political criminals of the nineteenth century were usually given better treatment than ordinary criminals; the house in which Lenin lived in exile in Siberia would represent luxury to the large majority of Soviet citizens today. The many times more numerous Soviet political prisoners have been regarded as much worse than ordinary criminals and so treated. Easygoing tsarist prisons were schools for revolution; Soviet labor camps conduct political education.

The Leninist-Stalinist state also owed much to the changes brought to Russian society. The de-Westernization occasioned by World War I was only the beginning. Isolation was much more extreme during the civil war; foreign trade was almost nil between 1918 and 1920, and the Soviet state was more or less at war with the leading Western powers. The resulting emotional reaction against traditional Western cultural and political patterns was used and fostered by the Bolsheviks, and they wove it into their ideology.

As the economy reverted to primitivism industrial production collapsed to a fifth of prewar levels and agriculture to a half. The cities were half depopulated because millions fled to the villages for food and warmth. The civil war itself was messy and confused, with many parties, much terrorism, and widespread banditry, which flourished for years after the Bolsheviks had defeated the organized opposition. Not until 1923 did recovery really get under way. For half a dozen years material survival was the main concern; the Russians were far too desperate for food and fuel to think of civil liberties. Starvation, disease, and terror reduced to a small fraction of their prewar numbers the educated classes who had formerly leavened tsarist society. Education was also practically in abeyance for the better part of a decade; not until the year 1927–28 did the number of schools return to the low level of 1920–21.[4] A generation grew up with the meagerest of learning.

Culturally, economically, and socially, Russia was pushed back many decades; in isolation and hostility to the West, it reverted practically to pre-Petrine days.

It was during the hardest years that the Bolshevik regime took shape. But political primitivism rose to its full height only after the passing of the Western-trained revolutionary leaders who had lived abroad. Then the crudity of backward Russia, the Russia of bitter, homebred men and crude careerists, unsoftened by significant exposure to Western culture, came to the fore.

Autocracy ripened slowly because there is much inertia in institutions; the Soviet state took time to evolve its methods. It was feeling its way into unknown political landscapes; there had never been a comparable regime mixing despotic and modern motifs. Later Leninist states, following the vaunted Soviet model, have moved much more rapidly to set up the full panoply of party-state absolutism.

NEW FAITH

The Leninists introduced a systematic self-justification much more thorough and purposeful than anything the tsars had attempted, a unifying and ordering compulsory belief system, an ideology in the most authoritarian sense. This was a *sine qua non* for an absolutist state under modern conditions: where there must be education and extensive communication, the people have to be given a plausible interpretation of the ordering of society; where the heretical outside cannot be physically excluded, it must be morally excluded. Lenin said correctly, "Without a revolutionary theory there can be no revolutionary movement." [5] Theory, or a coherent answer to questions of purpose, was necessary to hold the movement together and give it self-conviction to act decisively. Ideology was essential to legitimate the arbitrary regime and to enable a bunch of outsiders to claim the rights of the sacred tsars and to act with self-confident ruthlessness.

The ideology that Lenin used to replace the tsar by the party was well embedded in the Russian intellectual background. Since the 1880's, Marxism had been the most powerful inspiration of the intelligentsia. To those who hated the injustices and class differences that made a mockery of tsarist pretensions of equality, Marxism said that existing privileges were based on force and fraud and promised a classless socialism. Ideas of socialization of the economy were welcome because many large enterprises were Western-owned, state intervention was already customary, the middle classes had little prestige, and anticapitalism ran through Russian thought, both radical and conservative. Few Russians were ever so Westernized as to embrace economic liberalism. The Marxian primacy of collectivism over individualism was agreeable for a society which was long accustomed to the supremacy of the state and which idealized community, both in the communal institutions of the peasantry and in the togetherness (*sobornost*) of the empire. The idea of government and law as only the command of the strong was fairly descriptive of the Russian reality, and the doctrine of the future withering of the state appealed where the government was blamed for nearly everything. The universalism of Marx, whereby nationalism was a backward manifestation destined to disappear in the economically integrated society of the future, was superlative for the multinational empire. Marxism not only rationalized the gathering of many nations into a single political body but made it easier for radicals of dissatisfied minorities—the Balts, Poles, and especially the maltreated Jews, who furnished disproportionate numbers of revolutionaries—to join in such a party as Lenin's. It was an impressive and widely accepted theoretical basis for the order and authority of the revolutionary movement.

Marxism was balm for Russian inferiority feelings, making poverty virtuous by ascribing it to exploitation and promising that historical justice would overturn the smug bourgeois order and give the future to the presently oppressed. It accorded with the Russian ambivalence by rejecting as decadent the Western form of society while esteeming its material achievements; the Marxists had the same reasons as the Slavophiles for despising the West as rotten, but a better excuse, since they used an edifice of impressive Western scholarship and scientific-sounding dialectic to justify their revulsion against Western values. Marxism pointed to the advantages of backwardness; Russians could identify themselves emotionally, although not very logically, with a proletariat, and hope that Russia, by adopting socialism when the West rejected it, could yet realize its special destiny, skip over the detestable era of capitalism, and leap into the utopian order.

In mentality, likewise, Marxism satisfied the needs of the Russian intellectuals. It bespoke the superiority of the partly Westernized adepts of the creed. It lent itself to the scholasticism and theory-splitting of which they were fond, and the dialectical ideas of unity of opposites and progress through contradictions fitted the Russian milieu wherein extremes met or at least were confused, autocracy flowing into freedom, the tsar standing for the people, and backwardness signifying progressivism. Claiming absolute and potentially complete truth, Marxism gave grand answers in the black and white of the authoritarian mentality, without compromise or doubts. Viewing history as progress through the clashing of opposing forces from each era to the next and looking to violent dispossession, it harmonized with the extremism and violence characteristic of Russian politics and thought.

But Marxism was more fitted for the Russian milieu in its emotions than in its theories, several basic aspects of which were inconvenient. Since each stage of progress was to be built atop the preceding one, socialism should come first to the advanced West; and there was no glorious role for Russia nor for Russian Marxists. Similarly, Marxism was inapplicable to peasant Russia because it looked to the industrial proletariat as the class to make the future. Marxism was basically democratic; for the Russians, this was excellent in theory but unsuited to political traditions and the practical situation.

It was Lenin's masterwork to retailor Marxism to fit it for the conquest of power in Russia, turning logical inconsistencies into political assets. By his theory of imperialism he placed exploited countries partly in the place of the exploited class: with profits derived from investment in colonial and semicolonial countries the leading capitalist nations maintained their economic advantage and bought off their own working class. Therefore revolution should come to the exploited countries, among which Lenin counted Russia by virtue of the substantial foreign investment in its industry. This gave Russia and Russian Marxists a role in the Marxist-Leninist scheme and the potential glory of leading or at least beginning the world socialist revolution. That Russia had a small proletariat to make a socialist revolution was philosophically embarrassing but tactically advantageous. Since the proletariat was a minority, it was licit to overrule the majority. It was also essential and proper for the party to guide the workers and speak in their name, gripping power more tightly because of the perils of relaxation in a largely nonproletarian country. The democratic bias of Marxism was reversed; by using some democratic forms Lenin made his co-optive leadership more difficult to challenge.

The socialist revolution was thus to come not by the largely spontaneous breakdown of the most advanced capitalism but by the leadership of an élitist political party in a largely peasant country with only the beginnings of modern industry. This was more Russian than Marxist; Lenin practically equated Marxism with revolution in Russia and modified it as seemed appropriate for that purpose. The Bolsheviks were Russian revolutionaries who found Marxist approaches and the Marxist theoretical framework useful. In Lenin's party, the leadership, not the membership, was important; Marxism became a doctrine not for the proletariat but for bourgeois intellectuals. Lenin thought of himself as a good disciple, revising interpretations only as required by new realities. But the real issue was power, and Leninism was never a literal creed but loyalty to the political cause. Lenin was consistent in his way as he developed a set of ideas suited to the making of revolution in Russia and nowhere else.

That the Leninist doctrines were strained and garbled Marxism, which itself suffered grave logical weaknesses, was less important than that it met the emotional needs of a Russia torn between its ancient dual needs. Yet Leninism was so extreme and untraditional that it could not have found a large following in Russia except in times of desperation and stress. The Russian world was collapsing. The old autocracy had been discredited not only by military failures but by stupidity and degradation evident in the power of Rasputin and, in the popular mind, by treasonous elements. The new regime of freedom had been hailed with wild optimism and hopes for radical improvement; instead, the war had grown worse, the army was falling apart, the countryside was seething, and the workers were suffering unprecedented hardships and seizing factories. The old Russia was rejected, and the West had shown itself bankrupt by floundering in a terrible war for reasons hard for common folk to understand, murdering men by the thousands and millions, with no end in view. Under these conditions, the Bolsheviks claimed for themselves a monopoly of truth and propounded as the latest revelation and the height of political wisdom a series of propositions nearly all of which would have been rejected in normal times as mischievous and absurd. In the disorder and misery the most glowing promises aroused most hope. Yet once they had gained power, the Leninists could require universal acceptance of this faith; nor were they to be satisfied with outward compliance, as their predecessors had been, but demanded that the people internalize the correct beliefs to make their realm governable.

NEW UNIVERSALISM

The most unrealistic yet most appealing note of the Leninist message was its promise of salvation. A Russia bruised and bent, humiliated and suffering dire want, would assume the leadership of mankind and open a new era of history, ending not only the horrors of the World War but all wars. In the new order of socialism, there would be abundance for all, with brotherly harmony replacing the greed, envy, and quarrels of private property. The state, no longer needed to keep order among the virtuous citizenry, would of itself wither away. Russia was to leap from backwardness to the most advanced condition of civilization, from weakness to headship, from impoverishment and depression to utopian bliss.

It is questionable how many took the daydream for concrete reality, but it was more powerful than sober truth because it supplied a new foundation for the Russian empire—a renewed universal rule of justice, peace, and happiness, destined by the laws of history to prevail everywhere and last forever. Rejecting the evolution of Russia toward integration into the Western state system, Lenin and his fellows regarded their new regime not as a member of the international community but as a movement for its complete overthrow. "The goal of socialism is not only the liquidation of the fragmentation of mankind into little governments and of any sort of division of nations, it is not only the bringing together of nations but their merger." [6] At first they had no idea of regular diplomatic relations, although they were always open to practical dealings with class enemies; they took it for granted that the proletarian socialist revolution had to spread broadly or else fail entirely. In token of their convictions, they trampled on everything cherished by the despicable "bourgeoisie"; they confiscated property, repudiated debts, tore up treaties, laughed at international obligations, and poured scorn on traditional virtues. They despised patriotism, that inestimable virtue of the nations; Lenin, himself a consistent antipatriot, found no worse epithet for the nonrevolutionary Social Democrats than "social patriots." The Bolsheviks persecuted churches and reviled religion, and they claimed the right to terrorize persons who had belonged to well-to-do classes. They even challenged the existence of the traditional family, some of them wishing to dissolve these private associations in the new universal community.

The meaning of Leninist idealism was that the Russian empire, threatened with dissolution, was to be extended on a higher plane.

Russian national pride was decried; there was to be loyalty only to the cause. The name was broadened to Soviet (in a move reminiscent of Peter's renaming of Muscovy as Russia in 1713, in order better to claim dominion over the Ukraine and Belorussia), implying the adherence of all who should adopt the new form of government, nominally by workers' councils ("soviets"). It was assumed that Soviet Ukraine and other Soviet republics would be united not in a restoration of the tsarist state but in a world Soviet state, as promised by the first constitution of the Soviet Union.

At first the Bolsheviks saw their chief business as propaganda, the publishing of leaflets and broadcasting of proclamations; when the workers of the industrial states heard the glad tidings, they would surely overthrow their exploiters and join their Russian brothers. The Bolsheviks were so possessed by their ideal that after the Revolution they continued their dissolution of the Russian armed forces; on December 21, 1917, Lenin decreed a halt to war production and reconversion of factories to peacetime production within one month.[7] Compelled by military realities to enter conversations with the Germans, the Soviet delegates tried to talk over the heads of the German generals to the German proletarians. This failed, and the Bolsheviks had to reconcile themselves to a peace which renounced extensive non-Russian territories in order to hold to power in Russia. They then set about organizing a state and rebuilding the military forces.

But they gave up neither pretensions nor hopes. Revolution of some kind was the order of the day in Europe in the aftermath of the war; and during the dark days of the civil war, the Leninists hailed Communist regimes in Hungary and Bavaria and continually saw strikes and riots as harbingers of the spreading revolution that was to transform their almost hopeless struggle into utopian triumph. In the spring of 1919, when the tide of civil war was running strongly in favor of the Whites, Zinoviev was thus uplifted:

Now as we write these lines, the Third International has as its foundation-stones three Soviet republics—those in Russia, in Hungary, and in Bavaria. But no one will be surprised if at the moment when these lines appear in print we shall have not three but six or more Soviet republics. . . . Perhaps we shall see—for a few years and side by side with communist Europe—American capitalism will continue to exist. Perhaps even in England capitalism will continue to exist for a year or two, side by side with communism in the whole of continental Europe.[8]

Such musings came easily because world revolution seemed the chief hope for personal as well as political survival of the Bolshevik leaders, who could not hope to be spared if defeated.

As the broadcast word failed to bring the triumph of Sovietism, the Bolsheviks tried to organize it. Failure must be due to slackness and the weakness or treason of many leaders in the movement; to put it in order, it had to be welded into the tight organization that Lenin always cherished. In 1919 and 1920 he set up the new Communist International, or Comintern, with strict conditions of membership. The old idea of the Third Rome may have influenced Lenin's desire for a Russian-led Third International to replace the heretical Second International and inaugurate the new day. The overt purpose of the Comintern was to achieve a Soviet world. It was set up as a superstate to which the parties, representing the proletariats of various countries, promised obedience, the Russian being de facto master. The Comintern had an executive committee in permanent session and its own administrative and propaganda apparatus; it was once proposed that it should have its own general staff and troops.[9]

Chief hopes were laid on Germany, a land with a large Marxist party and Europe's biggest and best-organized proletariat, revolution in which would most directly benefit Russia. The Bolsheviks seemed convinced that they could revolutionize Germany as they had Russia, and poured in agents and propaganda. But this, like Comintern efforts elsewhere, had to be largely abandoned after a few years. The Comintern, applying Leninist patterns in countries where they were unsuitable and subordinating the revolutionary movement to a foreign body, hurt the cause politically much more than it could assist materially. Although the Bolsheviks for a decade after seizing power claimed to be heading not a state but a world revolutionary movement (a claim which has not been entirely surrendered), the Soviet Union settled down to a more modest role which would have been incomprehensible on the morrow of the Revolution, constructing (as Stalin put it) "Socialism in One Country."

If the universalist vision failed in the industrialized countries where by Marxist teachings it should have succeeded, it succeeded admirably over almost all of the former tsarist empire. Whether because of dislike for Russian domination or repugnance for the character of the Bolshevik regime, peoples of all non-Russian parts of the empire opted to accept the Bolshevik invitation to self-determination. In 1918 and 1919, not only did historical nations, such as the Ukraine, the Baltic states, Finland, Poland, Georgia, and Armenia break away; many others, even Tatars long submerged in Russia and various Cossack groups, tried to assert independence. As a result of this general exodus and the fortunes of the civil war, Soviet Russia was at one time stripped of empire, not only the western borderlands and the Baltic states but the Transcaucasus and much of Central Asia seeming to be lost.

But by a combination of military action with political subversion and division of their opponents, the Bolsheviks recovered one after another of the separatist areas. The Ukraine was Sovietized, brought into close treaty bonds, and rejoined to Muscovite Russia without great difficulty, as were other Slavic areas. Central Asia, where Russian colonists turned Bolshevik to assure Russian ascendancy, was made into "People's Republics" somewhat like those of Eastern Europe, and a few years later incorporated. Georgia, a nation of different traditions from the Russian, caused more difficulty. Under moderate socialist leadership, it became the world's only democratic socialist republic. The Soviet government recognized its independence in 1920 and established diplomatic relations, but in 1921 the Red Army was sent in and a Bolshevik government was set up. Various Bolshevized parts of the former Russian empire temporarily acted somewhat as sovereign states, but they were pulled closer and closer together until they were joined in a nominally federal but really centralized Soviet Union in 1923 and 1924. In Mongolia, the Bolsheviks regained the former tsarist sphere of influence; but out of respect for nominal Chinese sovereignty and the borders of the old empire they kept it as a satellite. Only peoples on the western fringe of the former empire, Finland, the Baltic states, and Poland, managed to make good their independence thanks to their national traditions and help from the Western powers.

The visible instrument of the regime was the Red Army, but restoration of the empire would have been impossible without the universalist cause, the message of hope and destiny carried by the Bolsheviks. Everywhere they were able to find at least a few dedicated, often fanatical converts to open the gates, to confuse and immobilize the nationalist or anti-Bolshevik cause, or to furnish an excuse for Soviet Russia's coming to the assistance of the people. In Georgia or Armenia, among Tatars or Ukrainians, there were always pro-Soviet partisans who could turn the scales as soon as the military situation became favorable. Nowhere except in Poland did the Red Army encounter a decidedly united people fighting for freedom. As the Soviet forces approached Warsaw, Lenin and the Comintern delegates assembled in conference thought the Polish proletariat would rise to greet them and make Communist Poland, under leaders nominated by Lenin, the gateway through which Bolshevism would flood over Europe and conquer the world. But the workers fought with instead of against the capitalists, and the Red Army faltered and fell back in defeat.

The Red Army marched into non-Russian lands avowedly as the vanguard of the world socialist revolution, not to impose the Russian state or any state, but to liberate from the yoke of capitalism, to help the peoples set up their own sovereign and independent states. Immediately after the Revolution, Lenin proclaimed the freedom of secession and right to autonomy or independence of all the peoples of the former empire. While the Whites alienated minorities by the slogan of "Russia Indivisible," Lenin came forward as champion of free nationhood.

But this represented only the doctrinal elasticity that was Lenin's political genius. For Marxists, the proletariat was naturally united and international; nationalism was the work of the bourgeoisie for its own interests. If some among the minorities opposed the proletarian Soviet cause, this could only be because they were misled by antiproletarians; Soviet interference, inherently selfless as it represented the unselfish working class, was always licit, whereas opposition to it was interpreted as antisocialist, antiproletarian, and antiprogressive. In a more sophisticated fashion than in earlier centuries, Russian intervention was held up as liberation.

It was the Leninist political virtuosity to permit, even encourage, formal statehood for minority peoples while calling on class unity to keep them together when divisive capitalism had been abolished. The Bolsheviks did not, however, rely on proletarian sentiments. Lenin insisted on the supreme right of his party as leading sector, so called, of the proletariat; and he insisted that the party remain firmly centralized. Thus, the Ukrainian, Georgian, and other parties were organized as mere sections of the All-Russian (subsequently Soviet) Communist party. Lenin, in the very message in which he acknowledged the independent sovereignty of the Ukraine, demanded that it establish a Bolshevik government, that is, place itself under the Russian-dominated party.

The universalism of Marxism-Leninism thus furnished a basis for the mobilizing and enveloping party organization and was a bond of restored empire while permitting the necessary pro forma concessions to Western-style nationhood. It gave a common purpose in the civil war, which was portrayed as a contest of socialism against the forces of world capitalism. By placing the Russians in the leadership of the overtly internationalist movement, it enlisted Russian patriotism in the universal cause and furnished an outwardly nonnational vehicle for Russian hegemony. By diverting minority nationalism into harmless channels and conceding forms while retaining the substance, it greatly assisted Soviet centralization. Minority people to this day complain that Lenin's nationality policy is not being correctly followed, ignoring the reality that it was designed to minimize their real autonomy.

INVERTED WESTERNIZATION

If the revolutionary tide of the Bolsheviks had succeeded completely, it would have solved the old Russian dualism by eliminating the threat from the West. If it had failed entirely, the dualism would have been ended by relieving the Russians of the burden of empire. It did neither, succeeding only over territories roughly corresponding to the old tsardom. The result was that Lenin had to give up in practice the goals he had to maintain in theory. He wanted to cure the Russian ambivalence by making a truly universal community; in fact, he increased the gap between political pretensions and reality, between the modern, Western side and the non-Western, imperial side of Russian society.

Lenin, however, was only following the secular Russian pattern of using Western tools and ideas for the strength of a non-Western empire. He was not at first concerned with technology, as Peter had been; the Russian problem was not so much technological, how to borrow useful knowledge, as political, how to control the borrowing. Lenin's feat was to appropriate Western political ideas, vocabulary, and institutions, and to put them to Russian uses. Thus he called "party" an organization which began somewhat like a conspiratorial society of the Populists and became a self-selected governing corporation. In the West, a party was part of the electorate, a grouping primarily for contesting elections and so an element of representative government; in the Soviet state it became the chief means of holding a monopoly of power and the instrument of dictatorship—in which usage it was later copied by many authoritarian states, anticommunist as well as communist.

The central doctrine of the party, Democratic Centralism, well illustrated this duality of appearances. It included a democratic-seeming provision for submission of the minority to the majority, but in practice those in power could say that the party majority was whatever they desired. It provided for elections to party positions, but the elections were thoroughly managed and served to legitimate the co-opted authority. It provided for free discussions of issues, but only insofar as the party, that is, the rulership, was undecided. It called for leaders to give an accounting of their actions to lower bodies, and it held up as a manifestation of democracy that higher party figures appear at electoral meetings; the ordinary effect was a call to work better. And, unsatisfied with these rules, it required all frankly to obey the superior party organs. The "Democratic" part of Democratic Centralism amounted to a requirement of close relations between bosses and followers for maximum effectiveness of leadership.

Lenin's democracy was only for the workers, or the party, or the ruling nucleus of the party, or for the leader alone. It meant not consulting any more people than necessary but taking power and securing the acquiescence of the majority. "Democracy" in the Soviet Union has become practically a synonym for the broadest participation of the people in carrying out the policies of the rulers. Recently, some 25 million persons were said to be engaged in various control organs,[10] in the flowering of the Leninist concept. Overtly democratic moves can also further the concentration of power, as Stalin promoted his dictatorship by recruiting proletarians into the party. In such usage, elections soon ceased to "elect," or choose, even in pretense; the obligatory voting for the official candidate might better be compared to an Oriental potentate's gathering the people in the public square, where they bow in manifestation of loyalty.* Correspondingly, the

* The approach was old. A revolutionary proclamation of 1862 stated: "Elections for a national assembly must take place under the surveillance of the [revolutionary] government which will at once make sure that no partisans of the old order—that is, if they are still alive—make up the composition of this new assembly." [11]

"legislative body" so "elected" was not to decide policy or the composition of the government, or even to ventilate opinions, but (aside from use as a showpiece) was made an adjunct of administration (especially on the lower level) and a means of carrying party policy to the people. The difference between Soviet and tsarist "elective" organs, which were at least forums of discussion, is striking. Similarly, Soviet courts were made instruments not of rule of law, as in tsarist days, but of party rule and psychological control. The old Russian question, why should we not have freedom like other countries, was answered by appropriating "freedom" as the proper description of Soviet compulsion; indeed, only in Russia was there true freedom, while alleged freedom in the Western world was only a cover for exploitation. The whole set of democratic forms, rights, and terms developed by generations of political contest in the West was put to use as cover and legitimation for the new authority, depriving opponents of means of attack, preempting their concepts, and immunizing against subversive Western influences. As Marx claimed to have stood Hegel on his head, so did Lenin with the whole Western political pattern. Not only did the Bolsheviks make Western concepts, like freedom and democracy, their instruments; they denied their validity in the lands of their development.

The Western idea of socialism itself, long the aspiration of Russian intellectuals, was similarly adapted. Organization and will took the place of the Marxist laws of historical development. "Treason to the workers" became an effective substitute for *lèse-majesté*. Unions were put to use to control workers and increase production, working with instead of against the management, unions and management alike being instruments of the party. The central concept of socialism, the alleged ownership of the factories by the workers, was turned around: since the worker was working for himself, he had to work harder. The good of the toiling masses became the best excuse for violence against the masses. This was part of Lenin's paradoxical approach that treated the workers, the historically appointed leaders of society, like sheep to be led by the party.

Lenin used federalism, a Western device for securing rights of self-government, as a means of rebuilding the empire and better controlling national minorities; removal of irritations, concessions in appearances and in nonessentials, facilitated the thorough centralization that the Soviet system imposed. He put the empire back together in

the name of freedom and anti-imperialism; the peoples had to be protected against heathen capitalism. In the name of internationalism the
people were isolated as never before from the outside world and
placed under Russian domination. Characterizing the Western state
system as the "world capitalist system" gave reason enough to reject it.

Part of this was merely Lenin's skillful and unscrupulous show-
manship. From the beginning, he made apt use of labels, using the
name "Bolshevik" (or "Majorityite") for his party, and "Mensheviks"
(or "Minorityites") for his opponents in Russian Marxism. In 1917,
Lenin employed slogans to gain support or disarm the opposition; thus,
"Land for the peasants" and "All power to the soviets" were no less
effective for being contrary to his ultimate intentions. The party was
to use words, not to be restricted by them. This led to what may at
best be called loose language, whereby in an Orwellian sense words
could stand for their opposites. For example, Stalin could claim the
objective of the withering away of the state as justification for the
strengthening of state power.[12] *Pravda* commented on the Soviet
attack on Finland in 1939:

Only the Soviet Union, which rejects in principle the forcible seizure of
territory and the enslavement of peoples, could consent to lend its military
might, not for aggression against Finland and for the enslavement of her
people, but to secure Finnish independence . . . to establish friendly relations with Finland.[13]

In this vein, Soviet authorities can deny the existence of censorship
and claim that Soviet citizens are free to travel abroad. The outer
ideology of Marxism and democratic pretenses has at times been a
rather fluffy garment covering the inner levers of power.

But it would be wrong to assume that the practitioners of Marxism-Leninism have been merely hypocritical; they have evidently been
motivated, as were tsarist governors, by a felt need to build the
right kind of political structure, ornamented with the most modern
features insofar as consonant with Russian political needs. Pure deceit-
fulness would not have been nearly so effective. As Diderot remarked
to Catherine II, "When an idea is transplanted from Europe to Russia,
it altogether changes its complexion," [14] and this was true to a higher
degree in Lenin's restructuring of the empire. If Dostoevsky would
use the sword, if necessary, to spread brotherly love, Lenin could consider violence and fraud justified by the ideal of eliminating them from
the life of nations. Like Catherine, he was probably sincere in desiring

an enlightened, democratic state controlled by himself and his hench-men in the interest of the people. It is fair to suppose that he really believed that he could, thanks to the restructuring of Soviet society, bring ultimate freedom by coercion.

This application of Western ideas had the additional utility of facilitating more borrowing of Western technology. It was another contradiction of Leninism that the state which set itself off from and reviled the bourgeois West set about taking advantage of its achieve-ments far more systematically and energetically than its tsarist fore-runner. The superficial modernization of the state encouraged the modernization of production; and useful ideas could be imported more freely as ideology served as a barrier to subversive ones. Lenin laughed at the willingness, as he saw it, of the capitalists to help, for a few pieces of silver, the force that would destroy them. In the flush of the revolution, he was eager to get Western investment in developing Russian resources, in order, as he said, to "overtake with the aid of foreign capitalism," [15] a policy Russia had been following for cen-turies. So many foreign experts, especially Germans, were engaged that by 1927 they represented a threat to Bolshevik control of the economy.[16] Soviet economic development up to 1945 rested on spe-cifically borrowed technology; no major plant or project was a purely Soviet undertaking.[17] Borrowing has continued uninhibited to this day; in February, 1972, an aide of Leonid Brezhnev came to the United States to study data processing technology to assist in party management;[18] and the party proposes that indoctrination should be computerized.[19]

Leninism was not especially designed for industrialization—this problem was to be solved by revolution in the most advanced coun-tries—and the industrialization program was more Stalinist than Len-inist. But Leninism gave a means of industrialization without making an individualistic society like those which created modern industry. Forced industrialization by the state was in the logic of the Bolshevik Revolution and accorded with secular Russian policy of using state authority to modernize and strengthen the state by borrowing achieve-ments of the West. Marxism-Leninism appealed to both sides of the Russian character, the scientific-practical as well as the ideological-utopian.

The result has been to build a kind of supercapitalism called so-cialism, in which the ownership of means of production is concentrated as nowhere else and the state-enforced monopoly creates the most favorable conditions for extraction of surplus value, high levels of saving and investment for rapid growth, and the use of ideology, law, justice, and the arts for the benefit of those who control the means of production. The Leninists gave the world new lessons not in social justice but in the effective organization of power. If before 1917 Russia was a pillar of antiliberalism in the world, afterwards it continued to be so in a different way but more strongly. The most striking successes of the Leninists in Russia and elsewhere have always been in those areas where state power was most effective—in propaganda, not literature, in education rather than science, and above all in the military, in battle and mobilization of resources for war, from the Russian civil war to the remarkable showing of Asian communists, Chinese, Koreans, or Vietnamese, against heavy mechanical and numerical odds.

Lenin's vitalization of the Russian empire answered deep emotional needs of renewal, enabling it to take up the ideological and resume the political offensive against the West. It was a work of high genius, a tour de force achieved in the face of pressures which have undone other empires, a splendid fusion of modern appearances and concepts with primitive political drives. But it had costs in meeting the severer problems of the new age. The Russian ambivalence was heightened as never before, and the gap between pretense and reality became much more extreme than under the tsars. For this reason the system became potentially vulnerable; if too many of the élite should cease to believe in it, it would become mere unprincipled coercion and might rapidly collapse. It became brittle, raising fears that a concession in any direction might lead to the opening up of papered-over fissures in Soviet society, cracks that would widen and lead to more cracks until the whole fell apart. The Leninist regime much more than the tsarist had to point to some sort of success in order to make credible its exalted view of itself. The Leninist fusion of opposites permitted far more arbitrary force than had the tsarist government. But it also required stronger instruments for survival, leaning more than its predecessor on police power, censorship, propaganda, and the whole panoply of dictatorial controls excluding or denaturing Western ideas. A modest freedom of political organization and of expression of dissident opinions like that tolerated by the old regime would doubtless be fatal to the Soviet synthesis, because the myths would quickly become unsustainable. It became especially indispensable to curb movement of persons and communications as never before in order to sustain the official version of reality on which the Leninist system rested. But it is not clear how long the Soviet state can maintain such controls in the modern world.

However brilliant, the Leninist renewal brought little that was truly new. The Soviet state was prefigured in the tsarist, not only in respect to general characteristics, such as authoritarianism mixed with equalitarian pretensions, the imitation of Western institutions within the framework of autocracy, and universalism and sense of mission, but also in doctrines, usually with the difference that the old traits and ideas have become much intensified in Soviet times. If the Bolsheviks have been self-righteous and anti-Western, so was for centuries the chief bearer of tsarist ideology, the Orthodox Church. Populists argued for a dedicated élite of the enlightened and believed that socialism should bring an end of national differences. Lenin's theory of inevitable war between capitalism and socialism was like Danilevsky's assumption of conflict between Germanic Europe and Slavism. Russians in the nineteenth century saw hypocrisy, oppression, and misery in the West rather than in their own land, much as the Soviet press does nowadays. Before Lenin, Plekhanov taught scorn for "bourgeois" rights, and before Plekhanov the Populists; the Slavophiles saw the West as riven by class conflict and derided parliamentary democracy as worthless or decadent. The supposed superiority of the Russian spirit to Western rationalism paralleled the superiority of Marxism-Leninism to "bourgeois objectivism."

Despite immense social differences and privileges, Russians see and saw theirs as a nonclass society. It was assumed in the 1870's that a Russian parliament would contain no parties because Russia had no social castes; [20] it is the standard Soviet argument that under socialism there should be only a single party because there is no class conflict. Non-Marxist Russians in the nineteenth century foreshadowed Lenin's theory of imperialism, postulating that England was the great bloodsucker of nations, strong by exploitation of colonies and other countries as well as by sale of cheap goods, while British society was much less just than Russian. By a typical view,

We Russians, on the contrary [as against the inequality induced by British laissez-faire], are genuine democrats and the representatives of modern ideas. We think that legal equality in your sense of the term does not suffice, and that the law ought to struggle against social inequality. Feudalism in all its forms is our special abhorrence. . . . Hence if fate should ever bring Russia into a country organized on English principles, she will be welcomed as a deliverer by the great majority of the lower classes. [21]

5

Soviet Ambivalence

UNIVERSALISM FOR ONE COUNTRY

With the passage of time and the settling down of the postrevolutionary state, the Soviet Union looks ever more like tsardom updated; the universal mission becomes more of a rhetorical shadow than an inspiration. The Soviet Union came to deal as a state with other states. The wholeheartedly universalist approach that inspired the Revolution hardly outlasted the shouting but retreated within a few months in the face of German power. In the debate over the peace terms offered by Germany in 1918, the majority of Lenin's party wished to refuse compromise and to continue by every means and everywhere possible an all-out struggle for the universal revolutionary cause, sacrificing the Soviet state, if necessary, for the world proletarian movement. But Lenin's soberer view prevailed, and from that time it has been Soviet policy to conserve and build up strength while waiting for the situation abroad to become more favorable. From March, 1918, when Lenin came to terms with Germany, or from August, 1920, when the Soviet invasion of Poland was hurled back, Soviet policy was basically "Socialism in One Country," although this was not official doctrine until 1924.

During the civil war, the morale of Soviet leaders was sustained by daily signs that the workers of the advanced countries were coming to their rescue. Even then, however, Lenin insisted on a nondogmatic approach to the capitalist world, offering concessions to the ideologi-

cally unappeasable enemy, going so far as to welcome foreign investment—the use of concessions to lure foreign investors was suggested as
early as December, 1917. He also supplemented revolutionary propaganda with diplomacy, overtly playing upon the divisions that were
inevitable because of capitalist greed and shortsightedness, in the spirit
of Chinese emperors using barbarians to defeat barbarians. In April,
1918, there were moves toward getting Allied officers to train a new
Russian army. After these fell through, the Leninists looked toward
alliance with Germany; in August, 1918, Soviet Russia came to an
agreement whereby 6 billion gold marks were to be paid to the Germans,[1] perhaps to help them continue the war against leading capitalist
states of the West.

With victory in the civil war, world revolution lost urgency for
the Leninists. It was still hoped that a socialist Germany would give
material help to impoverished Russia, but the normalization of relations with nonsocialist industrial powers gradually came to seem more
promising. In 1920, the Allied blockade was lifted; the Baltic republics,
the independence of which was recognized by Soviet Russia, became
a channel for commerce. Trade talks were opened with the leading
capitalist-imperialist nation, Britain, in 1920. In March, 1921, there was
a trade agreement with Britain; in May, with Germany. At the 1922
Genoa Conference, the Soviet delegation pressed for economic collaboration with the class-enemy states. After wearisome negotiations,
Britain and Italy extended formal diplomatic recognition in 1924, and
most other major powers soon followed. Through the 1920's there
was a strong effort to secure Western aid through inducements for
foreign capital, technical assistance contracts, and hiring engineers;
foreign managers participated in Soviet enterprises, as, for example,
General Electric directors on the board of the Soviet electrical trust [2]
—part of the past ignored by Soviet historiography.

The duality of Soviet foreign policy thus became explicit: one
hand worked through movements, subversion, parties, and propaganda
within foreign countries and against their official interests as well as
their values and social order; the other dealt with foreign governments in a fairly conventional way for advantages of trade and security. The two aspects contradicted each other nearly everywhere. Iron-
ically, the two countries that the Soviet government most wished to
cultivate, Britain and Germany, were those against which most revolutionary activity was directed. Britain was at first the chief hope

for credits and favorable trade terms, yet the revolutionary call in Asia was to fight not capitalists or even landlords but British imperialism. The huzzahs of the representatives of Oriental peoples gathered at Baku in 1920 were not for social revolution but for war against foreign colonial overlords. Mustapha Kemal Ataturk, leader of the Turkish revolution, was treated as an ally because he was anti-British, although he threw Turkish communists into the sea. King Amanullah of Afghanistan was "progressive" to the degree that he was useful, like many a Third World leader since. The Bolshevist campaign in Asia seemed to be little more than the old Russian drive provided with new weapons, and it was the biggest cause of friction between Britain and Soviet Russia for some years of the 1920's, as Russian expansion had been between Britain and tsarist Russia at the beginning of the century.

Germany clearly had to follow the Russian Revolution if the Marxian scheme was valid, and the Comintern interfered shamelessly in German politics. But Germany and Russia, both defeated and pariahs on the international stage and antagonistic to their common neighbor Poland, were natural allies; and the Rapallo Pact of 1922 helped both countries from their isolation. Military collaboration, whereby the Reichswehr used Russian territory to build and practice with weaponry forbidden by the Treaty of Versailles, was also useful to both, although the Reichswehr suppressed German communists whom the Russians were arming. Trade prospered because Germany was eager for the Russian market and readier to extend credits than any other Western power. Germany was by far the most helpful power to Soviet Russia in the 1920's; but the attention lavished on the German proletariat was counterproductive.

Of the two aspects of Soviet foreign relations, that represented by the Comintern was considered much the more important by Soviet leaders, whereas the agency of state dealings was a sideshow. Lenin and his fellows hovered around Comintern congresses, glorying in the guidance of the transformation of the world. Even Stalin consulted and opined frequently on issues of revolution abroad and relations with foreign communist parties. The Commissariat of Foreign Affairs, first taken by Trotsky on the supposition that no work was involved, was placed under a former tsarist diplomat, Georgi Chicherin, who had no standing in high party circles. For a few years when Soviet Russia was moving back onto the diplomatic stage, he had a fairly free hand because his business was not considered of sufficient importance to warrant the attention of the top men in the party (or, increasingly after 1922, Stalin).

Beyond such housekeeping matters as trade, it was the business of the Commissariat to offset the bad results of Comintern and related activities. Soviet missions abroad were largely divorced from party and revolutionary activities. Although a Bolshevik by ideals, Chicherin was a cultivated man of the old school, rational and accessible to argument as subsequent Soviet foreign ministers were not. The West was agreeably surprised when the Bolshevik delegation showed up at the 1922 Genoa Conference on war debts, the first Soviet appearance at a meeting of great powers, in top hats and gloves with protocol manuals in their pockets.[3]

Chicherin publicly joked about the Comintern. The Soviet official position, reiterated in countless treaties and statements, was that the government was not responsible for the deeds of the party, the propaganda and subversion of international communism. This was a thin pretense, since party and government were hand and glove. But the Foreign Commissariat did its best to assuage the irritations of Comintern provocations by presenting an image of conventionality and promoting peace and coexistence. There was much talk of improvement of relations with the states that the Comintern was promising to demolish. In 1923, Chicherin promised that the Soviet government would "do its utmost to remove all obstacles to a close and durable cooperation between America and Russia."[4] Disarmament became a Soviet theme. Lenin once derided the idea on grounds that disarmament talk lulled the masses and distracted from revolutionary passions, but as revolution receded he came to believe that disarmament negotiations could improve the Soviet position by strengthening pacific inclinations in the West and so protect the Soviet Union, whether or not they led to any specific results. The ideological posture was saved by contending that capitalism made disarmament impossible, but the Russians claimed credit for willingness to accept disarmament if only other powers would agree.

The reentry of Russia into the community of nations was, withal, slow and incomplete. Until after the advent of Hitler, Russia remained resolutely opposed to the League of Nations, which it regarded both as the creature of the leading interventionist powers, Britain and France, and as a sort of reactionary "international," in opposition to the Communist International. Basic attitudes of distrust persisted, hardly lessened by the passing years. As soon as they could pay them, the Bolsheviks began importing foreign technicians; but foreign trade remained much behind hopes because the Bolsheviks wished to mini- mize dependence on capitalist markets and suppliers. To this day, the volume of Soviet trade outside its sphere is small in relation to the entire Soviet economy, despite some effort to use trade as a political weapon. Although the Comintern gave up the overt fomenting of revolution, it did not cease to bother Western leaders by its unconven- tional activities and inflammatory statements; and the Russians admitted no retreat from revolutionary principles. Soviet diplomatic manners were (until after Stalin) in many ways crude and unpleasant. Utili- tarian relations did not mean normal relations with Western states.

In the latter 1920's, in fact, the Soviet Union turned more inward and accented the unbridgeable differences between itself and the world without as though in compensation for the giving up of dreams of world revolution. Stalin swore by the memory of Lenin to keep aloft the banner of world revolution and claimed legitimacy, like Lenin, as leader of the party of the working class. But his was a postrevolution- ary Russia, weary of failed utopias and frustrated messianism, ready to turn away from the agitator-politicians and revolutionary intellec- tuals under the rule of the crude but crafty boss. Stalin knew no for- eign language, took little part in exile politics, disliked superior intel- lects, and had little interest in the writings of Marx and Engels. He had no interest in the victory of communism abroad unless he could control it. Communist parties in the West were not to make revolu- tion but to weaken their countries. To Stalin the only value of the communist movement was the contribution it might make to Soviet (his own) power. He never bothered to address a congress of the Comintern, and he regarded world revolution as an empty slogan.

Asserting "Socialism in One Country" as doctrine, Stalin accepted practical reality as ideologically correct, acknowledged that there was no proximate prospect of proletarian revolution, and called for "new forms of the proletarian movement"—the consolidation of the Soviet government and the economic modernization of Russia. As Stalin made his power absolute after 1927 and began his "Second Revolution" of collectivization and industrialization, the antithesis of socialism and capitalism and the need for struggle were emphasized as they had not been since the civil war in order to provide a doctrinal rationale. But the emphasis was entirely internal, even isolationist. World communism was made more leftist-dogmatic, but a Soviet tractor was considered more valuable to socialism than a host of foreign communists. The press gave less attention to foreign affairs. Foreign contacts were cut down, and the economy was built toward autarky; if trade for a while increased, it was to procure machines to make imports unnecessary. In the mounting xenophobia, opposition was increasingly blamed on imperialist machinations, subversion, and sabotage. From 1928, political trials stressed the foreign connections of the accused. Foreign technicians, German, British, and French, were also put on trial as spies, in detriment to the already poor state of Soviet foreign relations. In the absence of a real external threat, internal political considerations outweighed the needs of foreign policy.

International communism reflected Soviet needs and tensions. The 1928 Congress of the Comintern (the next last to be held) professed alarm at the danger of war, although the world was at its most placid, and accused the League of Nations of preparing an attack on Soviet Russia. The world proletariat was called upon to prepare violent revolution when the prospects for violence were at their nadir. But leftist talk covered factual abandonment of revolutionary aims; the Comintern had ceased to weigh significantly in Soviet party considerations. Aside from acting as agents of division and disruption abroad, the parties were to serve Stalin as a claque to uphold his prestige as leader of a world movement, and to attack counterparts of his rivals in Russia, non-Stalinist leftists and Social Democrats, who were now promoted from "social patriots" (Lenin's term) to "social fascists," betrayers of the working class. To the old Leninist reasons for hating moderate socialists—rivalry for leadership of the workers, belief that they were more of an obstacle to victory than outright class opponents, and so on—were added new Stalinist ones: dislike for equalitarianism, democracy, and proletarianism, and paranoid hatred of any suggestion of a challenge to the primacy of Stalin as chief of the world's workers.

NATIONAL SOVIETISM

As anticommunist Germany became stronger and more assertive of its need for Lebensraum, and also as anticommunist Japan continued its expansion on the Asian mainland, it was evident that the Soviet Union faced a real danger instead of the old bogey of renewed capitalist intervention. The Soviet outlook accordingly changed abruptly in 1934. Perhaps in imitation of Hitler's successful example, Stalin reverted to nationalism as a force to mobilize his subjects and brought back much of the Old Russia which had been submerged by revolutionary mission and ideology. Patriotism, which had been held a reactionary deceit to smother class consciousness, was now exalted. "Russia," previously not an acceptable word, became semisacred. Marxist historians who had condemned tsarist imperialism along with other imperialisms were purged. Feudal princes and conquering tsars were glorified, and imperial generals who had won their spurs in repressing popular revolutionary movements became Soviet heroes. The expansion of Russia was fused with the mission of communism, as the Stalinist regime consciously identified itself with historic Russia and its foreign policy goals. Russification of minority areas, set back in the 1920's, was resumed. The Red Army, swearing to fight not for the working class but for country and victory, was made increasingly professional, and ranks and privileges of officers were restored. Marxist spirit was cast away, as equalitarianism was contemned and social transformation was attributed to individual genius. From the latter 1930's, anti-Semitism, concomitant of tsarist chauvinism, crept into Soviet attitudes and policies. Internationalism turned national; the Soviet Union became a supernation dominated by Russian culture and traditions, something of a militarily ordered society, ruled by a new class of technicians and party professionals.

Whether because of awareness of danger or because of the evolution of the Soviet mentality, the Soviet Union entered the power politics of the nations as never before, seeking security and advantages in the traditional way of the balance of power, by combination with one side or the other. First Stalin moved toward collective security, the formation of a broad antifascist front with the Western democracies, England and France. In 1934, the Soviet Union entered the "alliance of world bandits," as Lenin had characterized the League of Nations, replacing the departing Germans; and its status was recognized by a permanent seat on the Council. The Soviet Union became an emphatic supporter both of the League and of the sanctity of treaties, particularly that of Versailles, which had long been anathema. In May, 1935, the Soviet Union signed an alliance with France; although both sides were hesitant and the bond remained ineffectual, it was a deroga-

tion of Marxism-Leninism to link the supposedly revolutionary workers'
state to a class enemy, very "bourgeois" France.

The Communist parties, perennial irritants in relations with governments they were supposed to overthrow, were not discarded but
turned partly around. In August, 1935, the last congress of the Comintern was given the new line: capitalist states could be either aggressive
or pacific, and Communist parties should cherish bourgeois democracy
for the time being, sink roots in the native land, build on national and
patriotic traditions, and form a broad movement against the fascist
danger, joining any willing leftist or moderate parties in a Popular
Front. The Comintern was directed to reverse the radical leftist directions of the preceding years and become the defender of democracy,
moderate change, and the interests of the whole people. It is a tribute
to the discipline Stalin had imposed upon his foreign adherents that
these changes were accepted with little protest.

Neither in the party nor in the governmental sphere was the new
collaboration successful; differences between Stalinist Russia and the
Western democracies were too deep. The Communist parties could not
give up their aim of combatting the capitalistic basis of Western society, the aim which was their chief claim to existence, criticizing and
trying to undermine those with whom they wished to form an alliance.
Trust was also hindered by the fact that they were controlled by the
Stalinist state, which was becoming increasingly oppressive and violent.
Just as the Popular Front was coming to its zenith, there began in
Russia the nightmarish purges of 1936 to 1938, which incidentally
struck down most foreign Communists in Moscow.

Few Popular Fronts were formed, and nowhere were they lasting.
The most successful one was in France, where leftist parties won a
great electoral victory in the spring of 1936, the Communists increasing
their seats sevenfold. But the Communists still did not conceive of
sharing in the responsibilities of a bourgeois government (in contrast
to their attitude after World War II, when they were eager for any
share of power in practically any government). Frictions grew, mostly
over the Spanish Civil War, as the government followed the cautious
British lead and denied help to the Republican-leftist cause. In Spain,
Soviet policy was cautious and desirous of minimizing risks. The Communists in the Spanish Popular Front were instructed not to reach for
power or to attempt to make a social revolution. They left it to the
anarchists to act as a Leninist party, forming revolutionary committees

and confiscating and collectivizing land and industries. In a reflection of Soviet politics, it became a major purpose of the Spanish Communists to combat non-Communist revolutionaries, especially those of Trotskyite orientation.

Soviet moves toward collective security also failed. The Franco-Soviet treaty of 1935 and a supplementary alliance with Czechoslovakia (conditional on French assistance for that country) remained little more than a façade of solidarity, which crumbled in each crisis. A major test was the Spanish Civil War. Britain and France could only suspect that the Soviets were motivated at least partly by the hope of saving a regime in which the Communists were strong and potentially dominant, or of involving the Western powers in war with Nazi Germany and Fascist Italy; the Soviet Union denounced the effort to isolate the Spanish conflict as de facto aid to fascism. Similarly, in the crisis over the Czech Sudetenland, Russia was excluded as though not really a member of the European community; and the Munich agreement was interpreted by the Russians as an effort to turn Nazi ambitions eastward.

In the spring of 1939, Hitler turned against Poland and offered the Soviet Union an opportunity to play the game of Realpolitik for the highest stakes; and Stalin accepted with complete disregard of ideology. Having suddenly become a much desired partner, in a position to swing the power balance, he bargained publicly with Britain and France and privately with the Nazis. The latter could offer not only an opportunity to stay out of a future war or come in as Stalin pleased but also a hunting license to recover most of the territories the tsarist empire had lost on its western edge—the Baltic states, part of Poland, and Bessarabia. The Nazi-Soviet pact was surprising only because most people took propaganda more seriously than did its makers. The Soviet Union seems to have felt more comfortable in dealing with the authoritarian, albeit anticommunist, Nazis than with the more liberal and ideologically more dangerous governments of Britain and France. Stalin was reluctant to regard Germany as hostile even after Hitler came to power on a platform of anti-Bolshevism as well as anti-Semitism, and he never closed the door to improvement of relations and made it clear that ideology was no bar. When in 1939 Germany became the wooer, Stalin raised his price; but agreement was not difficult to reach, and the pact of August 23 was signed in an atmosphere of cordiality.

Thereby was inaugurated an interlude of friendly relations, for a time of near-alliance, between the two great autocratic powers. It was a period unique in modern Russian foreign relations. Russia could associate and trade with and borrow from an advanced Western country without fear of ideological-political contagion. Nazi Germany was about as antiliberal as the Soviet Union, and it made some show of being anticapitalist; like Stalin, Hitler was something of a revolutionary despot, a purger, and an eminent cultivator of his personality cult. Nazis and Bolsheviks agreed in their hatred for democrats and moderate socialists, while the nationalistic and racist aspects of Nazism guaranteed that it could have no appeal for Russians. The political accommodation was preceded by a trade treaty, and commerce soon swelled, promoted enthusiastically by the Russians, who not long before had been trying to minimize their exchanges with the outside world. Communist parties in the West turned defeatist, in effect working for Nazi victory. When the Germans proposed peace on the basis of recognizing their conquests, the Soviet Union, which had taken about half the territory of Poland, loudly supported the idea. Soviet leaders have never been so cordial toward a major power not actively fighting on their side as they were toward Nazi Germany in the latter part of 1939 and the first months of 1940.

In September, 1939, Joachim von Ribbentrop, the Nazi foreign minister, was received in Moscow for the second time with expressions of warm esteem, and a larger trade pact was signed. Like many of the more leftist Nazis, von Ribbentrop believed that Stalin, having turned away from world revolution, was turning to something like a Russian version of German National Socialism; why, after all, should national Bolshevism be far apart from National Socialism? Stalin, although morbidly suspicious of decent people, seems to have had real trust in Hitler; he replied to the gushing birthday greetings of von Ribbentrop in December, 1939: "The friendship between the peoples of the Soviet Union and Germany, cemented by blood, has every reason to be solid and lasting." The Soviet government provided, especially in the first months of 1940, large quantities of oil, grain, and minerals, and gave facilities for transshipment to defeat the British blockade. In return, Stalin sought German technical collaboration, especially in warships.

In October, 1940, Foreign Commissar Viacheslav Molotov went to Berlin to return the visits of the Nazi foreign minister and to consider the proposal that the Soviet Union join the German-Japanese-Italian alliance. He was received with manifestations of solidarity, but the negotiations failed. Hitler regarded himself, with an army unchallenge-able on the continent, as a world conqueror; but Molotov treated him as an equal, and Stalin seriously overestimated his own strength and bargaining position. As payment for neutrality, he had already pocketed the areas assigned to him by the August, 1939, agreement, acquiring some 23 million new non-Russian subjects. But he raised additional territorial demands in a spirit of Oriental dickering as his price for joining the Axis. Hitler, no longer feeling any need for Stalin's good will, gave orders to proceed with preparations for the invasion of Russia, which had been planned since shortly after the fall of France. But Stalin was too pleased with Soviet-German collaboration to believe the innumerable warnings of the impending assault of June, 1941.

During this period, the Soviet Union behaved strictly like a state acting simply out of self-interest. Although the vocabulary of Marxism-Leninism was not discarded, official declarations took a nonideological tone. Molotov frankly excused the pact with Germany on grounds of national interest, without any mouthings about the proletariat. When Soviet forces entered Poland to take over the area assigned to them, this was justified by traditional ethnic reasons, the kinship of the majority of the inhabitants to the Belorussians and Ukrainians of the Soviet Union. The Baltic states were required to admit Soviet forces on strategic grounds and because they had once belonged to the tsarist empire. Negotiations with Finland were carried on entirely in the spirit of a great power squeezing a small one, without idealistic pretenses, although after the Russians attacked they proclaimed themselves liber-ators of the Finnish workers. In the same spirit, Stalin supported not the Chinese Communists but the Nationalists, whom he judged better able to distract the Japanese. The chief direction of Stalin's territorial aims, the Balkans and the Straits, was traditionally Russian and had nothing to do with communism.

Several reasons for this change of mentality suggest themselves. The Revolution and its emotional impulse were worn out. Stalin's social transformation, for which an ideological basis was necessary, was also finished by the latter 1930's. The need was for stability, not change. At the same time, the interest of the leadership visibly shifted toward the foreign scene. In diplomacy, ideology was a hindrance, and the rewards on the world stage were to be gained not by promoting a cause but by ruthless Realpolitik; this could not but affect the mental-ity of the leadership. Moreover, the most obviously successful states of the West were dictatorial and supernationalistic; many persons, and perhaps Stalin, looked upon fascism as a wave of the future. Liberalism and nationalism, which have always represented the chief philosophical threat to the Russian empire, were less threatening when Hitler's was the most obviously successful Western state.

More concretely, Stalin's Soviet Union was behaving more like a national state and less like an empire because it was in fact more of a national state than the Russian-dominated polity before and after. Non-Russians formed about 56 percent of the Russian empire in which Lenin came to maturity. Because of loss of the western border regions, non-Russians were only 35 percent of the population in 1939 prior to the renewal of expansion, and this decrease was the more significant because the peoples lost were among the most culturally advanced of the empire.

It seems probable that the Soviet Union, with little more than a third of its people non-Russians, many of these relatively backward Asians, could have fairly soon come to feel that no internationalist rationale was necessary or desirable to maintain its unity. It might thus have become much more like the nation-states of the West. But this possible evolution was aborted by events. Thanks to his accord with Hitler, Stalin raised the proportion of his non-Russian subjects to 44 percent, including many more relatively advanced peoples, who were more difficult to govern than Turkic peoples of Central Asia. As of 1970, the percentage of Russians in the U.S.S.R. had declined (because of differential birth rates) to about half the total population. And it is the more difficult for the Soviet Union now to revert to a nationalistic position because of its de facto empire, the satellite states over which it has hegemony, containing some 85 million persons. In the empire so understood, Russians comprise about 37 percent; and the problem of maintaining their supremacy is perennially acute.

WESTERN ALLIANCE TO COLD WAR

In June, 1941, attack came from the power that Stalin had assiduously courted, a party-ruled, ostensibly anticapitalist state. Immediately thereafter, Stalin received the support of Winston Churchill and the power long regarded as most hostile, arch-capitalist Britain. The war was a complete contradiction to Leninism and the old Soviet stereotypes, for the Soviet Union found itself not the victim of the antisocialist coalition that Lenin expected to return to the attack but the ally of the leading capitalist powers.

In the fight for life of the "Fatherland of the Workers," the internationalism cultivated for a generation proved a complete failure. There was no significant workers' resistance in Hitler's Germany as long as it was winning, and the Communist parties elsewhere in Europe made headway only when they united the Communist cause with a national one. In 1943, the Comintern was dissolved. The action was mostly symbolic, as this body had been inactive for years; but it meant burying Lenin's beloved creature. Within the Soviet Union, too, where indoctrination had had full sway for more than two decades, internationalism failed. Stalin did not wait for the Volga Germans to evince disloyalty before scattering them. Wherever Nazi forces entered minority areas, they found anti-Soviet feeling; only their haughty philosophy and brutality prevented them from using these sentiments as a powerful, perhaps fatal weapon against Stalinist Russia. In the dark days the Soviet government could feel fairly sure of the loyalty of only the ethnic Russians, the Jews, and perhaps the Armenians.[5] Like previous rulers in times of national peril, Stalin called upon the people to fight not for ideology or the regime but for Russia and survival.

Relations with the West were fundamentally altered. It was no longer necessary to conjure up a picture of a hostile capitalist world for internal purposes; the Nazis were enemy enough. The chief "capitalist" powers immediately offered support and became allies. The stream of Western supplies for the Soviet armies gradually grew to dimensions no Russian could ignore. Cordiality waxed and waned from time to time, and the repeated postponement of the Second Front caused friction. There were many irritations, caused chiefly by the old bureaucratic and xenophobic habits of the Stalinist state. It remained unthinkable (except at the time of direst need) for British or American forces to operate on Soviet soil, and only with the greatest difficulty could arrangements be made for American planes to use Soviet airfields. But top Soviet leaders, such as Stalin and Molotov, were more reasonable and accessible than many of their woodenheaded or fear-ridden underlings. Many Allied leaders were convinced that if ignorance and suspicion could be overcome, the Russian outlook would not be fundamentally different from their own.

If Soviet leaders turned a friendly face to the West, this cannot be ascribed to mere expediency. They no longer felt sure of the inevitable

hostility of the capitalist world, and they perceived possibilities of cooperation with the more "progressive" countries. A Soviet economist,
E. Varga, concluded that the American government represented not
just the bourgeoisie but all classes; therefore the Soviet Union could
have good relations with it. Literature was practically freed of ideological bonds; it had only to support the war. The Communist party
was opened to good soldiers without requiring them to become Marxists. Emphasis on historical Russian values was made stronger, although
it was balanced by some concessions to minority national feelings and
by the image of the Soviet Union as an ideal superstate. Pan-Slavism
was revived. Stalin, who had nearly destroyed the Church, made peace
with it. Orthodoxy blessed the war, and Pan-Orthodoxy was mixed
with Pan-Slavism as a means to unity (and in time to expansion in the
Balkans). Russian patriotism, outraged by Nazi brutality, won the war
for Stalinism.

Soviet leaders made very un-Leninist statements. A deputy foreign
minister spoke disparagingly of the "old ideology of leftist trends" and
preferred the "tradition of the Russian and Ukrainian people." [6] Stalin
in his victory speech, May 9, 1945, spoke in non-Marxist terms: "The
centuries-old struggle of the Slav peoples for their existence and their
independence has been concluded by victory over the German invaders
and over German tyranny." A little later, Stalin gloated over victory
over Japan in a spirit of pure nationalism:

But the defeat of Russian troops in 1904 [in which Lenin had rejoiced] in
the period of the Russo-Japanese War left grave memories in the minds of
our peoples. It was as a dark stain on our country. Our people trusted and
awaited the day when Japan would be routed and the stain wiped out. . . .
For forty years have we, men of the older generation, waited for this day.
And now this day has come.[7]

By this date, however, a countercurrent had already set in. The
compulsion to a realistic estimate of the world diminished as victory
approached. At one time, almost all non-Russians in the western part
of the country, including the Ukrainians, were lost to Russia because
of enemy occupation. But as Soviet forces began moving back into
minority areas, the old problems of control began to loom again. Attention was turned anew to political education, and there began a retight-
ening in philosophy and literature. The war was given a more Marxist
interpretation, Nazism being analyzed as an outgrowth of German

capitalism. When the Soviet army advanced beyond the Soviet frontiers, ideology became more necessary to facilitate control of occupied
areas. The broader the extension of Soviet control, the greater the
reliance on local Communist parties and the Proletarian Internationalism which entitled them and through them the Soviet state to govern
the formerly independent nations of Eastern Europe. The Stalinists
knew well that freely elected governments in Poland, Hungary, Germany, and other occupied lands would adopt a stance more pro-
Western than pro-Soviet. Thus when the Western powers, particularly
the United States, pressed for democratic freedoms in the area of Soviet
control, the Russians could only see it as a threat to their position and
responded by intensifying ideological claims and political repression.

Soviet armies advanced into southeastern and south central Europe
not only to defeat Axis armies but to fill an area of weakness, in the
old Russian manner. Having achieved after World War II approximately what Russia had dreamed of in World War I, Stalinist Russia
faced the problem of maintaining and solidifying itself against insidious
Western influences, these being the more menacing as Russian hegemony was unwelcome to peoples of satellite countries. Particularly after
the Marshall Plan (1947) offered help in reconstruction through cooperation with America, and the defection of Yugoslavia (1948) created
an attractive communist heresy, Russia faced, perhaps more acutely
than ever, the problems of discipline of the multinational empire.

The means adopted were traditional. The Soviet sphere was sealed
off. Unofficial travel in and out was practically halted, and the movement of officials and journalists was stringently controlled. Foreign
trade was held to a minimum. Propaganda rose to new truculence, de-
nouncing everything that smacked of the West and bourgeois decadence in literature, art, music, even biology and other sciences; many
nonconformist intellectuals were purged. The enmity of America was
projected backwards, sometimes as though America had been the chief
evil since 1917, organizer of intervention to choke the Soviet state.
Blame for World War II was partly laid on American intrigues; and
the Second Front was seen as an attempt to crush popular resistance
movements and assert American hegemony. There was enormous self-
glorification, of Stalin personally, of the Soviet Union, and of Russia
past and present. As though to solve the problem of the Russian technological lag by denying its existence, all manner of basic devices, from

the steam engine to the radio, were attributed to subjects of the tsars. Soviet man was upheld as a superior species, the maker of the future.

Without revolutionary idealism and with no faith in the international proletariat, Stalin cared only for what he controlled. Communist parties were put in charge of administering the satellite countries, but there was little interest in communism outside. Nonruling Communist parties were regarded as expendable tools, used to battle American influence and to disrupt as far as possible, by strikes and protest movement, countries of the anti-Soviet alliance. "Socialism in One Country" became "Socialism in One Camp," broadened to include occupied and controlled lands but kept essentially isolationist. To draw the line sharply between the sphere of Soviet light and the outer darkness, foreign powers were rather indiscriminately regarded as evil, with little distinction between those more and less unfriendly to the Soviet Union. Neutrality was hardly admitted, just as it was held treasonous for Russians and satellites to refrain from chanting the praises of Stalin. Even revolutionaries and anti-Western nationalists, in India, Egypt, and elsewhere, were branded as agents of imperialism for accepting independence peacefully. Stalin concentrated on consolidation of the great gains achieved, for which foreign friends were not needed or (unless they became unconditional adherents) much desired.

The Stalinist state, however, was quite willing to extend its control wherever this could be done without undue risk; and it probed outward in several directions. Molotov repeatedly pressed for part of the former Italian colonial empire, preferably Libya; but the Western powers refused to permit Russian power thus to be installed in the Mediterranean. Stalin also demanded a base on the Straits, as though obsessed with that historic Russian longing. In addition, the Soviet Union claimed two provinces of eastern Turkey, which had been taken by Russia in 1878 and recovered by Turkey in the disorders following the Revolution; unofficially, the Russians called for the cession of much more of Anatolia on the grounds that it had once been held by the kingdom of Georgia. Having entered Iran in cooperation with the British in 1941 to secure the supply route, Soviet troops declined to depart as agreed from the northern part of the country. As they had done a generation earlier at the time of the Russian civil war, the Soviet forces sponsored a separatist movement in a region adjoining the Soviet Union, from which they withdrew only under pressure from the United States and the United Nations. Blockading Berlin, Stalin sought to sound out and solidify dominion over the Soviet share of Germany. Finally, Stalin took advantage of apparent American indifference and attempted the conquest of the noncommunist part of Korea, thereby to fulfill the Russian aspiration of 1904.

Unsuccessful war in Korea, coming after failures in Iran, Turkey, Greece, and Berlin, and the ability of the Yugoslavs to make good their independence, seems to have contributed to a reappraisal in Stalin's last years. There was a budding appreciation that trade might be more useful than dangerous, that truculence was counterproductive, and that the Soviet Union was neglecting opportunities to expand its influence by conciliating potentially friendly states and groups.

PEACEFUL STRUGGLE

By the time of Stalin's death, the Soviet Union had mustered sufficient strength to regard the outside world without paranoid defensiveness. At the same time, the complexity of the economy was compounding the difficulties of completely centralized management, innovation was increasingly necessary, and it was patently desirable to foster contacts with the West. With the departure of the tyrant who was the symbol of past transformations, the shaper of the Soviet bureaucratic order and of Russia's greatest historic victory—and also of the terrorism that was hard reality for Soviet citizens—there was need for a new legitimation and rationale of authority. The Soviet leadership moved to adjust philosophy and policy to the new age.

The new leadership—headed first by Georgi Malenkov and from early 1955 increasingly dominated by Nikita Khrushchev—quickly moderated the asperity of Stalinism, giving more consideration to welfare and less absolute priority to heavy and defense industry. Propaganda became less shrill, claims on Turkey were dropped, and the war in Korea was halted. Soviet diplomats spoke more reasonably, and in 1955 many conciliatory steps were taken, including the settlement with Austria, renunciation of the Porkkala base in Finland, and Khrushchev's trip to Belgrade to apologize to Tito for Stalin's maltreatment. Although no previous top Soviet leader had left Soviet-controlled territory, Khrushchev and his prime minister, Nikolai Bulganin, made a grand tour of India and Burma, meeting people and shaking hands like ordinary politicians.

To adapt ideology to the new age, Khrushchev introduced the largest set of explicit revisions since the Revolution. The starting premise was the inadmissibility of nuclear war. Lenin saw war between major states and between the Soviet Union and the capitalist world as inevitable, but in the atomic age it had become unthinkable. "States of differing social systems" (as the Russians put it) had to get along with mutual respect for rights and sovereignty. "Peaceful Coexistence," which had previously been accepted as an interlude, was recognized to be necessary indefinitely. As a corollary, the conversion of the world to socialism, still seen as inevitable, should or could come peacefully, Lenin to the contrary, by evolution or parliamentary process. This further implied, and it was explicitly acknowledged in the case of Yugoslavia, that there might be different socialisms traveling different roads toward the same distant utopia. The world dichotomy was tempered by the acceptance of neutralism, at least as a way station to Soviet socialism.

Khrushchev recognized the need to admit more of the intellectual currents of the West for economic, cultural, and scientific progress; hence Peaceful Coexistence. But it was necessary as ever to continue to exclude Western political ideas; hence Peaceful Coexistence was coupled with ideological struggle. The world was still depicted as dominated by struggle between socialism and capitalism, only war between great powers being excluded ("wars of liberation" being permitted or encouraged). In principle, there was no compromise or genuine collaboration; in practice, there was confusion. There should be struggle for peace, but peace was really possible only under universal (Soviet) socialism. The Soviet Union subscribed officially to the United Nations and used it politically and propagandistically while fundamentally rejecting its principles of national sovereignty and an open world order. Thus the Soviet Union accepted international law while denying its ultimate validity.

Khrushchev vacillated between regarding the United States as a potential co-ruler of the world or (more commonly) as the chief enemy. Desirous of advancing the Soviet Union by cooperation with the United States, he wished to be free to attack America by any means short of direct violence. Even this seemed hardly excluded; Khrushchev periodically tested the world's nerves with rocket-rattling crises, as in Berlin and Cuba. Yet on returning from his 1959 American tour, he told his people several things at variance with the conventional Soviet picture of the capitalist world: an American leader could be a man of peace and representative of many people and interests; the

American economy did not rest on armaments; and the American government was not merely the creature of monopolists and Wall Street.

Peaceful Coexistence promised slow death for the capitalist world system, but this death was not to come in the Leninist way, by revolutionary action of the proletariat, but through the economic and cultural superiority of the Soviet way, in which Khrushchev seems firmly to have believed. Thanks to space exploits, which gave an impression of a Soviet technological lead, and rapid economic growth in the 1950's, it seemed not unlikely that the Soviet Union would emerge as the world's dominant economic as well as military power in a fairly short time. In 1958 Khrushchev proclaimed his timetable for catching up with the United States in gross industrial output by 1965 and in per capita production by 1970. But the Soviet growth rate slowed. The Soviet system, pouring resources into heavy industry, could achieve impressive results in the first stages of industrialization, but it was less capable of innovation than the American. As the Soviet impetus wore out, Khrushchev tried more capitalist-style incentives and decentralization; but these were politically dangerous, and recentralization was called for before the end of the Khrushchev era. Meanwhile, economic growth in Western Europe, the United States, and Japan made the prospect of Soviet supremacy remote.

Khrushchev's other grand strategy was the old Russian one of expanding in Asia (or the less developed nations in general) to draw strength to fight the West. As soon as revolutionary hopes in Europe began flickering out, Lenin had turned to the colonial and semicolonial lands adjacent to Russia. According to his theory, the way to revolution in London and Paris was through China and India. The colorful Congress of the Peoples of the East at Baku in 1920 sent out a vibrant call for all the oppressed to ally themselves with the young Soviet republic. Subsequently the Comintern attempted to infiltrate or convert the nationalist movement in China, but Chiang Kai-shek nearly wiped out the Chinese Communists in 1927. The consequent disillusionment may have killed Stalin's interest in non-Communist nationalist movements for the remainder of his life. But Khrushchev had no such inhibitions, and by the time of his accession to supreme power, the time was ripe. The Soviet Union felt secure enough at home for excursions abroad, and it had resources for military and economic assistance to influence weaker nations. Soviet penetration was also facilitated by the fact that the Western powers, in contradiction to Marxist-Leninist theory, had largely withdrawn or were withdrawing from former colonial empires.

Khrushchev consequently initiated in 1955, concurrently with Peaceful Coexistence toward the West, a campaign to encourage less advanced nations of Asia and Africa in their hostility to the Western powers, and to lead them to reliance upon economic and political cooperation with the Soviet Union. They would, it was hoped, become neutralist in the East-West contest, then gradually be enticed into the "socialist camp" because this represented peace and justice. Thus the Soviet Union would become leader, if not effectively hegemon, of most of the world's peoples. Insisting on no particular definition of socialism, seeking converts almost anywhere, Khrushchev seems to have envisioned himself as leading a procession of nations toward the true path. As he said to the American ambassador, "We Bolsheviks are ravenous people. What we achieved through our struggle in the past is not enough for us. We want more—tomorrow." [8]

His optimism was not entirely unfounded. Marxism had considerable appeal for intellectuals in the less developed countries, much as it had for those of tsarist Russia. It answered their doubts, assuaged feelings of inferiority, and gave focus to accumulated resentments against the Western powers. Since much of the economy in these countries was foreign-owned, anticapitalism merged into nationalism. The success of the Russians in industrializing and mustering great power under an anti-Western doctrine made an attractive example. When the Soviets came bearing gifts and offered an alternative to dependency on the West, they found ready takers and made many friends. Castro's Cuba showed that it was not necessary for a leader to begin as a Communist. He could, if it suited, declare his country socialist and himself a Marxist-Leninist; and the Soviet Union could hope that his dependence could be made irreversible.

Yet the mixture of ideological universalism with Russian expansionism and the old civilizing mission had little success. Extreme nationalists, such as Ahmed Ben Bella in Algeria and Kwame Nkrumah in Ghana, were attractively anti-Western; but they had little idea of subjecting themselves to Soviet direction; and they had scant interest in Soviet ideology. There was always a contradiction between support for local leaders and support for Communist parties. The Russians could never fully dissociate themselves from the latter; to do so meant to weaken the general Communist movement and to cast doubt on the whole idea of a universal vocation. The Russians had to be in favor both of established governments and revolutionary change, of nationalism and international socialism, and hope that the inconsistency was not too conspicuous. More critical, in respect to the Third World they lacked the advantages they enjoyed in going into Central Asia; technically superior as they were to the less developed countries, they were far less able to supply economic needs than the West. Hence the cause was successful only where there were special reasons for antagonism to the West and a consequent desire for Russian protection, as was the case with Cuba and with the Arabs, whose enmity toward Israel overrode all other considerations.

While Khrushchev was hoping to swing at least some of the less developed countries into the Soviet orbit, difficulties arose in keeping neighboring satellite countries of Eastern Europe obedient. Shortly after Stalin's death, restiveness came into the open in East Germany and Czechoslovakia; and some relaxation was deemed necessary to calm discontent and foster economic progress. A graver threat to Soviet control impended after Khrushchev in 1956 told the Communist movement that the man it had been taught to worship was a criminal—vain, incompetent, and unbalanced. The exaltation of the leader had been an important element of Communist coherence and discipline ever since Lenin gathered a small sect in loyalty to himself, and it became relatively more important under Stalin because revolutionary idealism was left behind. Especially in the years after victory in World War II, the apotheosis of the leader was in practice the chief article of faith. When Khrushchev morally destroyed the dead *vozhd*, whom he could not replace, it was a little like the dethronement of the tsar. Fissures opened in the Communist world; people saw no more reason for blind obedience, and the organs of repression seemed to have lost the will to repress. Polish workers rioted in Poznan in June, 1956; and a little euphoria of freedom grew in Poland through the summer. In October, the Russians, with armed forces on the ground, went so far as to threaten force to check the movement toward more national self-determination. But the Poles stood their ground, and Khrushchev accepted a large measure of Polish autonomy in internal affairs. However, Poland remained tied to the Soviet Union in foreign affairs and defense, Soviet troops stayed in the country, and the special freedoms of Poland were whittled away in the next few years.

Stimulated by the Polish example, the Hungarians tried to do likewise. They were more anti-Russian than the Poles and less convinced of the necessity to rely on the Soviet Union for defense. The Hungarian Communist party fell apart; non-Communists were admitted to the government, which overplayed its hand by asking to be released from the Soviet alliance. Soviet troops returned and wrote a bloody end to this self-assertion.

In reaction to these threats of loss of dominion, the Soviet line hardened for a time, and liberal tendencies within the satellites were repressed. The Council of Mutual Economic Assistance (Comecon), which had been set up in 1949 mostly as a symbolic answer to the Marshall Plan, was brought forward to bind the satellites economically; Khrushchev had some Marxist faith in economic union. More life was also breathed into the agency of military integration, the Warsaw Treaty Organization.

After 1960, however, optimism for the Soviet-sponsored fusion of Eastern Europe faded, just as it did for the program of winning neutrals. Economic growth in most of the satellites was disappointing, and Comecon-sponsored integration lagged badly; it proved more difficult to integrate planned economies than market economies like those of Western Europe. Each country's planners wanted to control their own supplies insofar as possible, so there was much resistance to specialization. Since economic decisions were taken politically, misunderstanding and discontent were easily generated. For such reasons, the percentage of trade of Comecon members among themselves actually declined during Khrushchev's reign. Since the bureaucratized economies found innovation difficult, Eastern European economies found themselves hard pressed to keep up with world standards; and the West looked ever more attractive. But partially opening doors to facilitate modernization and the earning of hard currency (for instance, through tourism) to buy needed Western equipment only created new demands. Rumania, which had once been the most faithful of client states, managed to develop most independence, thanks largely to the withdrawal of Soviet forces in 1958. Everywhere in Soviet Eastern Europe there were tendencies toward self-assertiveness, and by the end of Khrushchev's tenure, Soviet rule seemed decadent.

The mounting quarrel between the Soviet Union and China also contributed to the destruction of myths of the great Communist wave of the future and utopian harmony in socialism. At the same time it furnished an example of deviation within the bloc and invited lesser states to play upon their differences. China seemed a faithful ally, if not actually part of the Russian sphere, until 1959, when the Russians took a neutral position in the border dispute between China and India, or 1960, when Soviet technicians were withdrawn from China. Causes of the quarrel included Chinese resentment at receiving less Soviet aid than neutrals, especially India, and Chinese demands that the Soviet Union use its strength more actively for the world revolutionary cause, in effect to help China against the United States and the American-backed Nationalist regime on Taiwan. There were ideological differences, and for years the dispute was stated only indirectly and in ideological terms. Maoism was essentially a peasant revolutionary movement, whereas Bolshevism was urban and took proletarianism and the special role of the workers fairly seriously. There were territorial issues; the Chinese still chafed at the loss not only of Mongolia but of large parts of Siberia ceded a century ago, and the Russians were reluctant to disinterest themselves in Sinkiang. Marxism-Leninism was no more effective than other creeds in maintaining unity in the absence of political or military control.

In 1963, after the Soviet Union signed the Nuclear Test Ban Treaty, the polemics turned into open name-calling. The "socialist commonwealth" lost—although the Russians were unwilling to acknowledge the departure of any member—two-thirds of its population. Dreams of a world socialist community headed by Moscow became hard to cherish when contradictions between socialist states were apparently as strong as those between capitalist states.

THE NEW STYLE

Khrushchev's approach seemed to have fallen short on all fronts by the time of his ouster in 1964, but the new leadership brought changes not of principle but of style. With no new ideas, it showed itself less bombastic, more rational and more effective, cautious and conservative. Soviet diplomats became more affable, regardless of the stridency of the press. Soviet foreign policy became still more conventional, or at least seemed to be more divorced from ideological imperatives. Outwardly, there was some return to ideological fundamentalism, with stress on the role of the party; terms such as "imperialist reaction," "workers' solidarity," "bourgeois nationalism," etc., became commoner. But Marxist-Leninism had clearly lost most of the limited intellectual significance it retained through the reigns of Stalin and Khrushchev, and the post-Khrushchev leaders did singularly little to adapt it to the demands of a rapidly evolving age.

The movement that was destined to overturn the world order had become ideologically defensive, stressing the dangers of infiltration of liberal-capitalist ideas. Revolutionary sentiments were replaced by authoritarian; in the world leftist movement, Communist parties became exponents of order. The post-Khrushchev leadership was obviously the most sophisticated the Soviet Union had ever had and perhaps ipso facto the one with least real belief in the official faith. Lenin sought to base the state on the idea of the inauguration of a new era of world history. Stalin, with all his unpleasant political methods, spoke in the name of a revolutionary transformation of Soviet society. Khrushchev believed that the Soviet Union was best qualified to lead the peoples to abundance and peace in the new age. For the colorless Brezhnev-Kosygin regime—after 1970 practically the Brezhnev regime—what little remained of the Soviet promise seemed to rest upon military power draped with ideological verbiage.

The new leaders, remembering the humiliation of the missile crisis of 1962, quietly and systematically went about building up long-range strategic power to match the American. This effort was successful, thanks in part to American preoccupation with war in Vietnam; by 1970 the Soviet Union had more or less closed the gap. The Soviet navy was also rapidly augmented, becoming equal or superior to the American by 1972 in most categories, except aircraft carriers and nuclear submarines. For the first time since the Napoleonic Wars Russia's military power was not substantially inferior to that of the West. The military was playing a larger part in the Soviet system, and military-patriotic themes loomed larger in education and the political culture.

Military strength was used to reaffirm the Soviet position in Eastern Europe. Whereas Khrushchev had counted mostly on economic integration to weld the satellites into the Soviet community, his successors looked more realistically to the military organization of the Warsaw Treaty and to the Soviet military presence to stem the erosion of Soviet authority. When Czechoslovakia, long governed by a Stalinist party but without Soviet forces in occupation, began moving away from Soviet patterns in 1968, Soviet armed forces entered to squeeze it back to conformity.

The Marxist-Leninist justification of the invasion was the so-called

Brezhnev doctrine of limited sovereignty. It was no innovation; Lenin had long ago asserted the supremacy of class over national interests, and in practice the doctrine was as old as the Russian empire. It was explained that the capitalist-imperialists, unable to attack militarily the socialist camp, resorted to subterfuge, subverting under pretenses of "improvement," "liberalization," and the like; therefore freedom of speech was inadmissible until the final victory of socialism.[9] The right of intervention to preserve socialism as defined by the Soviet Union overrode any considerations of bourgeois legality;[10] and it might be stretched to a right of intervention everywhere. "True revolutionaries, being internationalists, cannot refrain from supporting progressive forces in their just struggle for national and social liberation."[11] Rules of law being held subject to the class approach, the Soviet way was by definition right in a class sense and hence superior to law.

Whether or not such reasoning was convincing for Czechs, the judicious use of power sufficed to "normalize" the embittered land and return it to strict and dogmatic communist rule under leaders entirely acceptable to the Russians. Throughout the Soviet sphere, likewise, the Russians were able to resolidify their position. They had overwhelming force and had shown willingness to use it; it was made clear that whatever latitude Poland, Hungary, or other bloc countries might have was on Russian sufferance and that there could be no important deviation from Russian foreign and military policy.

In the effort to spread Soviet power in the Third World, the new leadership likewise relied less on ideology and economic ties and more on power and military means. Instead of scattering its attention somewhat throughout the Third World, it concentrated on lands of strategic interest and adjacent to the Soviet Union, from Turkey to India and south to Arab North Africa. Providing Soviet military aid and advisers to instruct in its use became the chief means of Soviet influence; economic aid shrank. The Soviet navy and air forces were ready to follow and make themselves at home. The Soviet leadership seemed more concerned with the image of Soviet power wherever this could be projected than with close application of the Soviet model of development,[12] favoring not so much Communists as local leaders disposed to lean on Soviet support. The socialization of the economy and the establishment of party rule could come, it seemed, in due time under gradual pressure. The collective leadership met the Khrushchev dilemma of supporting non-Communist governments by doing so where

Soviet power might hope to mold and sway the government, bringing it in line with the Soviet model and coordinating it with the Soviet apparatus.

In the post-Khrushchev years there occurred some growth of Soviet prestige and a widening of the sphere within which the Soviet Union was the preeminent power. But the old contradictions remained. From the latter 1960's the importation of processes and industrial installations was much increased, probably in awareness that the lag had been not diminishing but increasing during the previous decade. As never since the First Five-Year Plan, foreigners were invited to set up plants in the Soviet Union, many experts being retained for long periods to help operate them. There were numerous schemes like those of the 1920's whereby the Russians promised a share in their raw materials in return for production goods or capital investment, but on a much larger scale. Yet Western influences were as dangerous as ever; and as soon as barriers were lowered a notch, Western fashions and ideas began flowing into the Soviet sphere in a growing stream, from modern music and abstract art to heightened awareness of civil rights. Russia reacquired faddist youth and dissenting intellectuals. Rationalism, skepticism, and demands for civil liberties grew, threatening to erode the basis of the Soviet way of life. Minority nationalism was an ever-present, probably mounting menace.

It seemed consequently necessary to stress the separation between good and evil and the redeeming Soviet mission with its moral superiority. *Pravda* spoke almost in the same breath of good relations with "capitalist" powers, such as France and Federal Germany, and of the "socialist" countries standing firmly together in the struggle against capitalism. Soviet diplomats in the West were smiling more broadly than ever before, and the government made a number of pleasing gestures, such as agreeing to a lend-lease settlement with the United States, while the KGB cracked down on dissenters at home. As perceived by the Soviet press, poverty was a problem chiefly in the United States, Japan (the growth rate of which was disconcerting), or England, depending on the state of Soviet relations with them. The importance of discrediting the Western alternative was shown by the amount of space devoted to this in the press, regularly as much as a quarter to a third. Every opportunity was taken to belittle or downgrade the achievements of the West, even to comparing Shakespeare's alleged conceit with Pushkin's true Russian altruism. While making full use of American science, the relatively sophisticated *Literaturnaia gazeta* portrayed America as Gangsterland, and efforts to develop intellectual contacts were denounced as notorious bridge building, "ideological subversion against the socialist countries." [13] Soviet leaders and publicists characterized the present as an era of ever sharpening struggle between two diametrically opposed worlds, calling for greater vigilance against contaminating alien influences; this was the assumed major premise of hundreds of thousands of professional propagandists in the Soviet Union and their millions of part-time helpers and forms the permanent substratum of Soviet political faith. As Brezhnev said at a reception for Fidel Castro,

After having strengthened the principle of peaceful coexistence, we realize that successes in that important matter do not offer possibilities of relaxing the ideological struggle. On the contrary, we must be ready to see the struggle intensify, become an ever sharper form of antagonism of two social systems. And we have no doubt in the outcome of this antagonism, for the truth of history, the objective laws of social development, are on our side.[14]

Although acting ever more like a state on the international stage, the Soviet Union continued to express its cause in universalist terms. The victory of India over Pakistan in December, 1971, was seen as a victory not over another country but over the forces of imperialism.[15] It was insisted that "democracy," "freedom," and the like could be understood only in a "class" context, that is, as elements of the rule of the party. "Proletarian internationalism" was an essential virtue. Soviet patriotism "expresses not only love of the native land, of certain national-historical values, but dedication to the most progressive socialist social structure, scientific Marxist-Leninist ideology. . . . In essence, Soviet patriotism is an organic fusion of the feeling of love for the homeland, communist conviction, and proletarian internationalism." [16] The two aspects of patriotism were commingled, since Russianism appeared equivalent to international communism. "For us, Moscow is not simply a capital. Moscow is our history, our today, and our future. . . . The communist city, the city of communism. The city of the future. . . ." [17]

NONNATIONAL STATE

The Brezhnev-led collective leadership, like preceding rulers of the Russian domain, is unable to act fully like a territorial state nor quite like a universal or internationalist entity because it is a hybrid, a Russian-dominated entity imbued with Russian nationalism yet a multinational organization designed to sustain the loyalties of a hundred or more distinct nationalities (a number that raises images of chaos if the central authority should be dissolved). It is also a party-integrated multinational polity replacing the old Russian hybrid between a traditional Asiatic empire and a Western state.

> The Soviet people is not some sort of new nation, not a conglomerate of nations, but an international commonwealth of more than a hundred little and big nations. . . . The economic basis of this commonwealth is socialist ownership of the means of production. Its social-political basis is the Soviet government, led by the working class and its vanguard, the Communist party; its ideological basis is the ideology of the working class—is Marxism-Leninism. . . .[18]

The Soviet political system is *sui generis*. The nucleus is the Russian nation, comprising half the population of the Soviet Union, incorporated in the Russian Socialist Federal Soviet Republic. Consisting of Russia proper with Siberia, it has a large ethnic Russian majority, but it contains numerous so-called Autonomous Republics and other minority areas supposedly enjoying special rights. Outside this core, the other fourteen Soviet Republics of the U.S.S.R., the Ukraine, Georgia, Latvia, and so on, enjoy fictitious sovereignty, having joined, voluntarily in theory, to form the Soviet Union. They are constitutionally entitled to withdraw from the Union if they desire and to maintain their own foreign relations and defense forces. White Russia (Belorussia) and the Ukraine have their own membership in the United Nations, and various Asian Soviet Republics have entered into treaties with Near Eastern nations.

In fact, the Soviet Union has a highly centralist government which completely controls its supposedly sovereign constituents, their economies, financial resources, police, education, and everything except what may be left to local authorities for administrative convenience. But the basis of control is less the "federal" governmental organization than the all-embracing rule of the organizationally and ideologically united political party backed by integrated military forces. The Soviet Communist party has territorial divisions corresponding to the republics, but they are bound to obedience to the Central Committee. The omnipresent and absolute rule of the centralized party is the basis of the polity.

Legally all Soviet republics are on the same footing, but there are differences in status. Some republics, or at least some nationalities, stand higher than others. To be Russian or Belorussian is best, Ukrainian next best, with Armenian perhaps third. Under Stalin the Georgians were privileged, and since his day Georgia has seemed to enjoy a little latitude. Lowest on the scale are the mostly Turkic peoples of Central Asia. They are closely supervised by Russians or Ukrainians, and the Asian nationalities have very few representatives in the top layers of the political apparatus. Most discriminated against are the Jews, officially considered a nationality but denied any kind of corporate existence.

The rule of Moscow does not end at the official borders of the Soviet Union, and in the Soviet philosophy there is no real difference between the "commonwealth of socialist nations" which constitutes the Soviet Union, and the "socialist commonwealth" of the bloc; it is sometimes unclear which is intended by the frequently used phrase "socialist nations." The Mongolian People's Republic, which was under Russian control from 1911 and which became a Soviet satellite when the Bolsheviks won the civil war and gathered up the tsarist heritage, is close to being a Soviet Republic. It carries on diplomatic relations with a number of neutralist countries outside the Soviet bloc and is a member of the United Nations. But its economy is Soviet-controlled, it closely follows Soviet policies, and its armed forces are almost part of the Soviet. For it, joining the Soviet Union would change little.[19] Eastern European satellites have somewhat more autonomy, Bulgaria being apparently the most subservient and the German Democratic Republic the most dependent on Soviet support. Poland is slightly deviant, as in keeping an independent peasantry, but it is well aware of the potential Russian veto for any reforms it might undertake. Janos Kadar's Hungary, endeavoring to maintain some internal independence, refrains from any nonconformist gesture on the international scene. Czechoslovakia is reluctantly unfree with a wholly obedient government. Rumania seeks to keep as much independence as possible by pressing frequently near the narrow limit of Russian tolerance.

The satellites are thus semisovereign; they can privately argue, protest, or hope to influence the superior power, but they cannot oppose its will if it sees fit to act. Least of all can they conceivably have independent defense or foreign policies; their delegations in the United Nations behave as the representatives of a single power. Unlike the Soviet Republics, which carry on almost no foreign relations in the name of their fictitious sovereignty, Eastern European nations deal directly with the world outside; but they cannot swerve appreciably from the Soviet interpretation of world affairs.

The Soviet bloc in the narrower sense, including the Soviet Union, Mongolia, and the members of the Warsaw Treaty Organization (WTO) in Eastern Europe, forms a super-state looser than the Soviet Union itself but clearly set off from the outside world and effectively subject to a common direction. The Soviet Union has affirmed and reaffirmed the right of intervention in any part of this "socialist commonwealth." *Pravda* has called it a single "motherland" (*Rodina*).[20] The ordinary rules and categories of international relations, including defense and aggression, do not apply within it. Soviet relations with the components stand between conventional international relations and the dealings of an imperial capital with provincial authorities.

Farther afield, a number of other states stand in a looser relationship to the Soviet center. Countries such as Cuba and Iraq are associated by their own choice and might elect a different orientation in a changed international system; the Soviet Union may, on the other hand, hope to bring them into an indissoluble community. In a different way, Communist parties around the world are an extension of the Soviet polity. The Russians value them highly, whether for symbolic purposes, or as agencies promoting Soviet policies and views and disrupting "bourgeois" states, or as potential satellite governments. The Soviets have taken great pains to keep the movement together and to recement it after such shocks as the invasion of Czechoslovakia. The importance attributed to the foreign parties is shown by the fact that their representatives have made about half of the speeches at recent congresses of the Soviet party. The chief criterion of belonging is loyalty to the Soviet Union; "the question of relationship to the Soviet Union [is] the chief measure of the proletarian internationalism of each Communist and workers' party." [21] Some parties, especially the large Italian party, have ventured mild criticisms of the Soviet big brother. But most seem satisfied to act practically as part of the Soviet system.

The Soviet political system is thus not clearly defined because within it there are all shades of dependence and self-rule. But the law and right which must prevail over the many and diverse peoples, the rationalization of a single rule over them, must be general or universal. What is claimed as justice for the Soviet "brother-peoples" can only be absolute justice applicable outside as well as within the political borders of the U.S.S.R. The Soviet system must base itself on abstract principles, potentially applicable everywhere. "The defense of socialism is the international duty of Communists." [22] The community can only grow larger. "In close union, developing friendship and cooperation, the socialist countries are laying the foundations of the future worldwide brotherhood of peoples. And every year, every conquest of peaceful labor brings us closer to this great goal." [23]

To keep the entirety together requires the most elaborate political system ever devised, with countless intertwined formal and informal relations, a mélange of legal and de facto powers, of party and government, of ideology and interests. To stand over the whole is a demanding task for the predominantly Russian leadership. Yet few Russians doubt the rightness and necessity of holding onto it, if only because all might be lost if some part of the immense edifice should begin to crumble.

DUAL STATE

The entire Russian-centered political system is held together partly by governmental means, partly by the Communist party. The importance of the party relative to formal governmental bonds increases with distance from the center. Russians have an integrated state under party direction; but the ties holding the union republics are both governmental and party, with the former predominant in ordinary affairs. Legal means of control through the Soviet constitution are ample, and party bonds are mostly in the background. For the satellites, formal governmental unification, through treaties of friendship and alliance, Comecon and WTO, is substantial; but the real integration is through the Communist parties. Farther afield, the bonds with nonruling Communist parties are almost entirely of party nature; they belong only to the movement, with slight links to the Russian state apparatus. The government of the Soviet Union, on the contrary, stands apart from the ideologically oriented movement in its normal diplomatic relations with non-Communist countries. Soviet diplomats take pains to assure their "bourgeois" counterparts of their business-like practicality. In commerce, the Soviet Union deals very much like a capitalist, bargaining hard with friends and nonfriends alike and making deals according to convenience. The state also imports technology without prejudice as to origins.

It is a strength of the Soviet system over its tsarist predecessor that it has thus institutionalized its duality, charging the party with the chief universalist-imperialist functions, the state with administration, the management of diplomatic relations, and the acquisition and use of technology. In a small way, the Orthodox Church performed for the tsarist realm the integrative functions of the Soviet party; but the Church lacked purposeful organization, flexibility, and dynamism. In the Soviet way, the party is free to pursue universalist aims; it publicly proclaims itself (in the Preamble of its Rules) "an integral part of the international Communist and working class movement." It can be as arbitrary as it sees fit, making and applying the mythical-ideological views necessary for its rule. It can be the effective center of political purpose, purpose which is fundamentally irrational in terms of the pretenses to which the Soviet Union, as part of the modern world, must subscribe. Its central principle is unity, to be achieved by persuasion and coercion. The party is unhampered by law and little troubled by tradition or demands for logical consistency; it is beyond criticism, holds the keys of absolutism, and needs to make no concessions to pluralism.

The state, on the contrary, has the work of practical administration and conventional state relations; it is the legal, as the party is the extralegal, means of management. The government needs fixed rules of behavior in order to manage effectively; it is an enforcement agency, maintaining norms of conduct and securing the defense of the state, even while carrying out the policies of the party. It manages a great and diverse society; and everyone, in a sense, belongs to it with theoretically equal rights, whereas the party admits to its ranks only those devoted to its purposes and so separates the politically qualified from the unqualified. Hence the government is to some degree pluralistic, whereas the party can be in principle monolithic. The government can be formal, respectable, and outwardly dispassionate in its rationality; the party can be informal and passionate in its idealistic temper. The government conciliates foreign powers that the party in theory seeks to destroy. The government can subscribe to rights while the party, in the name of its higher mission, rules despotically.

The political system thus has two arms which can act independently but cooperatively; it has two voices which can be turned in different directions with different messages to different audiences. There are disadvantages, however. The ambivalence leads to conflict of jurisdiction. The party rules over the theoretically sovereign state, and it is no easier to draw boundaries of authority than to separate the actual from the theoretical. The areas of the General Secretary and Chairman of Council of Ministers, of individual ministers and sections of the Central Committee, cannot be demarcated. It is as under the tsars, when no one knew what the powers of a minister were because these depended upon his ever uncertain standing with the autocrat. A change in the status of a high Soviet leader is probably more atmospheric than formal in the basically anarchic conditions of the clouded political summit. For example, Stalin in 1939 was an absolute dictator with the same formal positions he had enjoyed in 1922, when he was a rather modest member of the Politburo. Khrushchev rose from second or third place in the Soviet hierarchy in September, 1953, to a strong first in February, 1955, without official change of status. Brezhnev seemed to have only a slight preeminence over his fellows when he became General Secretary in 1966. Still only General Secretary, he had become the dominant personality in foreign as well as domestic affairs by the middle of 1971; he might conceivably decline to equality with other Politburo members while retaining all his titles.

Party and state thus broadly represent of themselves the two sides of the Russian polity, the ideological-expansionist-imperial-Asiatic and the rational-practical-moderate-European aspects of the Russian state. But the institutions are also internally ambivalent. The party, the incorporation of arbitrary and unbounded rulership, was founded on the model of Western political parties and remains to some extent imitative of them. Thus, all authority is theoretically derived from the membership, through electoral process. But the devices developed to prevent untoward electoral results are so strong as quite to change the nature of the "elections." They are extremely indirect, so that the membership is separated from the holders of power by five or six stages, at each of which pressure can be exerted. Candidates are proposed from above, and representatives of higher bodies sit in on electoral meetings. Voting on individual candidates is open, so members can support a man unacceptable to the party hierarchy only at a risk to their party career; by secret ballot one can make only a general protest by voting against the list. It is forbidden to electioneer or organize support, except for officially approved candidates. Elections become a means whereby the authority of leaders is heightened and the party apparatus can gauge the effectiveness of leadership at various lower levels.

The trend since the Revolution has been generally toward less consultation and democracy in the party, while appearances have been maintained; the ordinary sequence is that party bodies grow larger, meet less often, and lose effective power. The party congresses met yearly through 1925, but then skipped first one year, then two, three, four, and twelve years. Now, after more frequent meetings under Khrushchev, they are to be held at five-year intervals. The gatherings have similarly evolved from a few dozen elected delegates before the Revolution to a few hundred in the early 1920's, to over 1,000 nominated delegates at the beginning of the Khrushchev era and recently about 6,000, who had to do nothing more controversial than to acclaim the party leadership. The Central Committee has followed a similar course of enlargement, with decreasing frequency of meetings and loss of importance, since the establishment of the Politburo in 1919; the latter, the nuclear body most remote from the membership, has alone kept its authority. In the same fashion, power gravitated to the Secretariat from the moment when, in 1922, it became the tool of an ambitious man. In theory designed only to assist in the execution of policies decided by the elected and consultative bodies, it became the principal, at times almost the sole, fountainhead of power.

Contradictions of form and substance are more striking in the governmental structure. For example, civil rights are abundantly guaranteed as in the best Western constitutions, with additions, including rights to rest and leisure and to education. Not only are Soviet citizens promised freedom of speech, press, and assembly, but the state engages to furnish paper, presses, buildings, and other requisites for their exercise. On the other hand, these rights are exercisable "in conformity with the interests of the working people," that is, at the pleasure of the party leadership. To indulge in even very restrained criticism of Soviet practice is likely to lead to another use of Western techniques for authoritarian purposes, psychiatric treatment for political irrationality. The constitutional freedom of political organization is balanced by police powers of extralegal repression. Another right, that to work, becomes a duty of employment by an officially recognized, that is, party-controlled agency; otherwise the Soviet citizen is subject to assignment to work or to forced labor. Such contrasts extend much beyond the constitution. For example, travel is supposedly completely free, but it is subject not only to stiff charges but to administrative and party discretion. In a different direction, a great deal is made of the equality and liberation of women, but in practice they do much more of the menial, often backbreaking work and hardly appear at all in places of power. They are conspicuous in the showpiece Supreme Soviet but absent from the omnipotent Secretariat.

The democratic forms of the state are closely parallel to those of the party, fuller in appearances and emptier of reality. Thus elections are all direct and by formally secret ballot, but the voters have no means, unlike party electors, of nominating or criticizing candidates. These elections are called "the most democratic in the world," but *Pravda* admitted [24] that free elections would destroy the "unity of the working class" and were hence inadmissible. The constitution provides (Article 49e) for plebiscites, but it has not been seen fit to use them even for show. The elected Soviets lack the limited authority of inferior party committees. The Supreme Soviet, meeting a few days a year to rubberstamp official measures, is more patently window dressing than the Party Congress, not to speak of the Central Committee, which at least brings together many important administrators who can exchange views. The Supreme Soviet is insignificant in part because it is pseudodemocratic, including champion tractor drivers, loom operators, nomadic shepherds, and so forth, persons less to be taken into account than party managers. The "deliberations" of the Supreme Soviet are much publicized, whereas those of the Politburo are entirely secret; it is a general rule that the more visible the workings of a Soviet political body, the less important.

It was not paradoxical but entirely natural that the "Stalinist" constitution, embodying full rights and providing for free and democratic elections, was proclaimed as the purges were demonstrating the fullness of arbitrary power. The democratic constitution contributed to Stalin's power by decorating it, and it was a suitable offset for the measureless abuse of power. The firmer ruler is in a better position to make empty promises than a weaker one. Nicholas II could not have made such a proclamation of freedoms without actually surrendering power. Probably the present leadership would also be afraid to go so far in extending guarantees for fear it would have to honor them. This may be a reason that constitutional reform, on the agenda for more than a decade, has made no progress. It should be noted, however, that the democratic appearances of the Constitution itself are ambiguous. The role of the Communist party is to be "the leading core of all organizations of the working people, both public and state," in effect consecrating the party's political monopoly. There is an impressive list of duties to counterbalance the rights, and a lack of means of making the latter effective.

The principles applied to the party and government are equally useful in secondary institutions. Unions, for example, have a similar pseudodemocratic structure under the control of the party. By this means, organizations nominally like those which in the West assert workers' interests against managers are in Russia devoted primarily to assisting management in raising production. In the same fashion, the outwardly democratically organized Writers' Union, a group which might be expected to stand for rights of writers and against controls, is an important adjunct of censorship, helping to fulfill "the duty of Soviet artists of the word to be on the front line of this struggle [between capitalism and socialism]. . . ." [25] Much the same is true of other Soviet organizations, which are invariably supposed to be "democratic" and responsive to their members yet guided by the party. The most significant exception is the relatively Western-oriented Academy of Sciences, where political power hesitates before the imperatives of science. Yet scientists, too, must follow the dictates of party and ideology, for they are subject to review for political as well as scientific qualifications; and party groups give scientists philosophical guidance.

In relations with non-Russians, similar principles apply. Subordination to the old empire was seen as liberation; now the extensive constitutional rights of Union republics are acclaimed propagandistically, and a state can only rise to fuller sovereignty, it is claimed, by joining the Soviet Union. Yet the sovereignty stated by the constitution is completely negated in practice, just as the republic sections of the ruling party, the Ukrainian, Georgian, and so on, are totally subject to the center. The minority peoples are theoretically encouraged in their own cultural development, but this is to be coupled with the spreading of Russian language and culture. The intermingling of political, economic, and cultural life of the "brother-peoples" is a "holy law of existence," wherein the Russians represent "internationalism"; thus, "The international working class of Transcaucasia is one of the militant sections of the Russian proletariat." [26]

The governments of satellite states are on a slacker leash. But control is exercised primarily in the same ways as in the Soviet Union, with reliance on the military, on Communist parties, and secondarily on economic and cultural integration. The precise legal situation is not important; in the Soviet way, power is not limited by law but is exercised by virtue of the mission of the party as representative of the working class.

The governing parties of the satellite countries are closely bound by tradition, ideology, and mandatory subordination to "proletarian internationalism," which is in practice synonymous with the dictates of the Soviet Union. Directives go primarily through the party. Whereas routine business proceeds through governmental channels, Brezhnev and company deal in political affairs with Gierek, Kadar, Zhivkov, and others, as party leader to party leader. The threats to Czechoslovakia before the invasion were not from the Soviet government to the Czech government. The negotiations at Cierna-nad-Tisou in July, 1968, were a strange species of diplomacy, with virtually the entire top party leadership of the two countries convening in something like a conclave of two branches of a church. Soviet ambassadors in satellite capitals are normally party figures, not regular diplomats of the kind sent to bourgeois capitals. One of the Soviet complaints against Tito in 1948 was that he treated the Soviet emissary like a bourgeois ambassador and failed to recognize his special authority. Within each of the satellite countries, the Soviet Union has projected its political style despite their different situations, and the institutions of façade and control are copied in detail, in party and state structures and means of management. It is in this line that they are all officially "Democratic Republic," or "People's Republic," titles unnecessary for democratic or popular governments but appropriate for new-style autocracies.

Such antitheses of borrowed forms and politically directed substance, of the Western and Oriental or of derivations of the pluralistic state system and the universal empire, are everywhere. For example, the organization of Pioneers, the schoolchildren, owes much in style to the Boy Scouts, including the kerchief and the motto "Be Prepared," although purposes are quite different. Among the most Western-patterned Soviet agencies is the court system, influenced by the Western legal mentality, as was the court system of latter tsarist decades. However, courts take account above all of the character of the accused, that is, his loyalty, while judges are party members, named by the party and subject to its discipline. Forms are to be observed according to "socialist legality," but they are not permitted significantly to interfere with the exercise of power; arbitrary and illegal actions are to be done legally.[27]

Marxism-Leninism, which belongs above all to the realm of the arbitrary, is likewise ambivalent. It is a mystic basis for power, whereby a certain political party, arbitrarily anointed as spokesman and guide for the working class, knows the will of the latter even when the workers themselves do not, and the works of a sainted individual become scripture. It is also a rationalistic, pseudoscientific structure allegedly resting not on revelation but factual evidence. It is a theory of history which becomes a program for ordering and governing society. It is a deterministic analysis melted into a voluntaristic rationalization. This leads to contradictions like those of the Soviet state, since directions of cause and effect are reversed. The political superstructure makes the economic base, and the authority of nonproletarians is justified by the rights of the proletariat. Hence, too, Soviet society must look to a utopia of freedom as goal, but the utopia cannot be allowed to come nearer. Although the logical basis of classes has supposedly been destroyed long ago, "socialism is a class society, and government under socialism necessarily bears a political, class character." [28]

The contrasting sides of Russian institutions can be characterized as appearances for appearances' sake and power for the sake of power, as was broadly the case with the comparable contradictions of tsarist times. Some such discrepancy between sanctimonious pretenses and less attractive realities is universal in politics and is perhaps inevitable wherever people feel some responsibility to standards not entirely convenient to their actions. But in the Russian reality this incongruity is especially prevalent, reflecting the tension between the two aspects of Russian life. This suggests hypocrisy, more or less cynical and deceitful covering up of realities. Certainly, such an interpretation cannot be entirely excluded. Soviet leaders are well aware that their claims of overwhelming public support are not factual. It is often admitted by implication, sometimes explicitly, that the Soviet system ("socialism") could not survive with freedom of speech and the press and democratic elections. It is revealing that democracy, according to the Soviet *Encyclopedic Dictionary* (1963), is "The form of government in which the will of the majority is legally recognized as the basis of authority, and freedom and equality are proclaimed"; Soviet democracy is indeed a matter of legal forms and proclamations. The entire system is designed, and skillfully designed, to concentrate power; and permitting freedom or democracy means conceding power outside the party. As Stalin said, "And what is meant by setting the kulak free? It means giving him power." [29] One may logically assume that the Soviet rulers did not take seriously the reasons they alleged for the invasion of Czechoslovakia, that they were summoned by Czech communists or that they were rescuing a socialist country. The fact that they did not speak out for several weeks indicates difficulty in deciding how to put the best face on it. At the time, Brezhnev is said to have told Alexander Dubček, captive in Moscow, "We have managed with other small nations, why not with yours?" [30]

But if colonialism is a duty for Russia, if democracy consists in the unanimity with which citizens are brought to make obeisance to the powers, this is not merely calculated two-facedness and cant. There is some parallel between the eighteenth-century aristocrats who aped the West in dress and styles and the party leaders who apply Western vocabulary and styles to their political machine. There is a felt need to do things properly, as long as or insofar as this does not interfere with the job of running the realm. It was surely a satisfaction to Stalin to have himself presented as a great democrat at the time when he was ticking off names of former associates to be executed.

Some or much of the unreality of democratic or pluralistic institutions may be quite unintended. It may be caused by exigencies of politics and contrary to widespread desires. Thus one may conjecture that there was no particular design of depriving the Central Committee of power after the setting up of the Politburo in 1919, but the smaller body was more efficient. There was also pressure to include friends in the Central Committee, thereby enlarging and incidentally incapacitating it. There was nothing in the Russian situation to hinder centralization, as there is, for example, in the American; but it has always seemed the easiest way, if not the necessary means, of preventing loss of power. The secretaryship of the British cabinet did not become a political force; if the secretaryship of the Soviet party did so, this was probably contrary to the intentions of everyone at the center except the secretary and his followers. But the secretary's office was suitable for the making of countless necessary little decisions, especially of personnel, which implied power for him who made them; and in the intrinsically antipluralistic society, no one was able to check the secretary. For Russia, the antidemocratic reality seems natural or inevitable;

Russians, instead of reproaching themselves for hypocrisy, are satisfied to pour authoritarian politics into democratic molds, as Catherine II took pride in the liberalism and progressiveness of paper rights and façade institutions. The dichotomy is not simply of sham and reality but of the two sides of the Russian character, and it is not to be overcome as long as the Soviet Union feels the need to make a bow to foreign models and the political philosophy evolved in the European state system while holding together a multinational empire.

DICHOTOMY OF POLICY

Just as institutions have their contrary aspects, Soviet policies have tended variably toward the realization of Western patterns and toward uninhibited exercise of centralized power. Repeatedly throughout Soviet history there has been debate, at first open and later mostly behind the scenes, over values and priorities; through them has run a common theme: restraint and legality versus arbitrary exercise of power; freedom and initiative versus management; free art versus "socialist realism"; local autonomy versus centralization; material incentives versus political drives; practical considerations versus ideological; receptivity and openness versus xenophobia and exclusivism; willingness to collaborate with others versus self-isolation. The two sides have been those of moderates and extremists in the party, of the more practical against the more ideological. They represent achievement by technology and initiative against achievement by order and authority. In the Soviet context, the difference is spoken of as that of "Rightists" versus "Leftists," although these terms lose the meaning conventionally given them elsewhere. In Western politics, Rightist parties have often been more inclined to condone the use of force by the state; in the Soviet this has pertained to Leftists.

The division in essence is a replay of the controversy of Westernizers and Slavophiles, the former urging the necessity of adopting Western values as well as tools, the latter pleading the special rightness of Russia. It is basically the same division that split official policy through the nineteenth century, between those who favored a constitution, civil rights, and the Duma against the partisans of autocracy, censorship, and the Orthodox faith—between those who would improve and strengthen Russia by importing more Western ways and institutions and those who would preserve Russian integrity through imperial

institutions. In a word, it reflects the old Russian ambivalence between
the Western and Eastern modes of strength.

Prerevolutionary Russian Marxists, too, suffered the duality. Some
turned revisionist and would have made Marxism a doctrine of reform
and economic progress instead of revolution; against them Lenin po-
lemicized violently. Among the Marxists who met to set in motion the
Russian Workers' Social Democratic party in 1903, there developed
this same split between soft and hard lines. In the terms of the day, it
was between those who emphasized "spontaneity" and those who
looked to "consciousness." The former saw Russian development pro-
ceeding naturally and following Western patterns; the latter wished to
push sluggish history into the maelstrom of revolution, in which Russia
should have a leading role. The actual issue over which the party split
even before it was properly born was insignificant, a slight difference
in wording of the statutes whereby Lenin wished to make it a little
harder, Julius Martov and others a little easier, to claim membership
in the party. But the Marxist intellectuals were ready to take sides in
the fundamental issue of Russian politics, most of them opposing Lenin.
As moderates and activists, Mensheviks and Bolsheviks, they pulled
apart, first forming factions, then separate parties on Lenin's insistence.
In 1917, the Mensheviks refused to move to take power, for the sensible
and logical but politically futile reason that Russia was not ready for
socialism. As usual before and since, the moderates were the more
numerous side, but their opponents were politically more effective,
better organized and more purposeful.

In the Revolution, Lenin took the Leftist side against the majority
of his own party, who opposed seizure of power as too dangerous until
the Bolsheviks should be able to gather broader popular support. Having seized the reins of power, Lenin insisted on an all-Bolshevik government rather than a coalition. In November, he wanted to cancel
elections for the Constituent Assembly, and in January he dissolved
the only democratically elected assembly of Russian history, thereby
turning his back on the libertarian side of the revolutionary movement.
Along with revival of absolutism (censorship, political police, etc.,
which he had once much decried) Lenin restored Russian utopianism
and universalism—the absurdity of stricken Russia promising redemption for the world being a demonstration of the prevalence of political
feelings over logical reasoning.

But Lenin, more than many of his fellows, was sensitive to facts;

and in February, 1918, he shifted to the moderate end of the spectrum in demanding acceptance of peace with the Germans, the class enemy with whom, in the imperial-ideological mentality, there could be no peace. After giving free rein to utopianism and universalism in the civil war, Lenin yielded to economic necessity when the conflict was over and reconstruction, with the help of the West, was in order. Subsequently, as recovery in peace proceeded, Lenin came to have misgivings about the compulsion accompanying his regime, especially in respect to the minorities, and favored substantial decentralization.

Stalin's first major contribution, his ideological espousal of "Socialism in One Country," was a step in the direction of nationalism and normalization. He renounced universalistic obligations, although not the corresponding claims to political superiority. But shortly after attaining full powers, Stalin embarked on a leftist-utopian-autocratic program, making rulership far more effective than for centuries past. He turned the foreign Communist parties onto a futile radical-leftist course of intransigent, pseudorevolutionary action and attacks preferentially on moderate leftists. By collectivization he subjugated the one sector of Soviet society with a slight degree of independence, the last actual or potential support for non-Stalinists in the party. He also brought the peasants into an organization like but more effective than the old peasant commune for extracting tribute, thereby more than reimposing the burden of taxation which had been largely lifted by the Revolution. He also proceeded in Russian fashion to forced-draft borrowing of Western agricultural technology.

The inauguration of Five-Year Plans did for industry something of what collectivization did for agriculture, placing industry in the service of the state and imposing by bureaucratic action the modernization generated elsewhere by private action. Like collectivization, planned industrialization destroyed remnants of private power in Soviet society; and it reduced production for private use, squeezing out artisan and small-scale industry, giving all priority to heavy industry and production for the state. More determinedly than any ruler since Peter, Stalin took over Western technology to strengthen the autocratic state against the West. This was accompanied by a mighty ideological campaign, which generated real enthusiasm; by political-economic action Russia was going to realize the utopia that the overthrow of the old order had failed to produce. Concurrently, Stalin mobilized culture in his service, ordering, with less success, that writers pro-

duce inspiration just as workers were mobilized to make steel. The
demand for compulsory dedication was general; a hero should love his
tractor and the party, not a mere maiden. Finally, in the purges Stalin
not only physically eliminated persons of any apparent capacity for
independence but psychologically crushed the remainder, so that savage
brutalities were accepted as passively as in the days of Ivan the Terrible.

Why Stalin was able to override opposition and carry out such
drastic "Leftist" policies, reversing secular trends and the tendency of
the first years after the civil war, is not easy to understand. His amo-
rality, suspiciousness, and unquenchable thirst for power contributed.
But Stalin's rise was only part of a general trend, the replacement of
the émigré intellectual leadership by men of the "lower depths," the
non-Westernized and more primitive layers of Russian society, not
only untouched by Western political ideas but positively hostile to
them. This did not seem decisive as long as top positions were filled
by the former exiles, men of some intellectual quality who had been
exposed for years or decades to the Western atmosphere. But they
were few, a thin frosting on top of the state apparatus. As the years
passed, attrition diminished their numbers, their influence decreased as
cruder men pushed upward on party and state ladders, their idealistic-
revolutionary mentality became discordant with the politics of the
settling bureaucratic state, and they were discredited by the failure
of the world revolutionary movement to which they were committed.
Stalin seems to have nourished deep hatred and scorn for them, and his
Socialism in One Country was a club to beat them down. As they lost
standing, Stalin and others equally harsh, like Lazar Kaganovich and
N. I. Yezhov, could come to the fore; many thousands of ruthless
collaborators were required to execute the Stalinist cruelties.

The growth and maturity of the apparatus of rule also made possible Stalin's leftist-dictatorial turn. The effort to drive the economy
by force and decrees during the civil war barely functioned by virtue
of strong dedication and rapidly broke down after the war ended;
illegal commerce filled the markets, and efforts, such as Trotsky's, to
rebuild by militarized labor failed dismally. The Soviet state was not
yet well enough coordinated to mobilize its citizens. But lines of authority in state and party were steadily tightened; the propaganda
machine was perfected and enlarged; party men came to take for
granted their exercise of power over the country. Idealists and doubters
were cast aside; and hardfisted bosses, happy to tie their will to Stalin's,
took charge.

While Stalin was carrying absolutism to bloody extremes, follow-ing the logic of Russian domestic primitivism, his government was responding to the international situation and reacting to the greater proportion of Russians in the state by turning to more nationalistic policies, internally and externally, as previously noted. Revolutionary license was replaced by a puritanical ethos and conservative family legislation, and education turned from experimentation to strict teach-ing. In the war, the Soviet Union became more than ever like a Russian national, albeit autocratic state. With territorial expansion after the war and renewed problems of imperial management, Stalin turned back to a more dogmatic dictatorial approach, demanding total conformity and unity around the leader under Marxist-Leninist-Stalinist doctrines of party authority. There were blood purges, and art and literature were made more sycophantic than ever.

But Stalinism had undercut the preconditions of its existence by educating a new class of engineers and qualified specialists; and it was becoming impractical to rule the economy by dictatorial fiat, especially in view of the growing need for Western technology in the electronic age. The necessity of relaxation to permit progress and further mod-ernization led to opening tendencies as soon as Stalin's hand was re-moved—there were hints of thaw even before his disappearance. Malen-kov softened the Soviet line both internally and externally. Khrushchev was able to use his position as party boss to turn the party against Malenkov because of the alleged dangers of such softening; but, having removed Malenkov from headship of the government, Khrushchev himself took measures in the same direction, as called for not by party requirements but by the needs of the country. He relaxed international tensions (despite crises off and on), increased trade and travel abroad, slackened controls on the economy, attempted some regionalization, paid more heed to the experts and specialists, and admitted that the writers knew better than the party how books should be written.

Through Khrushchev's tenure the old dichotomic controversies continued, between "steel-eaters" and proponents of more consump-tion goods, between the bosses who would keep writers in harness and those who would set them free to create. Khrushchev himself, with his modernizing of ideology (which was denatured by being mostly con-verted into an accessory of production) and de-Stalinization (which contravened the Soviet rule that unsuitable facts should be kept hid-den), leaned slightly toward the liberal side. A very human individual, he liked jokes, social affairs, and colorful nonbureaucratic language;

he permitted people to disagree with him. He counted on Soviet progress to defeat the West, but he saw that progress required easing of controls. He felt, too, the necessity of making more bows to democracy. In a few cases he permitted wide-ranging discussion of public policy issues, and proposed the use of plebiscites for legislation—an idea probably in effect vetoed by the party apparatus, for which public expression of differences is excessively dangerous. A significant gesture was to promote the party from representative of the proletariat—which had supposedly long since ceased to exist as an exploited class—to representative of the whole people, and "soviets of the toilers" became "soviets of the people." Basic Marxian notions were thereby pushed farther away.

The tide of liberalization swelled in Khrushchev's last years and contributed to his downfall. Changes of Communist party rules in 1961 were intended to make it less of an élitist secret society and more like a Western party, members being given more rights of communication and criticism. A monument was proposed to Stalin's victims. After the Cuban crisis, there was greater acceptance of the state system as an enduring reality. The high point came in September, 1964, with the posthumous publication of Palmiro Togliatti's frank analysis of Stalinism and call for "open debates on current problems." Yet concurrently Khrushchev shut most of the churches that Stalin had permitted, intensified atheistic propaganda, wanted all children educated in boarding schools, gave neighborhood meetings the power to banish undesirables, and imposed for the first time capital punishment frankly for economic crimes.

The Russian antithesis has become equivalent to that between party and popular interests, and the post-Khrushchev collective leadership stood more decidedly for the party apparatus interest than had Khrushchev. Aware that the ferment he had permitted to grow in Soviet society might become uncontrollable, the collective leadership sought to combat it by carefully applied controls and a heavy diet of indoctrination. It was possible to do so at least in part because of violence and tension in the world, particularly the effect of war in Vietnam in reinforcing the Soviet ideological picture of the world. After the Soviet leadership undertook a military response to the Czech liberalization of 1968, the fear generated, together with the success of forceful measures in halting solvent tendencies, led to a general hardening.

Yet the old controversies of liberalizers versus authoritarians remained. An economic reform program in 1965 reflected the differences by favoring both sides, giving more latitude for managers while returning centralized economic ministries. But the first was largely nullified, apparently by resistance of local bosses, and central control was reinforced, through the party itself as well as ministerial authorities. In the same spirit, much effort was made to supplement material rewards with "morale" incentives—honors and praise, which are psychologically akin to showpiece soviets. Relying heavily on means of persuasion, the state supplemented desiccated Marxism-Leninism with more traditional and authoritarian themes, especially the cult of Lenin and military-patriotic propaganda. It resorted, however, to forcible repression as far as felt necessary. Perhaps because of its emphasis on psychological factors, its special contribution was psychiatric treatment for dissenters. When Chaadaev was declared officially insane by Nicholas I, he was put under house arrest; under Brezhnev, mental hospitals were made prisons for sophisticated dissenters.

Yet the self-righteousness of the government seemed to shrink; it was a milestone that in December, 1970, several death sentences of Jews were commuted in response to world opinion. The number of Jews permitted to emigrate rose from zero under Stalin and a few dozen under Khrushchev to tens of thousands in 1971 and after. As the Soviet economy tended to stagnation and, no longer much propelled by ideological motivation, fell farther behind the innovative West, the Soviet Union became more cordial to foreign businessmen. By 1972, projects for joint development of Soviet resources became the order of the day, although realizations lagged far behind talk. In May, 1972, the chief of world communism, Brezhnev, welcomed the chief of world capitalism (as seen by Russia) to Moscow and signed a series of agreements, including a declaration of principles which, if literally followed, would have laid their antagonism to rest. Shortly afterward the Soviets began buying over a billion dollars of American wheat. In view of these developments, it was almost predictable that there should follow an internal crackdown, yet another campaign of ideological reassertion, arrests of dissidents, and an effort to wipe out the underground press, the so-called *Samizdat* circulating illegal publications. In June, 1973, Brezhnev, returning Nixon's visit, talked much more like a traveling salesman than a Leninist, and the man who lived severely secluded in Moscow and spoke mostly in

Communist clichés bantered amiably with American capitalists. At the time, Soviet press began treating the United States as a normal and interesting country instead of a morass of capitalist iniquity and emphasized as never before the importance of economic collaboration. Yet a few months later the old themes of dangers of subversion and the basic hostility of the two systems were again to the fore, and the little band of civil rights advocates was practically eliminated by the heightened diligence of the KGB.

The basic ambiguity of Soviet policy, the contradiction between requirements for imperial rulership of a state which in the way of the modern Western nation-state system would not be a state at all and the requirements of material progress in a rapidly developing world, remains little changed. But the responses to this situation continuously vary. Values of leaders differ, as do their ruthlessness in applying controls and boldness in permitting or fostering change. The international environment and the pressures of competition rise and fall—and the Soviet state has most relaxed restraints not when secure from foreign dangers but when most directly threatened. Some competing parties were permitted to exist (but hardly to function) during the civil war only to be eliminated when it was over. Stalin's "year of the great change," 1929, when he set out to subject agriculture and industry absolutely to the state, was a time of maximum tranquillity in the world. The great purges came to a halt in 1938 when the failure of the Western powers to restrain Hitler in Austria and Czechoslovakia showed that the Soviet Union faced not a bugaboo but a real danger. Censorship was slack in World War II and merciless after it. The Vietnam war evidently contributed to ideological fundamentalism, and American disengagement from Vietnam to more open attitudes. But Soviet policy, like tsarist, remains fundamentally polarized, one direction headed by party leaders, police, and bureaucrats, the other by managers, intellectuals, and technicians in general, the one stressing ideology, discipline, and production for strength, the other advocating openness, reform, and production for welfare. The relative influence of the two sides of the Russian character changes with circumstances and social development, but they must continue to wrestle as long as Russia seeks to maintain a non-Western empire by Western means.

6

Leninism Decadent

RENEWAL BY REVOLUTION

Democratic governments that have been too long in power grow stale and ineffective. They become smug and complacent, and exhaust their stock of ideas and drive to innovation; they develop bureaucratic rigidities and permit nests of privilege to form. The degeneration of the great authoritarian states, stiff, uncreative, incapable of real self-criticism, without means of checking or timely removal of the ruler, is far graver. They have always been subject to decadence, an often fatal disintegration of social order wherein common purpose is lost and corrupt self-seeking erodes the polity. Thus each dynasty of China's millennial imperial history lost vitality and dynamism, with ebbs and flows, eventually sinking into stupor. Likewise did the Roman empire, the Mongol, and all others which illuminate the pages of history. To restore the health of the state, it is seemingly necessary partly or thoroughly to submit it to the purgatory of violence, partially to destroy it in order to remake it. Again and again, after Chinese dynasties rotted to the core, there came a time of deep disorders and revolution; a new leadership took over and reconstructed a new, strong state, vowing to do differently and better than their evil and enfeebled predecessors. The Roman empire repeatedly found renewal and catharsis in civil wars and contests for the succession; after the long disorders of the third century there emerged a partially new empire enjoying renewed vitality under Diocletian and Constantine until decadence again overtook it.

Because of its continual relations with and borrowing from the West, the Russian empire did not become so calcified as self-sufficient empires. But it, too, had semi-revolutions which shook up and invigorated the élite. Ivan the Terrible slaughtered and degraded the old nobility and raised up a new class of parvenus prepared to follow his will and build a new state. Peter likewise carried out a virtual revolution both by renewal of the élite and by the introduction of new state forms. Ignoring traditional ranks and interests, he brought together able helpers of many origins, men dedicated to his new vision of Russia. As long as tsars were strong, each succession was potentially a mini-revolution. The tsar could and would dispatch the outworn and usually hated ministers and favorites of his predecessor and bring in a new staff to man the upper echelons of the state.

The increasing inability of tsars to wield useful authority in the nineteenth century caused a political vacuum; the regime became stiffer, more bureaucratized, and more alien to national life. But the collapse of traditional institutions in 1917, along with defeat in the World War, disintegration of authority, and years of civil war aggravated by banditry and economic ruin cast Russia into political and social turmoil almost without example in modern history. The plight of the Russians may best be compared to the travails of Chinese society in the generation preceding 1949. In Russia, as in China, the collapse made it possible for the most vigorous men to come to the top and make a new state, anathematizing the foul and unjust old regime, promising to end privilege, do everything better, and make a new Russia. It was a time of keen competition, when men had to struggle to survive, to excel if they were to advance themselves.

These were times of excitement and promise, the heroic period to which the Soviet Union looks back. The people, who had come to expect everything of the rulership and had reaped only disappointments, could kindle new hope. The promised perfect social order would bring a moral if not a material heaven on earth. The Bolsheviks proclaimed not only a new government but a new social order and family life, new values and new morality, a liberated art, all free from the poison of private property and selfishness. The prospect of making a fresh and better society inspired self-sacrifice and gave life new significance. Idealists and bold free spirits, who would never have made a bureaucratic career, surged upward in the revolutionary swirl. Young people, prepared to give their all for the sole reward of serving the cause, could rise to the summit of power instead of wearing themselves out in petty offices.

The accumulated discontents of generations gave way to equally fervent hopes of improvement. Shortly before the centurions of the French Revolution came for him, Condorcet could write, "The perfectibility of man is absolutely infinite." Similarly, Trotsky in 1924, when ardor had already cooled, predicted that in the new society, "The average human type will rise to the height of an Aristotle, a Goethe, or a Marx. And above this ridge, new peaks will rise." [1] Infused with all the millenarianism and messianism of the long-suffering people, politics became religion; and the more violent the disturbance the greater the hopes of redemption.

Particular interests were swept away in favor of general claims moralized in the interests of utopian harmony and happiness. The very idea of revolution became holy, desirable per se, like freedom, the symbol of all improvement. In the time of excitement, of passionate fears and consuming hopes, of new aspirations, ideas, and ideals, the Revolution evoked dedication on all sides, but mostly in those who believed they had the most to offer. Simplicity replaced ostentation; and the Bolsheviks prevailed in accordance with the Sukhomlinov rule, that the fancier uniforms lose the war. In the civil war, the anti-Bolshevik generals consoled themselves with alcohol and women, but Leninist leaders were abstemious and hard-working, ready to renounce material privileges and receive a workman's pay. They, and many among the masses, saw the sharing of material goods and life with minimal individual property as a great moral good and a promise of ending all the troubles of humanity.[2]

Because they feel themselves endlessly righteous, those who propose to reorder the world are prepared to use power without compunction, forcing people, if necessary, to be free and happy. Thus, the Russian Revolution gave the world a new political concept, totalitarianism, which is autocracy vitalized by idealization and fortified by modern instruments. Inhibitions were cast aside; Bolsheviks felt able to advocate not only the destruction of the Church and all religion but the abolition of the conventional family. They would make a new state according to their blueprints, introduce new codes of behavior and law. As in the French Revolution, reason could be enthroned, although not always heeded. Wealth could be divorced from position, the organs of the state could be modernized and shaped to fit new purposes. Society could be purposefully reintegrated as common people were given new dignity and women and persons of national minorities were brought into the mainstream of political and economic life. In the rush of change, everything could be modernized; symbolic were the 1918 reform of the Russian alphabet and the adoption of the calendar in use in the Western world—both changes paralleled in the reforms of Peter.

Like the French Revolution, which gave France strength to conquer nearly all Europe, the Russian Revolution had inevitably to age and lose potency. The élan of the first months and years, when people saw utopia glowing on the horizon and believed the imminent triumph of world revolution would compensate all their hardships and bring the era of harmony and abundance, could not last long. The misty visions were dissipated by harsh experience, years of hard work with poor rewards; and the excitement of novelty sank into the tedium of disillusionment. But Lenin's Revolution has maintained its spiritual vitality remarkably well; something of its spirit is still alive in grandchildren of its makers.

A number of circumstances have conspired to retard the aging of the Russian Revolution or to rejuvenate it. One is that ideology reinforced, systematized, and prolonged the idea of revolution. It was intellectualized and joined to modern ideas of science and progress to give more plausibility to its claims. Marxism made it not merely the ouster of the decrepit, rotten old system and its beneficiaries but the inauguration of a new era on the basis of a sophisticated and fairly plausible modern intellectual analysis. Marxism gave the Revolution the broadest possible meaning and a rationalization which excused the slowness of its results. It raised the struggles surrounding and subsequent to the renovation of the social order above mere self-seeking and schematized them in ideal and universal terms. The circumstances of the civil war favored this interpretation. Inasmuch as the young Soviet state saw and portrayed itself as victim of world capitalism and its victory as correspondingly glorious, it gained a philosophical basis for contempt for the enemy and exaltation of Soviet virtues. Hence the Soviets kept up by intensive propaganda the thesis of inevitable conflict between capitalism and socialism, the conviction that the Soviet Union was sure to be invaded again. To the extent that the government could sustain martial spirit the Soviets were morally at war for decades after the Revolution, and they remain propagandistically half at war today.

Marxism also made possible the formulation of policies in the class terms of the original revolutionary drive and so permitted a revival of the revolutionary transformation, a renewal of some of its spirit over a decade after the seizure of power. The socialization of agriculture could be presented as the completion of revolutionary promises of destroying the evils of private ownership and bringing people together. The industrialization program, calling for all together to achieve by economic construction what had not been attained by political upheaval, provided new inspiration. Now, in its socialist industrialization, Russia was indeed taking the leadership of the world and showing the way to the new Eden. Great cities rose where only a few herders had ranged. As John Scott relates it, tens of thousands of persons endured the severest hardships to fight the battle for steel in Magnitogorsk, many of them enthusiastically, with a sense of building a new world; the youth especially studied and worked day and night.[3]

The terror that followed was likewise made possible by the momentum that Marxist formulation gave to the Revolution. Comparison with the less rationalized French Revolution is instructive: five years after its beginning, the Reign of Terror and the fever of change were at an end; twenty years after Lenin's October, Stalin's purge was in full spate. Belief in the right of the party as representative of the workers, the class of the future, disarmed the opposition, especially the intellectuals, and armed the executioners.*

By the beginning of World War II, however, the despotic Stalinist state was clearly becoming decadent. The economic growth rate slowed, and the war with Finland showed up both diplomatic self-deception and extraordinary military incapacity despite large expenditures in previous years. Unpreparedness in June, 1941, likewise reflected the smugness of the leadership; and the disastrous losses of the first months showed up continuing military incompetence and widespread disaffection.

But the war retempered and revivified the Soviet state. Hitler thought the Red Army's losses of men and equipment sufficed to remove it as a fighting force, but the national danger brought back a sense of community and purpose, and patriotism mingled with ideology to make possible extremely effective mobilization. With a little stretch of logic, the Nazi attack was seen as confirmation of the revolutionary

* According to Nadezhda Mandelshtam, the conviction of having entered a new era amounted to something like a hypnotic trance.[4]

theses, and people joined in inspired but realistic dedication to survival through cooperation.

Russia emerged hurt but rejuvenated. The victory, the greatest of Russian history, seemed to justify everything that had been done and to compensate for all sufferings, especially of industrialization, even of collectivization and somewhat illogically the purges. The rightness of the Revolution was proved in the most convincing of all ways, by battle. Again, Russia was the elect of destiny, having saved mankind from the fascist scourge.

The experience of war made a committed and deeply patriotic generation, confident in their right and anxious to give Russia the power to prevent such danger and suffering in the future.* The élan of victory was apparently responsible for the very high growth rates of the first postwar decade, which occurred despite and not because of the suffocating centralized controls of Stalinism. The Soviet leadership appreciates the inspirational value of the war, for every effort has been made, through hundreds of movies, thousands of novels and memoirs, plays, innumerable grand monuments, and countless lectures and lessons, to keep alive its memory. Wartime comradeship is still appealed to as a social control. *Pravda* writes of a complainer, "How could he slander his former senior comrade, the director, a brave fighter?" [5] There are recurrent trials for war crimes, supposedly uncovered a generation later and vastly publicized; the resultant executions—some forty Soviet citizens from 1971 through 1973—are a means of sustaining images of wartime suffering and hatred for the common evil and presumably the spirit of heroism and sacrifice.

From 1965 through 1972, war in Vietnam, daily portrayed as the heroic fight of a small socialist nation against the aggression of the chief capitalist-imperialist nation, assisted this effort to keep the ideology alive. It served to discredit the Western alternative to the Russian way, since the Soviets had only to adopt the judgment of leading Western intellectual circles and to observe the moral disarray of the most advanced Western power to renew faith in Soviet prospects. The image of violence nourished feelings that are more useful than logic for the ideological view. "Imperialism" was effectively equated

---

* War experiences and suffering at the hands of the Nazis similarly tempered much of the Communist leadership of Eastern Europe. For the Chinese Communists, revolution, civil war, and world war were rolled into one; and the Long March furnished top leadership for some forty years.

with "capitalism" and to a large extent took its place as the designation of the enemy. Thus *Pravda*[6] quoted the Declaration of the 1969 Conference of Communist parties: Peaceful Coexistence "is a means of development of class war against imperialism on a national and world-wide scale." The Soviet press showed its attachment to the Vietnam theme by virtually ignoring the withdrawal of American forces and playing up the conflict in terms of atrocities and genocide as strongly in 1972 as in 1968. The cease-fire agreement of January, 1973, was treated as a great victory for the "socialist" forces.

Despite this fortuitous reinforcement, the aging of the Revolution can only be a little slowed, not reversed, by ceaseless incantation. A revolution must be fresh and young to be exciting; for it to come into old age is self-contradictory, if not tragic. Not only the battles against the Whites but the national struggle against the Nazis are far in the past; the much-abetted collecting of war relics can give them only a little reality in the eyes of the generation now pressing at the doors of power. The Soviet citizen may harbor to this day, or be able to conjure up on occasion, some of the emotions that made bearable or exciting the materially wretched life of the early years, the sense of belonging to a cause, with companionship and self-fulfillment in sacrifice. But after exuberance the spirit flags, in Russia as elsewhere. Controls accepted as necessary for mobilization become mere repression. The fever yields to calm, perhaps to disillusion, as expectations aroused make idealists more critical of deficient reality. In the French Revolution, the heroic champions of liberty gave way to the manipulators and speculators of the Directory. Other revolutions have undergone a parallel fate and more rapidly than the Russian since they were shallower and less fortified by a philosophic rationale. For example, it has been remarked of the Egyptian revolution which overthrew a corrupt monarchy in the name of national revival: "The revolutionary élan which existed for a brief time in the late 1950's and early 1960's has waned. Nowhere is this more evident than in the moribund Arab Socialist Union. . . . Its trademark has been rhetoric, not reform, manipulation, not mobilization."[7]

FADING IDEOLOGY

Unless they can maintain ideological conviction, the Soviet leadership cannot hope to avoid a creeping degradation. A utopia is as necessary to the Soviet system as heaven to conventional religions because it is the basis for a legitimacy that is dubious in the absence of expression of the popular will. Only a mission of transcendental improvement saves the Soviet system from sheer self-seeking and greed for power and privilege by the élite and lifts it above mundane tyranny. Without it, would-be bearers of a lofty cause become simple despots, single or collective. The leaders must themselves feel a higher vocation to keep from cynicism. Without a common commitment, it would be more difficult, perhaps impossible, to avoid serious divisions within the leadership. Ideology fills some of the role of a constitution in the allocation of authority, justifying the role of the party leadership; without it such potential power-wielders as the military would be difficult to repress. If people are not convinced of the virtues of the state, they must at least be impressed by its inevitability and irreversibility, which make conformity.

To keep all in a single pattern requires that the pattern be arbitrarily set at the center; this would be unbearable unless the élite shared a strong common purpose. Without belief in a cause, controls would be unworkable; the more integrated the state, the greater the need for an integrating faith. It is essential for the health of the economy, to overcome irrationalities of overcontrol, not that the people be enthusiastic but that there be a sufficient number of controllers desirous of making the system function. The defense industry is far more successful than light or consumer industry not only because the former receives more resources but because it has more inspiration. The Soviet state can better direct the writers than the tsarist because it has more positive ideas of what it wants. Ideology lies at the heart of the Leninist solution.

For this reason, the Soviet élite has made an extraordinary effort to sustain revolutionary-ideological conviction. Especially the post-Khrushchev leadership has made a major point of indoctrination. In 1971 for the first time there was promulgated a detailed, ipso facto formalistic and desiccated program for the ideological formation of university students. Political training of soldiers has been stressed as never before. The use of all media has been heightened, and propaganda has been made the full-time employment of hundreds of thousands, the part-time business of millions.

To make the message credible, an essentially very conservative élite keeps up something of a revolutionary stance, insisting that they truly represent a unique movement of social and political change. Only

they are true Leftists; it is a Soviet mannerism to refer to "Left" devi-
ations always with quotation marks. They insist on viewing the world
as dominated by class struggle, although logic is a bit strained: "But
the growth [of white collar workers] is above all evidence of the conversion of the overwhelming majority of the occupied population of
the developed capitalist countries (from 60–95 percent) into hired
hands." [8] The Soviet leaders are thereby made proletarians, and the
struggle long since ended at home is projected abroad to give an
excuse for mobilization and militarization. The expansion of Soviet
power becomes further vindication of the Soviet posture and ideals, a
substitute for realization of the Bolshevik social program. Propagandists
are to make the most of "the enormous influence of the building of
Communism in the U.S.S.R. on the whole course of world development." [9]

The Soviet rulership even makes gestures of proletarianism, as in
requiring scientists (but not party bosses) to leave their laboratories
for days of potato picking.[10] The editorial staff of a newspaper may
likewise be sent to the fields to raise their political maturity.[11] Every
effort is made to glorify labor. But the Nazis also glorified labor, and
it is at best a somewhat hollow exercise, at worst a piece of weary
hypocrisy. The basic idea of Marxism, solidarity with the oppressed
class, is inapplicable because the new possessors enjoy status and com-
forts. It was necessary at the outset to believe that more advanced
industrial nations would join the October Revolution; otherwise, the
Marxist class idea, or its application to Russia, was necessarily false.
As soon as the Bolsheviks found themselves in power and building
"socialism" in a nonadvanced country, Marxism became intellectually
irrelevant though still useful as state dogma. It was never emotionally
very relevant, except in the context of revolution; Marxism does not
address itself to the ultimate questions.

There has been a steady degradation of Marxist-Leninist idealism
from the time of the Revolution or the end of the civil war to this day,
broken only by World War II. Lenin's call for improvement by political virtue gave way to Stalin's promise of improvement by Western
machines. Lenin's revolution turned into the upheavals brutally imposed
by Stalin. As the Revolution lost immediacy, the "counterrevolution-
aries" of Lenin's day were succeeded by Stalin's "enemies of the people"; recently there are only "traitors to the Soviet homeland." The
failure to incorporate conquered lands into the Soviet Union after

World War II also betokened the evaporation of internationalist conviction. By Khrushchev's time, there was no longer much passion in the notion of social change, although there remained some confidence in Soviet socialism's outperforming the West and so winning supremacy. In the day of Brezhnev and Kosygin this had decayed to little more than a hope, at times nourished by news reports, that Western society would fall apart and the Russians would pick up the pieces.

In 1961, Khrushchev hoped to restore the Marxist-revolutionary-utopian component by the ceremonious adoption of a new Party Program pointing to the future; but the promise, much weaker than that of 1919, was for little more than an improved welfare state. The ideal of abolition of the state was reduced to a transfer of authority to the party. Even this pale utopia fell into the background and was soon largely forgotten, especially under Khrushchev's successors; the few experiments in communal housing ventured in the 1960's have been partly or entirely abandoned. In a final reversal of Marxism, it has been decided that the state is not to disappear but to grow with the approach of utopia. Social organizations are to take a broader role, "But this by no means lessens the role of the state as the principal agent of the building of communism." [12] There is no positive ideal or idea of importance to hold the Soviet system together, only a shared fear of loss.

Soviet publications amply testify that ideological decay has become a problem, as it was in the latter decades of tsardom. Declarations become pedantic and repetitious, because there is little new to say; even criticism of the West is almost entirely borrowed. Labels without content, such as "formalist" music, and talk of "class" positions become an empty routine. The censors no longer seem to believe strongly in censorship.[13] Posters are merely ornamental and devoid of political message.[14] As Yevtushenko said of the younger writers, "The decisive turn of history evoked in some of our generation a certain amount of skepticism, a tinge of political mistrust, turning at times into snobbish nonparticipation or snobbish contrasting of the self with society." [15] As *Pravda* sees it, "In literary criticism there are apparent subjectivism, favor for friends and associates, acceptance of ideological and artistic junk. . . ." [16]

Concern for material gain increases at the expense of civism, as *Pravda* notes unhappily.[17] The children of the top élite have shown a remarkable lack of political inspiration. The sons of the Politburo fail to follow their fathers' careers; exposure to modern influences and/or

familiarity with the heart of the power structure evidently incapaci-
tates young people for Soviet political engagement. The head of the
police, Iurii Andropov, is said to have his own collection of the abstract
art forbidden to ordinary people, probably not because he really appreciates it but because it is smart and Western.[18] The times when
Soviet citizens would not accept tips have irrevocably passed. Voluntary blood donation is successful in individualistic England, not in the
collectivistic Soviet Union. Idealism has so far withered that "obsessive
reformist delusions" is a regular diagnosis, according to the Medvedevs,
made by police psychiatrists of critics of the state; that a person "puts
the public interest higher than his own" and "believes he has to dedicate
his own life to the ideals of communism" was held to be psychotic.[19]
Abroad, the powerful Soviet Union of the 1970's has less emotional
appeal than the weak state of the 1920's; the attractiveness of its image
is now that of power, rather than social improvement. The KGB was
formerly helped mostly by sympathizers with the Soviet experiment;
it nowadays relies on buying cooperation.

The marcescence of ideology progresses as the basically nineteenth-century revolutionary creed becomes increasingly discordant
for the technological world of the 1970's. There are no new texts; the
sole canon of importance is the works of Lenin, mostly written before
the Revolution. But ideology, understood as the meaning the regime
attributes to itself, inevitably changes. It becomes more formalistic and
intellectually weaker; losing idealism, it decays to chauvinism and rationalization for power, a mishmash of Soviet patriotism, defense of
élitist rule, and self-congratulation. Ideology in the Soviet press appears
mostly in the foreign affairs section, "imperialists" or "reactionaries"
being loosely equated with enemies of the Soviet Union. As they did
a century ago, Russians are pleased to call the West selfish and merce-
nary, everything Soviet or "socialist" being superior to everything
Western or "capitalist."

The residue of ideology centers on a call to duty. "The honorable,
conscientious fulfillment of duty to the fatherland, the party, and the
people is one of the most outstanding traits of Soviet character. . . ."[20]
According to the General Secretary, "The very essence of communism
consists in the citizens' having a high degree of [socialist] awareness
and a feeling of responsibility to society."[21] The individual owes
everything to the party-led collective. "The collective is your family;
without the support of your fellows you cannot make a single step."[22]

This adds up to a rather simple-minded creed, even at the level of higher party schools. But it takes on a somewhat religious cast:

I love you, each oncoming day, I love you for all that life gives, and still more for what I truly know: today, as yesterday, I will accompany you with a ceaseless feeling of guilt before myself. I did not do as much as I wished, I did not say the weightiest words, I did not help all who needed support. . . .[23]

Generalization of ideology is inevitable as theory loses interest and applicability. But the Soviet state thereby leaves behind the doctrines of Marxism-Leninism which have particularly assisted in sustaining its integrity and drive.

SUBSIDENCE OF LEADERSHIP

The best-intentioned men and groups who remain long at the summit of autocratic power are thereby affected in their character. They easily lose their sense of proportion; most of all, they lose critical self-perception. The longer a man remains above correction, the more distorted his view of the world becomes.

This experience, common even in looser societies where leaders can be only partially sheltered from realities by their staffs, has run through Russian history. Tsars have regularly become more arbitrary and tyrannical, often cruel, through years of absolutism. Thus, Ivan IV began his reign as a rational and approachable monarch, only to progress to bloody, almost insane despotism; Alexander I, at first a genial and nobly intentioned ruler, became a mean tyrant. In Soviet times, Lenin in his few years of power prior to his disabling stroke (May, 1922) became much less accessible and receptive to critical views and more willful. The accumulation of power turned Stalin from a reasonable and moderate man into a paranoid mass murderer.

It is also ordinary and expectable that the men who dream of social betterment through revolution and devote themselves utterly to it are in time replaced by the gang which has managed by inside maneuvering and hidden means to squeeze or claw their way to the pinnacle of power. The Russian Revolution has been no exception. The change from Lenin through Stalin and Khrushchev to Brezhnev has been consistent, from the revolutionary intellectual to the consummate apparatchik. Lenin was competent in the headship of the new government, as he had been in the destruction of the old, and he had generally impressive men around him, men of originality and striking personality, such as Trotsky and Bukharin. But if Lenin was a revolutionary intellectual with pretensions as a thinker and student of society— he even ventured into metaphysics—Stalin was less of a revolutionary than a machine politician who hated Marxist intellectuals. Nonetheless, he was a man of parts who earned the respect of world leaders dealing with him in the war; and his writings, at least before he acquired autocratic power, are often much to the point, fairly well reasoned, and very quotable. Khrushchev was less impressive than Stalin; his flamboyance hardly disguised his shallowness. His chief contribution to ideology was some effort to prune it of obsolete doctrines; his big theoretical contribution, the 1961 Party Program, was remarkably lackluster. General Secretary Brezhnev has not much of Chairman Khrushchev's flair, dash, and verve. As they appear to the world, his associates have almost no individuality; there is no call for brilliance. Those whom the present leaders place in positions of succession are likely to be still less inspiring; they will, moreover, be the first generation that has escaped the tempering of the collective struggle for survival.

This progression is evident in various aspects. Thus, Lenin wrote voluminously and with learning and some originality in his interpretation and application of Marxism. Stalin's contributions were modest by comparison, both in volume and in ideological pretenses. Khrushchev's were much more so, as he dwelt on practical problems. But even Khrushchev's slight sparkle is missing from the trite, cliché-ridden utterances of the current General Secretary.* In parallel fashion, the means by which leaders have come to the top have become steadily more obscure. Lenin's formation of the Bolshevik party and his battles to secure conformity to his leadership are recorded in detail. Much less is known of Stalin's intrigues and the manner in which he built up a personal machine within the party, but his rise was entwined with policy issues and involved open controversy. It is far better documented than the manner of Khrushchev's elevation. Of this, only episodes are fairly well illuminated, especially the contest of June, 1957, on which a spotlight was turned by Khrushchev's efforts to secure the condemnation of his opponents. The rise of Brezhnev remains closely curtained; we know little more than the formal steps of his career.

* Lenin's works occupy fifty-five volumes (including much miscellany); Stalin's, thirteen plus three published by the Hoover Institution; Khrushchev's, eight; Brezhnev's, thus far, three.

In the social fluidity of the Revolution, the most ambitious, inspired, and capable characters were free to thrust themselves upward, like the driving capitalists of early industrialization. But as the state settled down, advancement came to depend primarily upon pleasing superiors; and rulers, especially those who feel insecure, rarely advance people capable of replacing them. They hardly need the advice tendered to Ivan the Terrible: "If thou wantest to be an autocrat, do not keep counsellors more clever than thyself; and so thou wilt be the best of all and quite safe on the throne." [24] Although Lenin fully mastered the party and could be fully confident in his position, he did not tolerate really independent minds. One reason for Stalin's early success was his conformity to the master's line. Stalin in turn destroyed everyone with any apparent potential for independence and regarded his aides as definite inferiors. As Stalin had removed Lenin's lieutenants, Khrushchev made it his task to get rid of former lieutenants of Stalin; he must have regretted not being more careful to promote harmless assistants. Brezhnev in turn managed to ease potential rivals, such as Nikolai Podgorny and Alexander Shelepin, out of the Secretariat.

Each leader has brought forward a more modest succeeding generation, men of less ambitious dynamism than themselves, in the degree that they could effectively select men of nonthreatening character capable of carrying out the tasks of controlling the party and administering the state; and the process of advancement by favor hardly selects and nourishes stalwart character. Nor is the situation improved in principle if the chief clerks of the dictator assume and manage power as a functioning collective for a longer or shorter time. The oligarchs are even less likely than a dictator to admit to their circle anyone capable of disturbing their equilibrium. The system of selecting leadership by pure co-option, without inputs from outside, has obvious built-in tendencies to degradation.

The selection of leadership is a problem for all states, but in the more pluralistic or constitutional states there are better chances for renewal from outside. The ordinary solution in authoritarian states, hereditary monarchy, is fairly workable. The realm at least gets a new, sometimes young, ruler from time to time, and heredity and upbringing may combine to bring forward capable individuals. The Soviet state has hardly tackled the problem, inasmuch as Lenin and company came to power not to design a better state but to put the party in power ("Dictatorship of the Proletariat") and to destroy the state.

There is no system of succession in the Soviet Union, and no thought, it appears, of devising one.

The problem is more difficult for the Soviet Union than it has been for traditional autocracies because of the basic ambivalences of the polity.[25] Use of an electoral process to check the leadership or renew it is excluded; at best, elections and associated criticism serve somewhat to restrict abuses by the lower cadres. On the other hand, democratic pretenses stand in the way of the institutionalization of an office of supreme leadership. If some sort of monarchy were set up and frankly acknowledged, it might be possible to arrange a regular succession, if not to define powers, and possibly provide a means of retirement or a limitation of term of office. As is, power at the summit cannot be defined and so is irregular. A would-be chief may be driven to try to increase his authority indefinitely if only for his own security; if Stalin had held a regularized and hence secure position, he would hardly have been impelled to slaughter everyone with a potential for independence. On the other hand, lack of definition of a supreme office makes those next to the center apprehensive lest anyone elevate himself to become threatening to them. Yet the system seems clearly to need a single strong leadership if it is to avoid stagnation and senile degeneration as the party and the entire system age. The post-Khrushchev oligarchy has shown itself practically unable to bring new blood into the inner circle of Politburo with Secretariat or to remove anyone who has shown himself ineffective.

The strengths that Lenin's Revolution and his party organization brought to Russia have been wrongly attributed to the political system. Impressed by Soviet successes and the efficacity of power ruthlessly wielded by Lenin, Stalin, and successors, the world has mostly ignored the fact that the Bolsheviks did not inaugurate a permanently viable state. They did not try to do so; their successors are unable to do so without attacking the basis of their own power.[26]

CONSERVATISM AND ÉLITISM

There is little more ideological urge for alteration of the social order in the Soviet Union, there are no changes of importance to stir political emotions, and there is no leadership for a renewal of the dynamism of the Revolution. The artificiality of the Leninist combination of intense autocratic control with democratic forms and appearances makes reform difficult and perilous. Having fulfilled, in Stalinism, the implications of Lenin's solution, the Soviet Union has settled down to bureaucratic rigidity. It cannot endanger any of its fundamentals. It cannot even admit a possibility that any essential part of the system needs change; to suggest such a thing would be to find fault with the system. Its program either has been carried out or has failed. The slogans are those of forty or fifty years ago, with no invention and little response to the changes that have come over the world. Stalin could be contrasted with Pobedonostsev as revolutionary against traditional authoritarian, but no such contrast is valid for the bosses of today. With some reason, Mao Tse-tung contemplated the Soviet Union and called for a new revolution.

After Stalin finished his "Second Revolution," he settled down to the maintenance of totalitarian power; there were no more consequential changes of institutions (until near the end of his life, when he seems to have been preparing a purge of the old guard) and few of personnel. Khrushchev saw the need for loosening and reshaping the system, but he was strikingly unable to move Soviet society. He decreed the transfer of the bulk of industry to a hundred-odd "economic councils" in 1957, but very soon their powers were being curtailed and broader authorities were being established over or instead of them. His effort to revive utopianism was futile. One of his initiatives for bringing nearer the communist society was the expansion of boarding schools, prospectively to take nearly all children away from their parents for a suitably socialized upbringing. But the program, which the élite probably did not like, was soon halted. Khrushchev's proposals for shaking up party ranks by limitations on reelection and requirements that certain fractions of committees be periodically renewed were likewise nullified, as was his division of the party apparatus into agricultural and industrial sections.

According to Brezhnev, "The Soviet people, by selfless labor, has built the developed socialist society of which Lenin spoke in 1918 and the future of our country." [27] Little, then, remains to be done. Almost nothing was changed at the 1966 Party Congress (except for some reversions to Stalinist ways) and less at the 1971 one. The chief innovation in 1971 was prolongation of periods between Congresses and regional conferences and extension of the terms of office of secretaries and committeemen. The boldest and most celebrated move, the economic reform announced by Kosygin in September, 1965, resulted in more reaction than reform. The economic ministries dissolved by

Khrushchev were restored, while enterprise managers were given more latitude and told to make a profit; but the liberalization was soon swallowed in new controls. The projected constitutional reform was shelved, as was the spelling reform proposed under Khrushchev. In 1918 it was possible (under the Provisional Government) substantially to simplify the alphabet, and a shift from the Cyrillic to the Latin alphabet was considered at one time.[28] By the 1960's, Khrushchev's proposal to drop a letter in a few words of the otherwise nearly phonetically spelled language was beaten back lest the great heritage be blemished.

The bureaucratic apparatus, the world's largest, would inevitably be ponderous and immobile of its own bulk; it is much more so as it tries to encompass everything, minimizes inputs from outside, and endeavors to avoid any dangerous beginning of division. No one can push policies offensive to the rulership. Soviet society should be kept bland and harmonious as far as possible. Since the regime regards itself as essentially perfect, spontaneity and idealism are per se dangerous.

The principal task of the apparatus becomes self-maintenance, as a whole and as individuals, with bosses at each level in the hierarchical society enjoying their status. As a writer in *Literaturnaia gazeta* said of the apparatchiks, "They bawl you out, and you bawl someone else out. As headquarters treats you, so you treat those below you. They don't trust you, and you don't trust others." [29] The director of an agricultural technical station has discretionary power to provide workers with meat, grain, firewood, and other needs, and distribute apartments.[30] Bosses get prizes and premiums, frequently unpublicized, whereas ordinary workers are to be satisfied with pennants and citations of merit. Incomes not only of the upper but of the middle élite are strictly secret. In the Soviet Union inequality of income after taxes is quite comparable to that in Western states, while inequality of authority is far greater. The Soviet Union leads the world in production of titles and distinctions; for example, there are eleven grades in the Procuracy, from Chief State Counselor of Justice (equivalent to General of the Army) down to Junior Attorney (equivalent to Second Lieutenant); coal miners have fourteen ranks, as in Peter's table.[31]

Even in science, the openest of the professions, senior scientists lord it over their juniors in a manner surprising to Western visitors.[32] Higher education is considered a prime mark of status, and it is held very desirable that persons in authority be so qualified.[33] On the other hand, young people are urged not to suppose that they must have higher education instead of doing manual work,[34] and the proportion of students in the population has not risen significantly for a decade. The influence of young people in the settled hierarchic order is minimal. Seniority plays an increasing part even in literature. As Yevtushenko complained to the Writers' Congress, young writers are given no status in the literary journals.[35]

The party is politically and socially set apart from the masses; "Communist" is a synonym for a person of importance.[36] Party position has become almost a kind of property, nearly as secure as ownership of shares in a corporation in the West. If a party man of medium or higher level gets into trouble, he appeals to his party organization. Unless he should by misfortune be chosen as an example, he is likely to be merely shifted to a nearly equivalent position, possibly promoted. A hospital director in Azerbaidzhan, having been discharged for incompetence, was placed in charge of all the hospitals of the county.[37] Far from living in fear of purge, the Soviet leader usually has much more security of tenure than his Western counterpart. Punishment of officials is seen as hurtful to state authority. There is a plaintive tone in Brezhnev's remark, "Nobody has everlasting title to leading positions." [38] The tsar similarly was likely to be tender to high-placed delinquents as long as they were ostensibly loyal.[39]

Much is expected of party men, and they count on corresponding rewards. Even during the years of World War II when there was strongest call for universal sacrifice, high party people lived vastly better than common folk; now they enjoy not only the psychological benefits of power but many material perquisites depending on positions held, from access to special stores, housing, and automobiles to travel and vacations at secluded resorts. Monetary rewards are used also; sealed special pay envelopes are known to be passed out to the deserving, and the mere fact of having been in the party for thirty years entitles one to two extra months' pay yearly.[40]

The party must be kept to a fairly small percentage of the total population so that it may regard itself as an élite, not as the people; pressures for democratic development are thereby curbed. A concomitant of élite privilege in a pseudodemocratic society is secrecy. Important people live in another universe, and no information is published that might indicate their fallibility or weakness; not even their illnesses are permitted to come to public notice. The increased shrouding of political life and decision making as well, especially since Khrushchev, is part of the growing separation of rulership from the people.

The status society stresses formality and convention. Proper Soviet horseback riders on promenade wear tailored jackets, bowler hats, and white gloves, in the most elegant Western fashion.[41] It was proposed that courses in conventional ballroom dancing be made compulsory in Soviet secondary schools.[42] Much has been done to develop new ceremonies where old ones do not fill the modern need. There are birth-registration ceremonies to replace baptism; children attaining age four, citizens receiving their (internal) passports, and newly fledged collective farmers have their rituals of dedication. Entrants to Soviet higher schools have a solemn inauguration, with a "Freshman's Oath." From 1964 to 1968, there were published eighty-one works on the new rites in Belorussia alone (seventeen from 1959 to 1963).[43] A "truck-drivers' oath" is suggested to curtail their drunken driving.[44] The solemnizing of vital occasions merges with the consecration of the past: "In the formation of new rituals and Soviet civil ceremonies special attention must be given to honoring the memory of those who died for the freedom and independence of our Motherland." [45]

Popular tradition, detested by the revolutionaries, has become a fine thing. *Izvestia* regrets that, in the view of some, "the sober economic manager has given way to the village grandfather, the guardian of age old traditions, finding 'spirituality' in the mystique of 'simple folk.' " [46] But *Pravda* takes a lyrically positive view of the people's heritage:

Now, at a time when one thinks more of future than past, unexpected thoughts come to mind, for example, about customs, traditions, cherished and excellent, undying traditions. Years go by and these beloved traditions, like the wisdom of the past, are handed on . . . they are inseparable from you and from time. . . . How many of them have grown up through the ages! The best of them retain their freshness today. Wise in thought and beautiful in form, they beautify our life and work.[47]

Along with Komsomol, Trade Unions, and Communist party, one of the "mass organizations" of Soviet society is the Society for the Preservation of Ancient Landmarks. It is exceptional in that its 6 million members neither are under pressure to join nor expect material or political compensation for their efforts. The principal business of the society seems to be the restoration of churches once looted or used as barns. Tsarist palaces are rebuilt in primitive splendor, and historic buildings that were torn down in less nostalgic times are to be reconstructed.[48] People love to read about the past; between 1966 and 1970, from 13 to 18 million copies of historical novels were sold yearly, twenty times as many as in the period 1930 to 1934.[49] Formerly reprobated writers are again fashionable; in November, 1971, the sesquicentennial of Dostoevsky was much celebrated. Even such idealists as Vladimir Soloviev and Nicholas Berdiaev have been readmitted as outstanding Russians.

Anti-industrial attitudes of the Slavophiles reappear. According to one author (decried by *Pravda*), "From a moral standpoint the peasant is the distinctive national type," a counterweight to "corrupters of national spirit." [50] There seems to have been something of a resurgence of religion, both within the traditional Orthodox Church and outside it. According to admissions in Soviet writing, by 1971 in some places half or more of the infants were baptized. The press and police give much attention to the alleged evils of the more evangelical sects, such as Baptists and Pentecostals. An avowal of religion is no longer deemed shameful. "On the beach during the summer one sees young boys and girls with crosses on their chests. Who are they? Believers? No. This is also a demonstration of devotion to that which is 'truly' Russian." [51]

The conservative society seeks order in the present and glory in the past. Military indoctrination is called upon to discipline spirits.[52] Stores are flooded with military toys, the television screen and children's books and magazines with images of warlike prowess and patriotic adventure. Teachers should imbue children with the "romance" of war.[53] Patriotism, coupled or not with socialism, has become frankly a value. The slogans in honor of the 1971 anniversary of the Revolution hailed "our great Homeland" and called on party members to lead the "patriotic movement." A poet in *Pravda* forgets proletarian internationalism and the working class to apostrophize,

> Fatherland,
> In the spirit's panoply
> No holy thing is holier than thou.
> Here we learned to know our strength
> And civil character.
> We stand in no militant pose,
> But build our lives by heart and sense.

We plan each step to benefit
Thy personal prestige.
Our works we do in love for you,
Our deeds we bring as a gift to you.
We will be always and in all things
Duty-bound to you.[54]

Pride is Russian; *Literaturnaia gazeta* headlines, "The Whole World
Studies Russian," reporting on a conference of Russian language teachers.[55] It extends to the distant past; relics of Novgorod show "the age-
old international authority of Russia." [56]

WEAKENING CONTROL

As idealism fades and men grow accustomed to looking out for
themselves, particular interests reassert themselves, and the welter of
unworkable controls offers countless opportunities for private gain.
The Soviet press tells nothing of the luxuries of the aristocrats and
gives only occasional glimpses of the abuses of the upper-middle echelons, their private villas, sometimes private factories; but much appears
in denunciation of the bribery, cheating, and private enrichment which
seem to have become epidemic on lower levels. Farmers frustrate the
intentions of the controllers by buying on the market what they are
required to deliver but cannot profitably produce; they may even
thereby overfulfill procurement quotas, qualifying for extra rewards.[57]
It seems quite accepted for truck drivers to use state-owned vehicles
and state gasoline to carry passengers for pay. Expediters are expected
to produce expensive presents.[58] Palm greasing, standard in tsarist times,
is evidently again the mode.[59] In Baku, it is said, to get permission to
drive a cab, to build a house or to qualify for an apartment, "either you
have to have a friend or it takes money"—several hundred rubles.[60] It
would seem that builders prefer to turn apartments over to tenants in
defective condition so that they can charge for fixing them. "A faucet
gets out of order, out with a three-ruble bill or you spend weeks on
the doorstep of the repair agency. They won't take a tape recorder at
the repair shop—lack of parts—get out a three-ruble note and the parts
are found." [61]

Such practices are not uncommonly denounced in the Soviet press,
but without real indignation; they seem almost taken for granted. There
is little severity against much bigger misdeeds, at least when done by

well-placed individuals. Punishment for defalcation may be merely
return of the stolen funds. If a factory manager is fired for embezzle-
ment, the enterprise probably pays. Shopgirls help themselves to merchandise, and reprimand is hardly in order unless quantities stolen are
excessive. A store manager, party member, whose accounts showed
shortages, was not even given a party reprimand but was shifted to a
different job.[62] When an engineer embezzled a few thousand rubles,
he was promoted to manager.[63] It is apparently regular practice, when
a party member is implicated in wrongdoing, for the party body
responsible for his appointment to take charge and decide what
measures, if any, are to be taken; and the party group can be expected
to deal gently with its own.

Swindlers stand together. As one said to the boss, "Let's all reg-
ister ourselves in your ring. Take us all with you. And let this ring
never come unsoldered." [64] Entrants to the circle may have to pay
an entry fee of several thousand rubles and to take an oath of loyalty;
in return they expect a guaranteed share of corporate earnings.[65] Oper-
ations may run into the millions of rubles, as in a case in Georgia.[66]
It is in vain that higher authorities seek to check abuses by encouraging denunciations from below. Tsars like Nicholas I gave rewards for
complaints against officials, but the ordinary result was punishment
for the complainers, and this is often the outcome nowadays. As under the tsars, the multiplication of controls today invites officials to
find ways of avoiding them and creates opportunities for extortion.
In the nineteenth century, corruption was worst under the firmest
ruler, Nicholas I.

Erosion of authority seems widespread. The director of a medical
institute, among other abuses, illegally discharged underlings; for years
he ignored court orders to reinstate them.[67] Some youths who learned
radio technology with the paramilitary organization, Dosaaf, put together transmitters from stolen parts and operated them freely enough
to interfere with aviation and naval communications.[68] The system
of internal passports and police control of movement seems no longer
rigorously enforced. In 1971 it was possible to organize in Riga an
all-Soviet congress of "flower children." According to *Pravda* in 1971,
the letters it received indicated that the most popular dances in the
U.S.S.R. were the disapproved twist and shake.[69] Parents paid 100 to
500 rubles to experts to take entrance examinations for élite universities in place of their children, but a lecturer who reported such prac-

tices was himself sentenced to seven years' forced labor.[70] Governmental agencies, too, have their own policies. In 1971, less than one-third of the state-owned housing was administered by local soviets, despite party and state decrees over the previous four years transferring all to them.[71] The Chief Administration of Higher Education demanded of the Russian Republic Ministry of Education that graduates of its Moscow institutions not be sent to rural schools.[72]

There are flourishing gray and black markets, wherein factory managers as well as private consumers find what the planned economy fails to furnish, not only forbidden books and Western phonograph records but also scarce industrial materials. Collective farms and institutions recur to private construction, probably using illegally acquired materials.* Workers go home by a privately organized bus service.[73] There seems little effort of police to interfere. Enterprises look out for their private interests. Some fix their prices willfully and illegally.[74] Others ship and bill for unwanted and unordered merchandise.[75] It was rumored that Soviet transportation agencies, eager to fulfill quotas and turn a ruble, had much to do with the greatly increased Jewish emigration of late 1971 and 1972.[76] A representative of the Soviet fishing trust insisted to Americans that his was "a private enterprise, and not an arm of the Soviet government." [77] There is probably some de facto growth of private ownership. City dwellers buy up houses in depopulated villages, and the party seems to have backed away from the policy of gradually squeezing out the peasant household plots. Measures are sometimes taken to help private agriculture.[78] "Today, as in the past, the state gives every kind of financial encouragement to people to build their own houses, offering tracts of land, designs, and loans on favorable terms." [79] The slackening of the reins may be positive; as managers see and use opportunities to make a profit, planned or not, the Soviet consumer benefits. But central power is diminished.

A more affluent population, less excited over social change, exerts pressure against economic regimentation; for example, huge quantities of old-fashioned, hand-wringer washing machines rusted in warehouses. After long resistance, authorities plan to increase automobile production sufficiently so that ordinary Russians can aspire to own a

---

* It is a sign of the vitality of the free economy that the present leadership, unlike Stalin, finds it necessary by legal and police measures to force people to take employment in the official sector.

car. On the one hand, this poses countless problems that the centralized economy is ill prepared to face, from traffic congestion to shortage of repair facilities; in all Moscow there was only one repair station
for the leading make, the Zhigulis from the Fiat plant.[80] On the other
hand, automotive mobility promises to make all kinds of regulations
more difficult to enforce. The automobile represents individualism.

A corollary of the strength of private against social interests is
that the state has lost the power to control the economy and move it
rapidly forward. In the civil war, total mobilization was fairly effective despite inexperience and the extreme crudity of the system. Reconstruction in the 1920's was phenomenally rapid by historical standards; and for a number of years under the First and Second Five-
Year Plans, the Soviet Union had by far the world's highest industrial
growth rate, despite the errors and crudities of Stalinism. Again in
World War II the application of all resources to the war effort was
exceptionally effective, and Soviet munitions production soared to
levels comparable to that of the American industrial machine. For a
decade after the war, moral momentum carried the Soviet economy
forward at a rapid rate, with claimed annual increases of industrial
production of 15 percent or more.*

The drive is now feebler, if not quite exhausted. The growth
rate has slowed to a crawl; thus, for 1972 the Central Statistical Bureau
recorded an increase of national income of only 4 percent; of productivity of labor, 1.4 percent. Housing completed, despite the serious
shortage, was below the previous year and amounted to less than half
a square meter per Soviet citizen. Since the 1950's, Soviet growth has
never been exceptional among industrial powers, and the Soviet economy seems to approach a plateau at a level where the average consumer receives only a third as much material goods as the American,
and most Siberians use outhouses.[81] Results decline relative to attention
and exhortation as well as material investment. The Soviet economy

* Rapid economic growth was claimed as a special virtue of socialism, but
fresh authoritarian regimes have frequently shown themselves capable of pushing
production vigorously. For example, the military government of Brazil which took
charge in 1964 was able to enforce some respect for law, collect taxes, give security to business, and hold down wages; it was consequently able to show a rate of
growth of GNP, 1968 to 1973, close to double that of the Soviet Union in the
same years. The military government of Greece, entering in 1967, could likewise
show high figures for increase of production and income; so, for that matter,
could Hitler's Germany.

moved rapidly toward catching up with the West when it had only a very small fraction of the number of American engineers; now it claims to have several times as many as the United States, yet the technological lag increases. It is deduced from the official statistics that the productivity of Soviet industrial labor in 1971 was 40 percent of the American, a figure which had hardly changed for fifteen years; in agriculture, the percentage was 11 percent. Despite the utility of data-processing for the controllers, the Soviets have had extreme difficulty entering the computer age, with a stock less than a tenth that of the United States and mostly a generation or two behind. Elsewhere, advancing technology has regularly raised the productivity of capital; in the Soviet Union, the return per ruble invested in industry has decreased over a long period.[82] Similarly in agriculture, the additional output generated by a ruble investment was 1.32 rubles for the period 1956 to 1960, but 0.42 for 1966 to 1968.[83] It does not avail greatly if more tractors roll onto the fields, for the average daily plowing per standard tractor fell from 5.8 hectares in 1963 to just half as much in 1968.[84] Soviet new fixed investment in 1971, at $187 billion, was slightly more than the American (at $182 billion), as it had been for many years, whereas Soviet increments to GNP were only a minor fraction of the American.

In the Soviet way, one arch buttresses another to uphold the gleaming façades and the more solid walls, and weakness in any one increases strains on others. Lameness of the economy robs the ideological world view of much of whatever credibility remains, but the enfeeblement of ideology undermines controls that are essential for the centralized economy, and weakening controls make it more difficult to sustain the indoctrination. The end of economic growth probably signifies practically the end of the Leninist-Stalinist state.

DISINTEGRATION OF LENINISM

By comparison with Western societies, the Soviet Union is still relatively monolithic and indoctrinated, with a uniformity of public expression, as of building styles, far beyond what is considered normal even in rather authoritarian non-Leninist countries, such as Spain or Brazil. But there has been a qualitative change since the departure of the last ruler closely associated with the Revolution, Stalin. From the military and the KGB to collective farms and writers, there are now countless groups and individuals pulling in their own directions, not directly opposing party rule but claiming a bit more autonomy for themselves. This has come about in part because of declining effectiveness of controls, in part because of the maturation of the economy, which has become more difficult to direct as its complexity—like the complexity of life in general—has outpaced the capacities of the controllers. It has also generated, as the tsarist economy did in its latter decades, increasing numbers of persons who do not fit into the political scheme, experts and professionals, newly self-assured and independent élites, who feel that they owe their status not to party generosity but to their own efforts. Their leisure and growing affluence mean more time to think and criticize, more political interest, and concern for freedom of political action and information. This course seems practically irreversible without a fearful convulsion. Because the ruling group wants rights and security for itself, it cannot reinstitute a reign of terror; and with neither terror nor idealistic dedication to cement them, groups and individuals assert themselves as far as they can, mostly quietly and privately, but increasingly openly and even in defiance of rules.

Possibly the most significant aspect of the disintegration that has overtaken the Leninist synthesis is the intellectual retreat not only to Russian sentiment and history, in the footsteps of the Slavophiles, but, as in the nineteenth century, to a multitude of tendencies. As educated Russians search for more satisfying answers to political and philosophical questions, some hold feebly democratic and pro-Western views, although it is difficult, as it was in tsarist times, to be democratic when the masses are conformist; and Soviet pseudodemocracy hinders idealization of the common people. More apparently turn to mysticism and religious themes. Psychic research, apparently conducted with much credulity, thrives in Soviet institutes.[85] Many look back to Lenin and criticize Soviet reality by reference to his supposed high standards and for failure to live up to the goals of Leninism. A few take Stalin for their teacher and want to overcome present troubles by his simplist methods. Many demand fulfillment of the promises of the Soviet constitution, especially those relating to civil liberties. Others take up the cause of national minorities; rights for the minorities mean rights for Russians, and vice versa. Ukrainian intellectuals seek more autonomy for their land, and Russians have come to the defense of various victims of illegality, such as the Crimean Tatars. Most are at least outwardly Marxist, a fact which arms them against the custodians of the official creed. The Marxist ammunition against the old opposition is impotent against the new. Even higher party schools, designed to secure élite philosophical uniformity, may have become centers of revisionism.[86]

The samples of dissident thinking that have come to the attention of the West are of uneven quality, some (such as those of the scientists Andrei Sakharov and Zhores Medvedev) of real caliber, most politically naïve. This is not surprising in view of the scarcity of unapproved books and journals and lack of means of interchange of ideas beyond the narrowest circles, together with many years' exposure to rigid indoctrination. There has been improvement since 1965 with the development of underground communication networks and publications—or their revival, since clandestine presses, even inside the ministries, were a regular part of the tsarist scene.[87] Many typed manuscripts and even a few regular "journals" make the rounds of some thousands of intellectuals, despite efforts of the police to crush them. Technology causes trouble; electronic copiers are kept in sealed and armor-plated rooms, accessible only to persons with special clearances.[88] *Samizdat* ("Self-Publisher") includes not only writings of political interest but literary works that fail to secure publication; in 1971 it was reported to have branched out into light and lewd creations in defiance of Soviet puritanism. The dissidents have been able to smuggle out thousands of documents and even to make and export sound films.

It is equally significant that the dissidents have acquired self-respect. They are no longer cowed as under Stalin, and they have shown a considerable ability to surmount lifelong indoctrination. In the Daniel-Siniavsky case (early 1966) writers were for the first time put on trial frankly for their writings; and they responded by asserting the rightness of their cause in unprecedented fashion. Their successors in the dock have usually used their own trials, although closed to the public, for a declaration of faith in the manner of tsarist revolutionaries. Thus Vladimir Bukovsky concluded his declaration:

Our society is still sick. It is sick with the fear which has come down to us from the Stalin era. But the process of the public's spiritual enlightenment has already begun and cannot be stopped. . . . I will fight for legality and justice. And I regret only that over the short period—one year, two months and three days—during which I was at liberty, I managed to do too little for this cause.[89]

According to a Russian scarred by the purges, "The political dissenters in Russia today are not going into the camps helplessly, as we did, without any idea why these things are happening. They go knowing what they believe in, and they are willing to take the consequences."[90]

Like the tsars, the Soviet state seems a bit nervous in the face of this numerically small but morally strong opposition. Outright terrorism being undesirable, it resorts to a variety of chicanery to ensure conformity: pressure on careers, withdrawal or offering of sundry privileges and opportunities, surveillance, lecturing, and harassment of dissidents; wiretapping is sanctioned since it is illegal to communicate anything over the telephone that the Communist party may dislike. Censorship becomes less effective as conviction becomes more watery, and a greater effort is made to encourage conformism by the crass means of generously paying compliant authors, such as Mikhail Sholokhov.[91] But the aging Writers' Union (its members averaging fifty-three years in 1971) has been brought to complete obedience, and writers are officially kept within narrow bounds. Paradoxically, at a time when writers as individuals are more restive, the Writers' Union has recently seen less open controversy than under Stalin. As a result, little interesting literature is published pertaining to the present; for heroic conflicts writers must look abroad or to the past. The level of official writing is suggested by poems which sound like unsophisticated advertising copy. A writer in *Literaturnaia gazeta*[92] elaborates on how he could not sleep because of eagerness to be among the first to vote in the pseudo-election; the depth of his emotion was uncontainable. The official press seems to hold little interest for the educated, as in tsarist times, when for many years the most influential of all Russian papers was Herzen's smuggled *Kolokol*.[93] The consumption-oriented society is overcome by boredom with slogans, campaigns, ceremonies, meetings, and political cant.

Good literature is a desirable frill, but science is a direct ingredient of power. The party can come nearer to telling writers how to write than to telling scientists how to think. It is possible to berate writers for holding to the principle, "That's the way it really is," thereby neglecting the deeper truth of the party.[94] But scientists cannot be told to be unobjective. Writers lack bases for self-assurance, but scientists know their own competence and importance and often credit themselves with broad understanding. It is a sign of the independence of scientists and the breadth of their social interests that physicists in 1970 set up the Committee on Human Rights. This was only a tiny nucleus, but it was the only open non-party-controlled political organization in the Soviet Union since before Stalinism, and it has defied official disapproval. Its prime mover, nuclear physicist Sakharov, made himself the most prominent and effective spokesman for intellectual dissent; his strongest plea has been that more freedom is necessary for progress.

Official controls are especially onerous for scientists, because authorities set not only goals but detailed means and stages toward goals; yet results are unpredictable. The temptation is for scientists to go through motions of following the plan or to shape results to fit it. Scientists are favored materially, and the overwhelming majority are doubtless entirely loyal. But they are aware of the much greater freedom of their colleagues in the West and of their achievements, which are usually superior to the Soviet. They are probably conscious of the lack of objective evidence for many ideological doctrines, and they are troubled by demands for unquestioning conformity. They are hampered by the secrecy that hinders communication not only with foreign scientists but within the Soviet Union and blocks the publication and utilization of results; they are suffocated by bureaucratic restrictions far beyond those which weigh upon American researchers.[95] Psychology and social science are subject to particular problems, because they clash immediately with Marxism-Leninism and party policies; yet social science becomes more necessary as social problems accumulate in the complex industrial state.

Physical science, like the economy, can function fairly well despite excessive controls as long as morale and purpose are strong. But in science, as in industry and agriculture, returns per unit of investment have markedly declined. Numbers of scientists and expenditures have swelled enormously, but the scientific output of the Soviet Union has grown much less impressive over the past generation. In the latter 1950's, it seemed undeniable that Soviet science, strongly supported and purposeful, was overtaking American; a decade or more later, there no longer seemed to be a race. Only in a few favored fields, as in power generation, have Soviet results been outstanding. The party seems as much concerned with the ideological outlook of the scientists as with their productivity. They are admonished to think properly, warned against "bourgeois" influences, and subjected to political checks on their careers; party groups are required to look more actively into the work of scientific institutes. Open manifestations are suppressed, as for instance in 1970 it was deemed necessary to close the famous Integral Club in Akademgorodok because it was a center of seditious talk. By 1962, Soviet science had emerged to a degree of openness, wherein scholars in all fields were able to ask broad questions. Khrushchev's successors seem to have felt this went too far, but they can permanently reverse it only at substantial cost. It is difficult now, as it was in the nineteenth century, to reconcile absolutism with rapid scientific-industrial change.

7

Russia and the New World Order

WESTERN INFLUENCES

Lenin's solution of the Russian dilemmas was brilliant and in some ways brilliantly successful. But as the traumatic times of Revolution and struggle recede, the Leninist answers become steadily less applicable. The erosion of the foundations of Russian dominion, which was becoming serious in the latter decades of the tsarist state, is again a problem, no longer overridden or disguised by revolutionary élan. To maintain strength in a competitive world it is necessary to admit ever more contacts, communications, and exchanges, to become dependent and concede dependence upon the ideological enemy. The breezy atmosphere of the Khrushchev days is gone, and controls have been stiffened in many ways. But the Soviet Union is unable to isolate itself, not only because of defensive needs and economic shortcomings but because of pride and the determination to play its role in Eastern Europe and the world. In the decreased efficacity of controls, it grows harder to bring in what is needed and exclude that which is damaging. Even as ideology loses effect, it becomes more necessary as a barrier against subversion.

The oft-expressed fears of bridge building as indirect imperialism are real; Russians have a fondness for Western ways and culture which can develop into an inclination to adopt Western criticisms of the Leninist state. The penchant of Soviet youth for modish Western articles and styles, from popular music and dances to chewing gum and clothing, must be attributed as much to the prestige of the originators as to the intrinsic merits of the things desired. Modes are smuggled in from the West, for stylish shoes, wigs, or what not. Eastern European countries had to put on their own programs of pop music and to permit (modest) miniskirts and hot pants, and the Russians follow at a distance. Western dietary fads and jogging have come to Russia;[1] and the Soviets, with little originality, take up Western subjects of social concern, such as environmental pollution and population problems. A tearoom on the Moscow-Voronezh highway is named in English "Russian Kvass"—and pictured in *Pravda*.[2] Santa Claus ("Grandfather Frost") helps celebrate the Soviet New Year, a holiday substituted for Christmas. The language is extremely receptive to borrowings from the languages of the principal ideological opponents.* But *Pravda* warns that fondness for things foreign and the English language is likely to lead into political trouble.[3] Yet there is a veritable passion among intellectuals for the study of that language.

Foreign radio broadcasts are an important means for Soviet citizens, especially the more affluent and educated, to supplement uninformative newspapers. Listening is said to be extremely common, especially among the youth; and the authorities respond by attacking frequently and violently such stations as Radio Free Europe and Radio Liberty, thereby calling attention to them. A journalist writes that, inasmuch as these stations exist, it is necessary to be franker in informing the public and to be more realistic in portraying the West.[4] Western influences are blamed for the philistine outlook of workers, their individualism and political apathy.[5] The Soviet TV network, on the other hand, feels driven to put on such Western fare as *The Forsyte Saga*.

The foreign contacts of science present a chronic and ever acute problem. It was probably hoped to reduce dependency on foreign research by a massive buildup of the Soviet scientific establishment, but this has not succeeded. Khrushchev felt it necessary to reopen doors closed by Stalin, and the number of Soviet scientists permitted

---

* A little reading of the Soviet press shows such recent infiltrations as action, aqualung, auction, avenue, champion, cocktail, comfort, container, credit, debut, devaluation, division, exaltation, fashion, hobby, interview, jeans, meeting, occasion, outsider, prize, reporter, reputation, speedometer, stewardess, stop, street, teletype, tennis court, vacancy, visit.

to go to meetings abroad increased twentyfold between 1954 and 1966, while visits of foreign scientists to the Soviet Union grew fiftyfold.[6] There is no reluctance to take whatever is useful from the opponent; although it treats the United States as a veritable gangster society, the *Literaturnaia gazeta* discusses the effects of smoking entirely in terms of American research, with no Soviet contribution.[7] Despite the ideological cost, the Soviet Union agreed in 1972 and 1973 to an extensive cooperative program with the United States on cancer, heart disease, and environmental and other problems.

But exchanges are still very limited by world standards; in theory, the Soviet Union rejects the idea of any contacts between its savants and foreigners that are not useful for the state. Soviet scientists are supposed to make political use of gatherings; psychologists should treat a world psychoanalytic conference as "the form of ideological struggle most necessary and important at present."[8] Western journals are censored and may be made available to Soviet scientists only after annoying delays,[9] with the result that many more Soviet discoveries than those of opener lands duplicate work already done elsewhere. Soviet scientists, particularly those of higher standing, are naturally aware of these irrational restraints on their productivity, and many of them are prepared to raise voices in protest, at least against political repressions of fellow scientists. They are also able to use foreign scientific opinion; thus, those exercised by the confinement of Zhores Medvedev in a mental institution threatened to bring up the matter at a world psychiatric congress.[10] American scientists have threatened to withdraw from exchanges, which are much more valuable to the Soviet Union than to the United States, if the dissident physicist, Andrei Sakharov, should be repressed.

To remain competitive with the ever developing West, Russia must import increasing amounts of technology; the need to secure innovation from abroad opens up innumerable points of contact. In the 1960's, the Soviet Union went back to the practice of the First Five-Year Plan of importing industrial layouts on a large scale along with experts to set them running and sometimes to keep them operating for a time. Western participation has been sought particularly in automotive but also in many other projects; there has been talk of billions of dollars of foreign investment, Japanese and American, in Siberian mineral production, to be paid for by a share of output. No longer prepared or able to deprive the population as Stalin could for political purposes, the Soviet government in 1972 bought 28 million tons of grain abroad for $2 billion in precious hard currency, mostly from the United States. Needs of trade also tend to break down the official monopoly of foreign trade, one of the pillars of the Leninist state, since organizations in Leningrad and the Soviet Far East have received authorization to deal directly with suppliers, respectively, in Finland and North Korea and Japan, thereby incidentally feeding black markets. Yet dependence on the capitalists more than half a century after the inauguration of socialism makes the Soviet system incredible as the model for the future.

The Soviet Union also finds opportunities for profit from collaboration with capitalism abroad too inviting to shun. The marketing of Soviet oil in the West has led to an intermeshing of interests with the much reviled Western "monopolies." The Russians sell oil through Western marketers, operate refineries in France and Belgium and service stations in England, and they export to Japan oil bought or swapped from Western producers in the Persian Gulf. A Soviet corporation makes tractors in Belgium in cooperation with Belgian capital. Soviet banks operate in many Western cities; and Soviet bankers behave much more like good international capitalists than Leninist anti-imperialist revolutionaries.[11] Soviet bankers have discussed participation in a large development project in Australia,[12] and there have been reports that the Soviet Union may, like its forebear before 1917 and some Eastern European states in recent years, raise money by selling bonds in the West. A growing number of foreign concerns, even American banks, have offices in Moscow, a real breach in the order of the total state. Soviet airplane salesmen are booking orders around the world; but to sell aircraft abroad in large numbers they must open Soviet factories to foreign inspection.

Commerce brings thousands of well-placed Russians into friendly and mutually advantageous relations with foreign capitalists and helps disintegrate the protective screen. For trade and prestige, the Soviet Union has acquired a large merchant marine, thereby at least slightly exposing many persons to subversive influences. Apparently mostly for the sake of trade, West Germany has been practically given up as an enemy, although it was by far the most useful of bogies. Japan has also ceased to be a subject of frequent abuse for reasons of commerce as well as Realpolitik. Forces of evil are requisite for the ideological picture of the world, but by 1973 the logic of agreements and trade with the United States led the Soviet press to write in friendly terms of the American "biznesmen" desirous of improved relations—assumed to be a large majority of the formerly denounced greedy, war-mongering "monopolists."

Foreign currency earnings through tourism become more necessary as import needs rise. Because of bureaucratic practices and lingering distrust, the Soviet Union has not profited as much from foreign visitors as Poland, Rumania, Czechoslovakia, and Hungary, which have had 2 to 6 million visitors in recent years. But foreign tourists to the U.S.S.R. increased from zero under Stalin to over a million in 1964 and over 2 million in 1970, half from outside the bloc. This is a growing problem for exchange controls and an obvious source of ideological contamination no matter how carefully managed. One effect of tourism to and within the Soviet Union, as well as of increased economic ease, is a whetting of the urge of Soviet citizens to visit the world without. This urge cannot be readily satisfied; free movement of people is hardly consonant with the structure of the party-state. Western and Eastern tourists can be admitted freely to Bulgaria or Hungary, and citizens of these countries can be allowed to travel abroad in large numbers, because the center of power is elsewhere; Russian travel even to satellite countries is severely restricted. But it is not possible to admit that the happy land of socialism is in effect a prison, and world opinion has contributed to the release of some 30,000 Jews yearly; if more are permitted to depart, it may be hard to deny exit permits to many other discontented folk.

Soviet leaders who travel abroad have contributed to the opening of society, and they indulge freely in Western luxuries. Lenin and Stalin, like true autocrats, never left the territory they ruled; when Khrushchev in 1955 undertook a barnstorming tour of India and Burma, acting not like high priest and divine Caesar but like an ordinary politician, he signaled a new Soviet outlook. Khrushchev's 1959 trip to the United States caused him to adopt more realistic views of Eisenhower and America. The post-Khrushchev leaders at first stayed close to the Kremlin; but, desirous of improving the Soviet image and probably of seeing the world, by 1971 they had become peripatetic, venturing outside the Soviet bloc to Canada, India, France, Denmark, Norway, Algeria, and so forth. When Western statesmen in Moscow are allowed to say a few words to the Soviet people, it detracts from the dichotomous world image; and when the Emperor of Ethiopia lays a wreath on Lenin's tomb, it must be counted a blow against the essence of Leninism.

Only abroad do Soviet leaders hear independent views, and it may have been that questions addressed to them while on tour persuaded Brezhnev and Kosygin to permit limited Jewish emigration. In independent lands, Politburo bosses cannot behave like little gods. To humanize his image with the French, Brezhnev gave an interview to *l'Humanité* in which he cast aside the veil covering his personal life, telling of his residence, work habits, hobbies, and vices—all of which it was held unnecessary to publish, before or then, for his Russian subjects. The habit of travel, moreover, may be contagious; what is right for dignitaries becomes harder to deny others.

The Soviet world role also erodes the mentality of the isolated empire. It is highly desirable to act as leader of a movement comprising eighty-odd Communist parties, but this nowadays requires some toleration of differing viewpoints, even a little criticism. Discipline is much laxer than in Stalin's days and to expel dissidents in Lenin's way would shatter the movement. Foreign parties hence serve to some extent as channels for varying and usually more realistic views. Soviet expansion into the Third World means foreign travel for many Russians, although service among persons whom they can regard as inferiors is less edifying than contact with those whom they must respect. Although the holding of a hegemonic sphere in Eastern Europe serves to stiffen the imperial system, it also has a contrary effect, because the satellites are not under the same compulsions of rigidity as the Soviet masters but are allowed some variation and experimentation. A bit of political satire in East Germany, private farming in Poland, some elections with competing Communist candidates in Hungary, and Western comedies on satellite television screens are examples that are difficult to reject categorically because they are in approved socialist countries. This is a reason for the border control between the U.S.S.R. and satellites, nearly as stringent as between the U.S.S.R. and "bourgeois" countries, and for censorship of printed matter imported from the satellites. But these restrictions cannot be complete, because they would excessively hinder not only the desired amalgamation of the "Socialist Commonwealth" but its management; and the influence of "brother socialist countries" cannot be excluded.

NATIONALISM

The Soviet leadership is evidently annoyed by the introduction of Western frivolities, the many trifles of the consumption-oriented society which raise expectations and distract from service to community and state; but the effects are not serious and possibly could be welcomed as a distraction from political concerns. Much more serious is the infection of ideals of political liberalism and the stimulus for demands for civil rights, genuine elections, and broader participation in decision making. But these yearnings are also probably manageable and no immediate threat to the status quo. There is little support for representative government in Russian tradition, the people seem generally to accept the right of authorities to decide without consultation outside, and the idea that multiplicity of parties means disorder seems to have been well internalized. Various other authoritarian states, such as Spain, have resisted the erosive effects of massive foreign contacts for long periods, and there is no reason to suppose that authoritarian Russia could not do likewise.

That is, Russian authoritarianism is fairly well armored, especially in the sophisticated Leninist version, against demands for constitutionalism and freedom. But it is vulnerable to another, more powerful Western import, the idea of national identity and the right of culturally identifiable groups to self-determination. This caused far more trouble to the Bolsheviks at the outset than calls for democracy and freedom in general. Lenin could reintroduce censorship of the press and arbitrary police action and could dissolve Russia's only freely elected assembly with hardly an audible murmur of protest, but he had to deal carefully with the national minorities. He brought them under factual control at the price of conceding in theory everything they asked for; and the workability of his solution depended on emotional acceptance of his theses of the priority of class (as represented by the party) over nation, the progressiveness of the Revolution and the Soviet state, and the rightness of union under the Russian-ruled party.

Consequently, since the stabilization of the Soviet state, the Leninist solution to the problem of the Russian empire has been subject to erosion. Toward the end of his life, Lenin was lamenting and combatting the rebirth of Russian chauvinism. Stalin undid many Leninist concessions to minority feelings, and he persecuted but could not end —perhaps under the surface exacerbated—minority "bourgeois nationalism." World War II was seen as a victory primarily for Russia and to this extent was a setback for the vision of an international polity. Nowadays, Russian nationalism, the exaltation of Moscow, and the turn to historical values are the obverse of the decay of Leninist internationalism. The Society for the Preservation of Ancient Landmarks is Russian only. The collecting of icons, restoration of old monuments, and sentimentalizing of the past are a Russian fashion only; they are not for minorities. Neo-Slavophilism is a prominent current in unofficial thinking; modern Slavophiles, like those of the nineteenth century, uphold the special virtues of the Russian people and the Orthodox Church and at least in part [13] resent what they see as unwarranted privileges for alien peoples. Some Russian nationalists are anti-Semitic in the old tradition; others would like the Russians to have a party and state of their very own.

The Communist party used to be truly international, with a large part of the leadership belonging to various minorities; a Georgian like Stalin, a Pole like Dzerzhinsky, Jews like Kamenev, Zinoviev, Trotsky, Radek, and many another non-Russian were quite at home in Lenin's government. All cooperated in the universalist cause; those who had most reason to feel slighted were the Russians. But by the 1930's Socialism in One Country had become in effect Russian socialism. Stalin himself became a great Russifier, and the role of non-Russians shrank through his reign. Lavrenti Beria, the Georgian whom Stalin trusted to control the police, was removed and executed in 1953, partly because of anti-Russification policies. Kaganovich, the last Jew on the Politburo (Presidium), left in 1957. The center of political control, the Secretariat, has been purely Russian since late 1965, and non-Slavs are represented on the Politburo as candidate members, that is, mostly symbolically. The power structure consists of Russians seconded by Ukrainians.

In practice, pride for Russia means neglect for others. Russianism is as contrary to Leninism as minority nationalism, no less dangerous, and more insidious. The two go hand in hand, and one is a reaction to the other, as in the last decades before the Revolution. Minorities resent Russian hegemony if not leadership, while Russians are troubled by minority self-assertion and more inclined to insist on central control and Russian leadership since they feel the unity of the realm brought into question. But public Soviet concern is exclusively for the "bourgeois nationalism" of the minorities, an almost unfailing topic in speeches at major gatherings and a preoccupation of the leadership—perhaps an obsession to judge from the frequency of references to the nationality question in public discourse. As *Pravda* put it, "The national question is one of the most complex and acute questions of socialist development."[14] It has been menacing since 1918–19, when minorities generally opted for independence. Lenin's modest concessions to minority feelings led to suggestions of national communism, and the Ukraine in the early 1920's practically tried to eliminate use of the Russian language. Stalin showed his estimate of the effects of a generation of Soviet education by removing the Volga Germans before they had an opportunity to commit treason, and he subsequently exiled several peoples, such as the Crimean Tatars, en masse. Despite the discredit of the Nazis, it was in many areas difficult to restore Soviet rule after victory. In Latvia, Soviet authority was at first so unpopular (as portrayed by a Soviet movie [15]) that Pioneers did not dare to wear their neckerchiefs to school.

Problems have seemingly become more acute in recent years, with something of a running battle between Sovietism and nationalism, between "proletarian internationalism" and "bourgeois" ideas.[16] There have been hundreds of articles on nationality problems and reports of incidents, protests, or arrests of nationalists, in the Ukraine and Caucasian, Baltic, and Muslim areas. Party housecleanings, usually with denunciations of profiteering scandals, have been found necessary in most minority republics in recent years. Economic growth is no longer sufficiently dynamic to silence discontents. The spread of Russian settlers, often occupying superior positions, has created frictions; the Latvian party boss wrote that some Latvians opposed industrial projects because they would bring more Russians into Latvia.[17] Even communist leaders quietly protest Russification in the Baltic states and elsewhere; an underground letter from seventeen Latvian Communists protesting Russification (and presumably sacrificing their careers thereby) was published in the West in January, 1972. In the same month, 17,000 Lithuanians signed a petition calling for religious freedom and defiantly giving addresses; subsequently there were self-immolations, riots, and mass arrests.[18] The Baltic, however, is marginal politically as well as geographically; most critical is the second largest of Soviet nationalities, the Ukrainians, control over whom is crucial to the Russian position.[19]

Soviet education in minority areas is designed to train a ruling élite to assist administration, to spread the ideology of the rulers, and

to wash out native culture. But it is only partly successful; it raises up
a new local apparatus and local intelligentsia with an interest in autonomy and a belief that Caucasian or Turkic peoples should deal with
Russians as equals and be responsible for their own affairs. It is true
that more and more people learn Russian and adapt themselves to the
Russian-dominated milieu. The Russian language increasingly envel-
ops education from the primary grades on, supposedly at the request
of parents.* But census figures indicate little assimilation over the whole
period of Soviet rule. For example, the percentage of Bashkirs whose
native language is Bashkiri has risen steadily from 54 percent in 1926
to 66 percent in 1970.[21] The percentage of Russians declines because of
differential birth rates as well as territorial acquisitions. Moreover, outward assimilation is no warranty of harmony; this is evident in friction
with the Jews, only about a sixth of whom consider Yiddish their
native tongue. The large numbers willing to accept severe sacrifices in
the hope of securing permission to emigrate testify to the imperfect
success of indoctrination, and it is notable that recent arrivals in Israel
hate socialism and can seldom be persuaded to enter a kibbutz.†

The end of national differences within the Soviet Union is post-
poned until after the worldwide victory of communism.[22] Meanwhile,
an official answer is to evoke "Soviet" nationalism; but "Soviet" does
not define a nationality in terms of language or cultural background.
The ideological bond is indispensable; the Soviet Union would surely
be unsustainable as a simple Russian empire in the modern world. But
Marxism-Leninism is less convincing for minorities, for whom it is associated with not only an overcontrolling state but with Russian domination. Nor is it certain that Marxism serves perfectly its purpose of
overriding national with class themes. "The great danger of nationalism
in our day comes from its disguise under Marxist philosophy," as *Pravda*
informs.[23] Governing parties, although called "Communist," can become vehicles of independent thinking and resistance to external domination, just as, on the larger scene, the Communist parties of China,
Yugoslavia, Albania, and Rumania have become. Lenin's solution of
defusing minority feeling by granting paper rights was clever but

---

* "As of 1970, the teaching of Russian was introduced everywhere [in Azer-
baidzhan] beginning with the first grade and, the voluntary principle notwith-
standing, there has not been a single case yet of unwillingness or refusal to study
Russian."[20]

† This is a remarkable turnaround; emigrés from Russia were prime movers
in the kibbutz movement in the 1920's.

potentially dangerous, for the minorities were furnished a basis for protest and organization whenever ideology and party control should weaken. It is felt necessary to bow to the worldwide ideas of freedom of peoples, even to reemphasize the vaunted "sovereignty" of the "republics" which compose the Soviet Union; [24] but this is an invitation to think, first privately and then aloud, that one's own republic might well exercise a little of this constitutionally guaranteed freedom.

With no new ideas, the Soviet state seeks to preserve itself by ceaseless propaganda, indoctrination, and institutional centralization. The latter is largely economic; it seems primarily for political reasons that it is impossible to give way to the imperative needs for economic decentralization and relaxation of the prohibitions against any sort of private enterprise. As *Pravda* put it in 1968, "Only under socialism is secure the firm unity of nations and nationalities in the framework of a united multinational government." [25] It is similarly inadmissible to relax central control of culture, censorship, education, the press, and police. In recent years, many concessions previously made in these areas have been retracted to supplement the less formal authority of the centralized party with the complete formal authority of ministries in Moscow. But the withdrawal of even the pretense of autonomy from the republics and the transfer of administrative power to distant bureaucrats cannot appease discontents.

CHANGING WORLD ENVIRONMENT

Since the first part of the nineteenth century, when Russia came to a zenith in leadership in the victory over Napoleon, the favorable configuration has been breaking down. The gradual infection of nationalism changed the imperial state from a truly international and hence viable polity to a national one, or, in the Leninist rehabilitation, a pseudointernational one. It was a sign of basic trouble that Nicholas I sought, not to foster Westernization, in the manner of Peter, but sternly to check it and so to hold Russia back as the West was racing ahead. In the second half of the century, the effort to exclude Western influences was given up; but the price was deep division of Russian society, the divorce of the intelligentsia from the regime, and the undermining of the ideological bases of the state.

Externally, likewise, the world situation was changing to the detriment of the Russian way. By the beginning of this century, prospects for easy expansion came to an end, because Russian power collided with

Japan's rising sun in the Far East and the British sphere in southern
Asia. The balance among the states on the Western frontier, essential
for the safety of Russia, was being undone by the upsurge of a single
threatening power, Germany. Despite rapid economic growth, Russia
was having increasing difficulty in keeping the technological gap from
becoming dangerously broad. Western influence was growing uncon-
trollably, and it was more than ever difficult to screen out corrosive
political and social ideas, constitutionalism, democracy and, still more
dangerous, nationalism, which threatened to make the imperial synthesis unworkable.

Leninism gave a new mission and new bonds; and it revitalized the
empire. World War II and victory over a dread enemy renewed morale and permitted the first major expansion in several generations, now
into Europe instead of Asia. But the world configuration that made
possible the growth of the Russian empire and basically shaped its
Weltanschauung—the peculiar mixture of nationalism and universalism
—has changed detrimentally into a quite different ordering of the political globe.

One factor has been the dissolution, mostly during the 1960's, of
the Western colonial empires, descendants of the empires built by the
maritime powers at the same time that the Russians were spreading
over northern Asia. Earlier, at the time of World War I, the big multinational states nearest Russia, the Austro-Hungarian and Turkish empires, were broken up. The end of the colonial empires (except the
Portuguese) has left the Russians in lone splendor as the world's imperialists and correspondingly more dependent upon an ideological-
universalist rationale. As the right of self-determination of peoples has
gained axiomatic acceptance, for Asians as well as Europeans, moral
pressure on the multinational Russian domain has increased, making
imperative potentially dangerous concessions of form and making difficult the denial of substance.

The relinquishment of colonies by major capitalist powers falsified
Lenin's basic theory, whereby the higher stage of capitalism required
colonies so desperately that competition in the grabbing of exploitable
territories necessarily led to war. By shedding colonial empires, leading
capitalist countries deprived the Leninists of their strongest accusation.
Stalin seemed simply unwilling to believe in the independence of the
former Western colonies. Khrushchev was more realistic, but he was
less troubled by theoretical implications than enticed by the opportu-

nity to resume at least symbolic and ideological expansion. He would take advantage of growing Soviet economic and military power, the disorganization of the West, and the anti-Western sentiments of ex-colonial peoples to swing them into the "Socialist Camp." This could amount, especially in areas adjacent to the Soviet Union, to a renewal of the old Russian expansionist-civilizing drive, using technology borrowed from the West to assert superiority over less advanced peoples, thereby justifying and legitimizing the Russian political system and (as Khrushchev emphatically hoped) strengthening it against the West.

This was in the logic of Leninism, which required vindication by growth; although the universalist order does not need to rule universally, it must seem to be advancing in that direction. But prospects are very poor. In the traditional direction, eastward and southeastward, the rise of strong, independent states, Japan, China, and India, has halted apparently permanently the Russian march. Many lands that seemed promising to Khrushchev were and are amply weak; but, unlike the Asian expanses that lay at the feet of the tsars, they are fully open to economic and cultural relations with the West, and the Russians were usually behind their competitors except in military wares. The Russians could bring gifts and make themselves welcome in many countries, but they could hardly aspire to gain (except perhaps by military means) the exclusive influence that would be profitable to them. Non-Western countries from Iran to Algeria developed their own nationalism, and they could seek support and favors from Western powers, who are better able to supply most developmental needs, or from the Chinese, who can speak more convincingly for the Third World than can the Russians. There seems no possibility of the Soviet Union's acquiring the economic preponderance that Khrushchev hoped would push the balance decisively in Russia's favor, and the ideological attractiveness of Sovietism is meager. Hence, despite some inviting areas of weakness, prospects for easy expansion in the old style have shrunk. Emphasis has been shifted from economic-ideological to military-naval expansion of the Soviet sphere of influence. This hardly seems more promising, as was shown by the failure of the Russians to win influence in Egypt despite billions of dollars worth of arms and several years' military presence.

The contest for influence in the Third World has also been erosive of ideology, since politics requires acceptance of political leaders, non-Communist or anti-Communist, as virtuous. Friendship treaties certified the virtues of sundry non-Leninist regimes, such as those of Egypt and India. Moreover, the Soviet Union has found itself in numerous non-ideological conflicts, wherein taking one side means antagonizing the other. The Russians were troubled by lack of Third World support for their policy of helping India against Pakistan in December, 1971. In various ways, as in questions of nuclear energy and matters of trade, the interests of the Soviet Union as an advanced power conflict with the purposes of the less developed nations and the Soviet solicitation of their favor.

Soviet frustration in the less developed countries has been intensified by the emergence of China from isolation and its 1971 entry into the United Nations. China is an offset to Russian influence, one that goes easily with anti-Western consciences, and a surety that Russian aid cannot be cashed into hegemony. A country like Sudan, finding itself at odds with the Soviet Union, can lean on China if it prefers to avoid a Western orientation. The Chinese have also been cultivating relations with East European countries since 1970 and directly or indirectly encouraging their independence. The self-will of Rumania has been expressed partly in terms of neutrality in the Sino-Soviet dispute; in all the satellites Communist leaders have a little more latitude because of the split between the giants of Communism. The Chinese can at least offer an ideological and moral alternative; against them, as non-capitalists, Soviet ideological weapons are dull.

The emergence of a dynamic and antagonistic China further complicates the situation of the Russian leaders because they no longer have to counter only Western ideological threats. The Chinese, with fewer compunctions than the United States, do their best to stir separatist strivings of Soviet minorities, such as the restive Ukrainians, and most of all the peoples of Central Asia, who have more in common, racially and in cultural background, with the Chinese than with the Russians. At the same time, the Chinese assert claims in their own name to a large part of Siberia, taken by tsarist imperialism a century or so ago; Russia is the only one of the nineteenth-century imperialist powers that still holds former Chinese territory. China is the only power that poses a continuing danger to the Russian realm; the Russians envision themselves again defending European civilization against the successors of the Mongols.

Since Marxism-Leninism is not a truly internationalist but a Russian-internationalist creed, the split between the two powers was practically inevitable. The Russians could not permit the Chinese, at least five times more numerous, to dominate their movement; even co-leadership with the Chinese would mean deep alteration of the system. On the other hand, it was not conceivable that the Chinese would long bow to the leadership of Russians, whom they regard as in no wise superior. In the Russian scheme, whereby an inner core dominates a larger group and this in turn manages a still larger circle, there is no place for divided leadership and no way to fit in another large and powerful nation beside the Russian. Consequently, even when the Russians and Chinese were most eager to display brotherhood they seem to have been quarreling behind the scenes—over conditions of aid and trade, border areas, nuclear weapons, "socialist" foreign policy, and the like. As quarrels piled up, the polemics became opener and sharper, until by the latter 1960's there were bloody border clashes, and each side became evidently the chief antagonist of the other.

Effects were multiple and mutually reinforcing. The Russian self-designated leaders of world revolution found themselves outflanked on the left and challenged in their theoretical radicalism. The "socialist camp" lost at a stroke two-thirds of its population—and the claim of representing over a third of the people of the world was one of the grander of Soviet boasts and the best support for assuming the rightness of Leninist historical destiny. The bitter dispute with a "socialist" state punctured the Soviet utopia, a major premise of which held capitalism responsible for conflict and assured harmony when it should be replaced by socialism. The results of the victory of the Leninist political style in China could only be profoundly discouraging for the effort to spread Soviet influence by ideological means. China also appeared as a barrier to Soviet expansion and threatened Soviet dominion in Eastern Europe, perhaps the integrity of the Soviet Union itself. Forming a solid and increasingly powerful nation, armed with nuclear weapons, China could neither be subverted nor divided nor at any acceptable cost conquered; it hence practically nullified any conceivable Soviet aspirations for indefinite dominion.

For this turn of affairs there was no credible ideological explanation. For a long time, the Soviet press ignored the Chinese, except for occasional verbose statements about "dogmatists." Subsequently, every effort was made to depict differences not as between Russia and China but between the "Maoist clique" and the Marxist-Leninist workers' movement. The Maoists were dismissed as militarists, nationalists, and ultimately as petty bourgeois, although China is more egalitarian and has less private property than the Soviet Union. But such free use of words deprives them of content. Some of the things said about the Chinese were applicable, perceptive Soviet citizens must have noted, to Soviet society as well. Soviet journalists denounced Maoist pretenses of democracy and rigged elections, and accused the Chinese of concentrating on military industry, of speedup of the workers and paying in terms of ideology instead of goods, and so on.[26] In China "Society was merely to be turned into a will-less, regimented mass, freely manipulable according to the secret intentions of the clique at the top." [27]

To attenuate ideological difficulties, Soviet propagandists continued for some years to treat the "capitalist-imperialist" United States as the main enemy, to the side of which China has defected. Thus the United Nations debate of December, 1971, in which most harsh language was between delegates of China and the U.S.S.R., was portrayed by the Soviet press as primarily a confrontation between American imperialism and the Soviet Union, the latter defending India and the people of Bangladesh. But in bitterness that China was looking to its own interests, the Russians had nothing to offer except their version of Leninism.

Beside China, Japan towered ever higher economically, a richer and technologically more advanced state to the east like the more advanced states to the west. Japan, with double the volume of exports in 1971, played a much larger role in the world economy than did Russia; the superiority of the latter was only military. The rise of Japan further strained efforts to interpret the world in Marxist-Leninist terms, which were conceived with reference to the European scene. It also hurt that nonrevolutionary, nonsocialist Japan could display the economic virtuosity that the Russians boasted but failed to achieve and maintain. In 1973 the Japanese GNP was already close to the Soviet level, despite a population less than half as large and nearly complete lack of industrial raw materials of domestic origin.

On the Western marches, likewise, the pattern turned against the Russians. The destruction of German power in World War II was a great boon, which permitted satisfying expansion. But the affiliation of the Western powers with the United States in NATO excluded possibilities of further gain in that direction; and the rapid recovery and economic growth of Western Europe in the 1950's and 1960's, though less remarkable than that of Japan, was hurtful to the Russian standing and to Russian control of Eastern Europe. Worse was the inability of the Soviet Union to check the unification of the Western nations in the Common Market. Russia no longer had the advantage of dwarfing a quarrelsome pack of small states, but faced an economically bound, potentially politically united Western Europe.

The defection of China and fears of complications on the Eastern frontier led the Soviet Union to soften attitudes in Europe, particularly to reach détente with the previously much berated West Germans. When the United States and China in 1971 and 1972 moved toward an understanding, it became imperative for the Russians to do likewise, inviting Nixon to Moscow and cooperating in the settlement of the Vietnam War, thereby practically losing the last really useful enemy. Impelled by economic shortfalls, and the need for huge grain imports and for ever increasing technology from the more innovative nations, the Soviet Union deemed it advisable to come to a fair degree of understanding with the United States, which has largely replaced Western Europe as the object of admiration, envy, and sometimes hatred, and the standard by which Russia measures itself. It was hence possible to mark the May, 1972, Nixon visit to Moscow with no less than ten agreements to reduce tensions or increase collaboration, including the first consequential disarmament pacts between the two nuclear giants and a remarkable declaration by which the two powers promised, inter alia, to avoid tension-producing situations, to resolve differences amicably, not to seek advantages at the expense of the other, to recognize the security interests and equality of the other side, to avoid interference in the internal affairs of all countries, to exchange opinions and hold meetings of leaders, and to carry forward efforts toward general disarmament.[28] With the end of the Vietnam war and the visit of Brezhnev to the United States in June, 1973, the way was opened to as normal relations as the Soviet state could admit with an independent power.

Yet a world of four or five truly independent superpowers or near-superpowers is entirely contrary to the Russian way. The inspirational value of the extensiveness of Russia is no longer so outstanding in the global picture. The political utopia is plausible only for a self-engrossed empire or for a polity with hopes of overcoming competition, but only its utopia separates Communism from ordinary dictatorship. The Soviet Union must represent itself as harbinger of historical justice, the flood tide which must sweep over all, a position which becomes unsustainable in a multipolar world. The Communist parties likewise have no special role if the Soviet Union is only one of several counterbalancing powers. Russia is and must be unconditionally opposed to the open pluralistic state system.

The Soviet Union hence holds stubbornly to the unrealistic image: the Soviet family of nations is upheld as the model of internationalism; and the world Communist movement, struggling for a single justice, justifies the unity of Soviet nations.

Soviet patriotism . . . means not only devotion to the native land, to certain national-historical values, but dedication to the most advanced, the socialist form of society, to scientific Marxist-Leninist ideology . . . an organic fusion of the feeling of love for the Motherland, communist conviction, and proletarian internationalism.[29]

The Soviet Union wants good relations and advantages of trade and technical cooperation with states which by ideology should be class enemies, yet it is unwilling to give up the ideological picture. Foreign Minister Andrei Gromyko expressed the ambivalence before the assembled delegates of the world's states in 1971. Speaking of the friendlier attitudes even of members of anti-Soviet alliances, he sacrificed logic to politics:

in recent years cool, even hostile relations between states with different social systems have in a number of cases been replaced by relations based on mutual understanding.

All this cannot in the slightest remove the historic opposition of socialism and imperialism, lessen the sharpness of the struggle of two opposites in world politics. . . .[30]

The litany is repeated endlessly for internal consumption: "Our era is characterized by the further deepening of the world revolutionary process."[31] Chief ideologue Suslov, to justify their commitment, told French Communists, "The strengthening of principles of Peaceful Coexistence in international affairs in no way signifies a weakening of class struggle on a world scale or a 'reconciliation' of capitalism and socialism."[32] Peaceful Coexistence, it is often pointed out, means ideological warfare.

As Alexander Solzhenitsyn pointed out, the Soviet system cannot get along without enemies; but it runs out of credible ones. In a world of several great powers, the interrelations, competitions, and antagonisms of importance on the world stage are between states, not classes; and the black-and-white view becomes increasingly empty as the revolution that gave it substance is buried in history. It was the good fortune of the Soviet Union that the world of the first postwar decades looked mainly bipolar, but the chief "bourgeois" power, chastened by troubles in Vietnam, has moved away from principled anti-Communism and taken a more flexible view of the world. It is with reason that the Soviet mentality detests the idea of balance of power with fanatical hatred. It is seen as a capitalist conspiracy to destroy Soviet socialism [33] —which may be its effect.

In an ever more close-knit world, where to shut oneself off is to decay, Russian exclusivism becomes untenable unless it can be ever broadened. Under the tsars, as today, the rulers could demand blind obedience in the name of the Russian mission (or "proletarian internationalism"), and service became more bearable with this rationale. For the Soviet Union, the end of expansion threatens disintegration, but further expansion has become impractical. As a universalist-type empire, not really internationalist but Russian-dominated, the Soviet Union is an anomaly in a world of strong nation-states. It requires more absolutist government than seems permanently viable under modern conditions, and it clashes with modern expectations of freedom and human dignity. It has a unique problem of legitimation, the maintenance of an artificial unity at home through an artificial antithesis to the world outside. It seems clear that if the multipolar world continues to develop, the Soviet Union must adapt itself to it; the Soviet system is not compatible with close relations with the world of nation-states. But so to adapt would mean leaving behind the Leninist synthesis. Lenin was probably right in his belief that his revolution must prevail indefinitely or fail. He only underestimated the time necessary for the dénouement. Soviet leaders, indeed, have never accepted in theory the permanence of the Soviet Union in a non-Soviet world. In Soviet terms, it is not possible to build communism without the final defeat of the capitalist enemy, and Soviet leaders have never acknowledged the peaceful coexistence of capitalism and the Soviet system as permanent.

THE RUSSIAN SITUATION

Many a writer, from Karl Marx to less celebrated journalists, has wondered at the consistency and purposefulness of Russian policy and its secular success in making the state ever larger, sometimes halting but practically never surrendering land acquired. This success has been often attributed to a special Russian cleverness, a conspiratorial acumen whereby other peoples were regularly deceived, Russian purposes were concealed, and Russian policy had an integrity and direction more innocent peoples failed to match. Such an interpretation, however, attributes to diabolical guile and cleverness or supposed racial attributes the effect of the favorable circumstances in which the Russians found themselves. In their position as beneficiaries of Western technology and neighbors of nonbeneficiaries, dominion fell naturally to them; and expansion fed on itself by enlarging the basis of power and nourishing mentality and institutions appropriate for indefinite rulership. Hence expansion continued as long as the favorable conjunction lasted, that is, until space ran out and the effects of Westernization became too difficult for the old Russian system to handle in the last decades of the nineteenth century.

By restating the old Russian mission to adapt it to this century and shaking up and reforging the rotten and calcified society, Lenin was able to give it new life. His efforts bore success, although different from that which he dreamed, rather of national power than international social change. Representing something of a new departure in the world, in many ways a rationally organized system, the Soviet Union has amply demonstrated its fitness by surviving, bringing numerous countries into its orbit (thanks in part to good luck in connection with World War II) and building an advanced superpower, acknowledged as an approximate military equal by the United States.

The Soviet state has also had internal successes. The Bolsheviks jerked and shoved Russia out of backwardness and poverty to considerable, albeit uneven modernization. They gave a new inspiration and vision of the happiness that might be achieved through a better social order. Most of the promises of the Revolution have been defaulted, but the Soviet state assumes much responsibility for its citizens; and its structured society gives security, both economic and psychological. The Soviet, unlike the American way, provides ample guidance for its people. It gives simple answers to many perplexing questions, relieving of confusions in the overwrought modern world. Its achievements in education and health care are generally esteemed. Its paternalistic collectivism suits most people. There is realism in calling factories and other enterprises "public" and insisting that they serve, at least in theory, general needs. The Soviet economy should be troubled neither by strikes nor large-scale manipulative speculation. The principle of "The responsibility of each to the collective and the responsibility of the collective for each worker" [34] is sound. If the Soviet state does not burden its people with political choices, few seem to regret it; Soviet citizens ordinarily regard a multiparty system as an invitation to anarchy and weakness. Many Americans who insist on freedom for themselves admire the orderliness and social spirit of Soviet children.

The Soviet Union has strengths in the world akin to those it displays at home. It is the big ostensible alternative to tense and distraught Western society, to inane commercialism and frivolity. It promises not so much revolution as harmony and order—the disunity and disorder of the West, especially in the years 1966 to 1971, were a Soviet bonanza. For states which suffer lack of coherence, as do many of the underdeveloped world, the Soviet Union offers a model of integration despite national and cultural differences. It profits from great concern for appearances and an ability to present its best face; and in international confrontations, the Soviets have the advantages of infinite self-righteousness, clear and steadfast purpose, and willingness to use force. They point to the Berlin Wall and the invasion of Czechoslovakia as acts of virtue, and the presence of Soviet forces in Eastern Europe is effective because people know they will not hesitate to shoot if their purposes require it.

It is the basic promise of Leninism to combine the advantages of the autocratic empire and the free pluralistic state—to couple strong, purposeful, and unhampered rulership and political drive with economic and technological improvement. It has been able to do this in past decades thanks to the dedication of the leadership and the power of its mythology, and so in effect to have the best of two worlds. But Leninism did not solve the dilemmas and contradictions of historical Russia, only papered them over, deepened the tension-creating ambivalences, and made Russia more dependent upon a pseudoscientific theory of history and society. The advantages are not permanent. The ideology, the power of which was dependent upon continuous movement, has worn thin in the routine of political life, so it no longer effectively cloaks the political realities; there remains a threadbare garb of chauvinism and self-adulation. Abilities decay in both directions: the state loses purpose and coherence, and economic innovation becomes more difficult. With the decline of revolutionary élan, the problem of renewal of leadership at the top becomes more severe, and no

solution is visible in the nonconstitutional order; there is not even the
regular order of a monarchic state. The bureaucracy grows more ponderous and unresponsive. Stability is inherently destructive of the Soviet
system.

The state has lost much of its capacity to rule and move society.
Censorship is less effective, and the police find it difficult to repress
underground publications. The intellectuals no longer stand in awe of
the state. An enormous effort, far beyond what Stalin thought necessary, is made to indoctrinate the people; but they may react oppositely
to the intentions of the propagandists.[35] Campaigns against tobacco and
alcoholism are of no avail, and petty crime flourishes.[36] Far more things
are smuggled in or out than a generation ago, manuscripts, records,
Western clothes. The gray market is immense, and illegal private enterprise flourishes.

It is extremely serious that the state can no longer propel the
economy rapidly forward. Several times in Russian history, after a
period of narrowing the gap with the West, the Russians have seen it
widen again; the cycle repeats itself. The system of centralized planning, once a means of rapid industrialization, has become an impedi-
ment to further progress, partly because the economy has outgrown it,
more because the spirit needed to make the controls effective has been
exhausted. Much as serfdom once stood in the way of productive agriculture, so now do the overlarge state-controlled *sovkhozy* and *kol-
khozy;* again, as did tsardom a hundred and fifty years ago, the regime
clings for political reasons to economically harmful institutions. There
is a growing demand for more, better, and more varied consumer goods,
and for more adequate services, which can hardly be met without a
substantial degree of decentralization or freedom for small-scale private
enterprise, as in several Communist countries of Eastern Europe. But
the leadership has given priority to controls over consumer interests
for fear of where a retreat might lead and what dire consequences it
might entrain for the entire system. The Soviet state increasingly faces
the old dilemma of tsarist Russia, that economic liberalization is called
for to keep Russia from slipping farther behind, but economic liberalization is inseparable from political. The other side of this dilemma
is the problem of contacts with the West, which become more necessary but more dangerous. The Leninist ideological sieve for admitting
needed technology while excluding heretical ideas no longer works so
efficiently.

As momentum is lost and drives weaken, the Leninist state is riven by internal contradictions as severe as those dogmatically attributed to capitalist society. Formerly submerged cleavages come to the surface, and new fissures appear and widen. As Academician Sakharov put it in a memorandum of March, 1971,

> The following problems should be noted: aggravation of the nationality problem; complications in relations between the party-government apparatus and the intelligentsia, and in their relations with the basic mass of workers who find themselves in a relatively poorer position as far as living standards and economic situation go and in relation to job promotion and cultural growth, and who experience in a number of cases a feeling of disenchantment with "big talk" and the privileged group of "bosses," a group which for the most part often includes the intelligentsia in the eyes of the more backward strata of workers because of their traditional prejudices.[37]

The collectives that the system fosters turn inward and defend their own interests. The cultivation of militarism and patriotism as supplement for Marxism-Leninism is dangerous because the military is a better embodiment of these virtues than the party. Russianism, too, undercuts the position of the party and its universalist image; the Church is a better vehicle of national sentiment. The official society and the practical world grow farther apart. Pressures for change visibly increase, both internally and from outside influences, as the ability to cope with them subsides.

The most crucial of divisions in Soviet society and the most threatening is that of nationalities. Despite the fullest means of control, even the local Communist parties develop some self-assertiveness. This is self-reinforcing, since the growth of self-awareness erodes central controls and permits the further growth of self-awareness; it is difficult to see how additional efforts to strengthen central control can be more effective in the face of systemic decay than tsarist Russification, the chief effect of which was to deepen antagonisms. But the Soviet Union rests upon the ability to get Georgians, Ukrainians, and other ethnic groups to work together in the Russian-dominated conglomerate. The permitting of some Jews to emigrate is itself an admission of failure and a loosening of the state; it becomes harder to deny to others this freedom of detachment from the Muscovite state.

The Soviet system is most vulnerable in its only partially incorporated fringes, in Eastern Europe, where it is overextended with consequent strain on ideological patterns.[38] Force may work in the short run; the Soviets showed in Czechoslovakia that they could reimpose their system in the face of almost unanimous resistance and shortly get large numbers of Czechs to assist in the "normalization" of Czechoslovakia. For the Russians, it is not essential to make people into good Marxist-Leninists, only to convince them that Soviet domination is unavoidable; but this becomes more difficult as contacts with the West steadily grow, and the effectiveness of Soviet troops on the ground decreases as Soviet attitudes soften.

The peoples of Eastern Europe are close to the West in traditions; and it seems that they are finding the Soviet Union more, rather than less, foreign.[39] The economic systems of Eastern Europe, especially Poland and Hungary, continue to diverge from the Soviet model, the magnetism of which is dissipated by Soviet economic stagnation. Satellite literatures and art also go a little way of their own. Poland and other countries want the American series "Sesame Street" for their children, and some leaders send their offspring to upper-class British schools. It is impossible to keep the workers from learning a good deal about their fellows in the West and consequently wondering why those who suffer under the capitalist yoke are so much better off. Western tourists come by the millions, and trade and collaboration with Western business interests on both sides of the border grow steadily.

Russian reliance upon indirect rule, for which ideology is essential, is unpromising as a permanent arrangement; yet it probably is no longer practicable to incorporate the satellite states into the Soviet Union, as it may have been shortly after World War II. Not only are concern for the world image and bureaucratic conservatism against it; admission of large blocs of advanced peoples would make Russian management of the Soviet apparatus more difficult. The Soviet minority problem is bothersome enough without taking in, for instance, 34 million nationalistic Poles. But it is difficult to see how Russian domination of Eastern Europe can be permanent unless it is institutionalized.

The incompleteness of the Sovietization of Eastern Europe requires separation between Russian and satellite peoples, separation that hinders absolute control. Probably Soviet rulership has in fact, though not openly, slackened in recent years. Apparently the Kremlin can no longer easily change the leadership of vassal states, as it could under Stalin; at least, it has seldom done so since Khrushchev. In Poland, a Soviet-favored ruler was forced out at the end of 1970 by popular pressures which army and police refused to suppress. Local leaderships can slowly carve out a degree of autonomy for themselves, and there is no legal bar to its indefinite increase. Territorial socialism, or strong governmental control of the economy and culture of an area, is divisive, not internationalist in spirit, since the rulers are disposed to assert their control of whatever is in their jurisdiction. In the absence of an overall political authority, it is thus harder to integrate planned than un-planned economies; each set of planning authorities prefers to manage its own resources, and decisions for specialization are complicated and difficult to reach. For this reason, the Soviet Union has felt unable to admit even a modest amount of economic decentralization. The world can only guess how much tension there may be beneath the fairly calm surface; Communist states can keep grave differences submerged for many years, as did China and the Soviet Union in the 1950's.

It is, moreover, somewhat uncomfortable for the Soviet Union to maintain its position in an Eastern Europe which seems increasingly to offer bad examples which cannot easily be ideologically refuted. If censorship is weakened in Poland, Soviet writers must become aware of it. If some elections are real contests in Poland or Hungary, the prac-tice might spread to Soviet elections. On the other hand, relinquish-ment of dominion there would be very difficult. Retreat is ideologically unthinkable and horrifying in principle, because it might not stop at the Soviet border; if Czechoslovakia can rule itself, why should not the Ukraine and Georgia? It is even painful to acknowledge departure from the "Socialist Commonwealth" of nations which have become fully independent; only recently has the Soviet Union conceded that relations of Peaceful Coexistence should prevail with China instead of Proletarian Internationalism. It is similarly inadmissible to yield any land of the Russian empire, such as the valueless tiny islands which stand in the way of better relations with Japan. Any territorial conces-sion would open a Pandora's box of claims and conceivably call the very existence of the Soviet Union into question.

Similarly, it seems to be felt dangerous to make any political con-cession lest a swarm of political demands be released and the entire brittle political order be endangered. The Soviet way is completely geared to concentration of authority and monopoly of force, of the economy, and of political organization. Its major premise is the absence of any organized opposition; a public political contest would mean the dissolution of the ideology and of the basis for party rule and rule of the nucleus within it.

An aging absolutist regime is likely to be brittle; if it begins to make concessions, demands multiply, all manner of grievances surface, the prestige of the élite sinks, and the whole social edifice may crumble. This was the case with the eighteenth-century French monarchy, which started an avalanche by summoning the Estates General. The tsarist government saw liberalization after the Crimean War spawn a massive Polish uprising in 1863. In 1905, after defeats thousands of miles away, the authority of the Russian government practically disappeared in major centers for a few weeks. In 1917, when no one had any idea of early revolution, the venerable government collapsed like a balloon at a pinprick. Repeatedly, when people of Communist societies have felt for some reason that it was no longer necessary to obey, the Soviet-sponsored order has collapsed. In parts of Czechoslovakia and East Germany in 1953 and in Hungary in 1956 expectations of relaxation led to riots that became more or less serious anti-Communist rebellions. In not dissimilar fashion, when Maoist China yielded freedom for the "Hundred Flowers," criticism rapidly became a deluge. In Czechoslovakia in 1968, as soon as it became possible to express demands for change they became overwhelming, and the old system of control fell to pieces. Riots or strikes that would be of minor importance to a Western country threaten in the Communist context the existence of the state. What if the police or army should refuse to fire upon demonstrators, perhaps turn their guns against their officers?

The Soviet system is held the more tightly by the fear that yielding anything means endangering all. Reform turns attention to remaining grievances. As the Polish leader Gomulka is quoted saying in July, 1968, "When one renounces an element of power, the result isn't a vacuum, but the enemy immediately takes over." [40] To give freedom means permitting agitation for more, and to open lines of communication and permit wider access to decision making is to allow demands to multiply.

It is doubtless partly for this reason that the Soviet state has remained refractory to change since Stalin gave it definitive shape. Perhaps less than any other has it responded institutionally to the massive economic changes of the past generation. Not only is the huge bureaucratic apparatus immobile and hidebound; apparently the Soviet leaders do not conceive that they could rule their realm otherwise, or do not dare to try. The reaction to troubles is usually simply to strengthen or slightly reshape controls. There can be no tampering with the essentials of party monopoly, opinion control, centralized planning of the economy, collectivized agriculture, and police repression.

As pressures continue to accumulate against a stiff system, for which concessions appear more dangerous the less dynamic it becomes, the outcome is wholly unpredictable. Conceivably, corrosive foreign influences might be largely excluded by a new isolationism. This would inevitably have an economic cost; but a political system, if it serves political purposes, need not be discarded because it is an economic hindrance. Many a state in the past has accepted backwardness. Old Russia could not do so for fear of weakness. In this age the pressure to keep up for the sake of security is less, so far as a few nuclear weapons suffice to deter attack. Withdrawal behind a Chinese Wall or an Iron Curtain like that which Nicholas I drew around Russia is impracticable, however.

The mentality of the élite will determine whether or how adjustments can be made. Internal ferment can lead to softening or to hardening of rule, in Soviet practice usually the latter; there has been less freedom when the Soviet Union was not under external threat and it consequently was more difficult for the regime to justify itself. In prerevolutionary times, "Although the Russians might listen to the siren call of reduced armaments or play with the idea of relaxing the bonds by which the subject races were held, no patriotic Russian could contemplate with equanimity the loss of power to protect or expand their possessions." [41] Dissolution of the empire still seems to be unthinkable, and concern for it is the basic factor in the stiffness of the apparatus of rule. As they have for centuries, the Russians regard themselve as bearers of a special world destiny, and now they are mostly prepared to tolerate Marxist-Leninist party rule in the conviction that this is the way to hold the conglomerate together under their hegemony. If the gains of so many victories were lost, the shock would be profound; Russians would have to alter radically their self-image.

Although empireship in the past has dictated caution in foreign relations and the avoidance of strains, it is not impossible that internal insecurity might bring external aggressivity, or at least refusal to accept setbacks. The Hapsburg empire did not wait to fall apart but reached out desperately to destroy the apparent source of trouble, Serbia. The decadent tsarist empire undertook expansion in the Far

East and war with Japan in 1904 in the hope of revitalizing itself. But one of the clearest effects of modernization is to increase the dangers and reduce the rewards of violence, and adventures abroad seem alien to the mentality of the staid and presenescent leadership. If more Russians come to see the freedom of the minorities as prerequisite for their own or regard non-Slavs as burdensome, the rulership may one day be persuaded that Russia can be reshaped to a loose association of free nations; or it might resolve, as the European maritime states have done, that hegemony is unproductive.

Less than ever can Russia escape the influence of the world milieu, and a strongly interacting multipolar world must deeply influence the mentality of all modern powers. The Soviet Union more and more forms part of the world system, and détente feeds upon itself and spreads through society; it is futile to talk of heightening ideological confrontation while enlarging all manner of practical cooperation with the enemy. But for the Soviet Union to fall in line with modern trends would mean a profound alteration of the relations of people to state and Russians to non-Russians, presumably a replacement of the official philosophy by that of the more enlightened intellectual critics of the regime. Sakharov, for example, has expressed the view that the "socialist camp" could only gain strength by admission of true equality of members.[42]

Adaptation to the contemporary world means acceptance of pluralism internally and externally, the recognition of contrary and independent rights. It also requires surrender of outmoded pretenses of universalism, which are discordant with the pluralistic state system, even though an integral part of the Russian way of the past. This would be a painful sacrifice; Russians could no longer see themselves as a chosen people. But it would also mean a great relief and release from the historical constraints imposed long ago by the geographic situation of Russia. The Russians have long borne the burden of empire; relieved of it, they would for the first time since the Tatar invasions be free to develop their true potential. The special gift of Russia might then be the humane and spiritual components of the Russian heritage, released from the authoritarian-imperialist shell formed in response to the opportunity of Eurasian expansion.

NOTES

1 EMPIRE

1. Georg von Rauch, *Russland: Staatliche Einheit und nationale Vielfalt* (Munich: Isar, 1953), p. 21.

2. Albert J. Beveridge, *The Russian Advance* (New York: Harper, 1904), p. 368.

3. Heinz Pächter, *Weltmacht Russland* (Oldenburg: Stalling, 1968), p. 15.

4. Von Rauch, *Russland*, p. 43.

5. Richard Pipes, *Karamzin's Memoir on Ancient and Modern Russia* (Cambridge, Mass.: Harvard University Press, 1959), p. 7.

6. Quoted by Sidney Harcave, *Years of the Golden Cockerel: The Last Russian Tsars, 1814–1917* (New York: Macmillan, 1968), p. 133.

7. Jan Kucharzewski, *The Origins of Modern Russia* (New York: Polish Institute of Arts and Sciences in America, 1948), p. 17.

8. Quoted by Anatole Leroy-Beaulieu, *The Empire of the Tsars and the Russians* (New York: Putnam, 1902), I, 406.

9. *Literaturnaia gazeta,* June 17, 1970.

10. *Pravda,* February 26, 1972, p. 1.

11. Nikolai A. Berdyaev, *The Russian Idea* (Boston: Beacon, 1962), p. 217.

12. Andrew Marshall, *Brazil* (New York: Walker, 1964), pp. 9–10.

13. Lysias A. Rodrigues, *Geopolítica do Brasil* (Rio de Janeiro: Ministério da Guerra, 1947), p. 20.

14. Thornton Anderson, *Russian Political Thought* (Ithaca, N.Y.: Cornell University Press, 1967), pp. 72–73.

15. Tiutchev is quoted by Hans Kohn, *Prophets and Peoples* (New York: Macmillan, 1946), p. 131.

16. Dinko Tomasic, *The Impact of Russian Culture on Soviet Communism* (Glencoe, Ill.: Free Press, 1953), p. 75.

17. Beveridge, *Russian Advance,* p. 368.

18. Kohn, *Prophets and Peoples,* p. 149.

19. Donald Mackenzie Wallace, *Russia* (New York: Holt, 1877), p. 199.

20. Fedor Dostoevsky, *Pages from the Journal of an Author* (Edinburgh: Edinburgh University Press, n.d.), p. 67.

21. Beveridge, *Russian Advance,* p. 369.

22. Thomas Riha, ed., *Readings in Russian Civilization* (Chicago: University of Chicago Press, 1969), II, 384.

23. Leroy-Beaulieu, *Empire of the Tsars,* pp. 238–239.

24. E. J. Dillon, *The Eclipse of Russia* (New York: Geo. H. Doran, 1918), p. 118.

25. Dostoevsky, *Pages from the Journal,* pp. 66–67.

26. Berdyaev, *Russian Idea,* p. 153.

27. Stuart R. Tompkins, *The Russian Mind* (Norman: University of Oklahoma Press, 1953), p. 148.

28. Wallace, *Russia,* p. 402.

29. Georg von Rauch, *A History of Soviet Russia* (New York: Praeger, 1967), p. 6.

30. Berdyaev, *Russian Idea,* p. 104.

31. Cf. Tomasic, *Impact of Russian Culture,* pp. 22–30.

32. Cf. George Vernadsky, *The Mongols and Russia* (New Haven: Yale University Press, 1953).

33. Michael Prawdin, *The Mongol Empire, Its Rise and Legacy* (London: George Allen and Unwin, 1961), p. 514.

34. Edward C. Keenen, Jr., "Muscovy and Kazan: Some Introductory Remarks on the Patterns of Steppe Diplomacy," *Slavic Review,* XXVI, 4 (December, 1967), 549.

35. Vernadsky, *The Mongols and Russia,* p. 344.

36. Omeljan Pritsak, "Moscow, the Golden Horde, and the Kazan Khanate from a Polycultural Point of View," *Slavic Review,* XXVI, 4 (December, 1967), 577–583.

37. G. Barraclough, *The Origins of Modern Germany* (Oxford: Basil Blackwell, 1949), pp. 277–280.

38. H. Seton-Watson, *The Russian Empire, 1801–1917* (Oxford: Clarendon Press, 1967), p. 75.

39. Riha, *Readings,* II, 281.

40. Sidney Harcave, ed., *Readings in Russian History* (New York: Crowell, 1962), I, 327.

41. Von Rauch, *Russland,* p. 179.

42. Stuart R. Tompkins, *The Russian Intelligentsia* (Norman: University of Oklahoma Press, 1957), pp. 249–250.

43. Marquis de Custine, *Journey for Our Time* (New York: Pellegrini and Cudahy, 1951), p. 117.

44. K. Waliszewski, in Warren B. Walsh, ed., *Readings in Russian History* (Syracuse, N.Y.: Syracuse University Press, 1959), p. 58.

45. Anderson, *Russian Political Thought*, p. 199.

46. Riha, *Readings*, II, 252.

47. Henry Norman, *All the Russias* (New York: Scribner, 1902), p. 36.

48. Custine, *Journey*, p. 93.

49. Norman, *All the Russias*, p. 36.

50. Ronald Hingley, *The Tsars, 1533–1917* (New York: Macmillan, 1968), passim.

51. Wallace, *Russia*, p. 589.

52. Harcave, *Readings*, p. 215.

53. D. S. Mirsky, *Russia, a Social History* (London: Cresset Press, 1952), p. 114.

54. Maxime Kovalevsky, *Russian Political Institutions* (Chicago: University of Chicago Press, 1902), pp. 93–94.

55. Anderson, *Russian Political Thought*, p. 139.

56. They are treated in some detail in Robert G. Wesson, *The Imperial Order* (Berkeley: University of California Press, 1967).

57. William G. Bray, *Russian Frontiers* (Indianapolis: Bobbs-Merrill, 1963), p. 24.

58. Harcave, *Years of the Golden Cockerel*, pp. 45–49.

2 RUSSIA: EUROPEAN STATE AND ORIENTAL EMPIRE

1. For a strong statement of the secular dependence of Russia, see Werner Keller, *East Minus West = Zero* (New York: Putnam, 1962).

2. Warren B. Walsh, ed., *Readings in Russian History* (Syracuse, N.Y.: Syracuse University Press, 1948), p. 130.

3. Sidney Harcave, *Russia, a History*, 6th ed. (Philadelphia: Lippincott, 1968), p. 83.

4. *Ibid.*, p. 117.

5. Tompkins, *Russian Mind*, p. 139.

6. Cf. Wesson, *Imperial Order*, pp. 1–12.

7. Kovalevsky, *Russian Political Institutions*, pp. 77–78.

8. For this and other projects of reform of the autocracy, see Marc Raeff, *Plans for Political Reform in Imperial Russia, 1730–1905* (Englewood Cliffs, N.J.: Prentice-Hall, 1966).

9. Tompkins, *Russian Mind*, p. 52.

10. Harcave, *Years of the Golden Cockerel*, p. 11.

11. Wallace, *Russia*, p. 452.

12. George Fischer, *Russian Liberalism, from Gentry to Intelligentsia* (Cambridge, Mass.: Harvard University Press, 1958), p. 61.

13. Ivan Turgenev, *Dreams, Tales, and Prose Poems*, trans. Constance Garnett (New York: Books for Libraries, 1969).

3 A CENTURY OF STRAINS

1. Sergei F. Platonov, *Moscow and the West* (Hattiesburg, Miss.: Academic International, 1972), p. 31.
2. Tompkins, *Russian Mind*, Chap. 4.
3. Paul Miliukov, *Russia and Its Crisis* (New York: Collier Books, 1962), p. 336.
4. *Ibid.*, p. 336.
5. *Ibid.*, p. 77.
6. Robert F. Byrnes, *Pobedonostsev, His Life and Thought* (Bloomington: Indiana University Press, 1968), p. 279.
7. *Ibid.*, p. 357.
8. Kucharzewski, *Origins of Modern Russia*, p. 89.
9. Albert L. Weeks, *The First Bolshevik: A Political Biography of Peter Tkachev* (New York: New York University Press, 1968), p. 87.
10. Tompkins, *Russian Mind*, p. 233.
11. W. H. Parker, *An Historical Geography of Russia (1968)* (Chicago: Aldine, 1969), p. 106.
12. Riha, *Readings*, II, 380.
13. Richard Hare, *Pioneers of Russian Social Thought* (London: Oxford University Press, 1951), p. 83.
14. H. Kohn, in Ernest J. Simmons, ed., *Continuity and Change in Russian and Soviet Thought* (Cambridge, Mass.: Harvard University Press, 1955), p. 514.
15. Wallace, *Russia*, p. 106.
16. Hans Kohn, *Panslavism, Its History and Ideology* (Notre Dame: University of Notre Dame Press, 1953), p. 195.
17. For a treatment of the nationality question under tsardom, see von Rauch, *Russland*.
18. Leroy-Beaulieu, *Empire of the Tsars*, I, 372.
19. Edward Chmielewski, *The Polish Question in the Russian State Duma* (Knoxville: University of Tennessee Press, 1970), p. 65.
20. Von Rauch, *Russland*, pp. 152–153.
21. *Ibid.*, p. 155.
22. V. A. Maklakov, *The First State Duma* (Bloomington: Indiana University Press, 1964), *passim.*
23. Jacob Walkin, *The Rise of Democracy in Pre-Revolutionary Russia* (New York: Praeger, 1962), p. 119.
24. Alec Nove, *An Economic History of the U.S.S.R.* (London: Penguin Press, 1969), p. 26.
25. *Ibid.*, p. 13.
26. William L. Blackwell, *The Industrialization of Russia* (New York: Crowell, 1970), p. 40.
27. Theodore H. von Laue, "Imperial Russia at the Turn of the Century: The Cultural Slope and the Revolution from Without." *Comparative Studies in Society and History*, III, 4 (July, 1961), 353–367.

28. Von Rauch, *Russland*, pp. 156–157.

29. *Ibid.*, p. 172.

30. Chmielewski, *Polish Question*, p. 163.

4 THE LENINIST RESYNTHESIS

1. Theodore H. von Laue, "The Chances for Liberal Constitutionalism," *Slavic Review*, XXIV, 1 (March, 1965), 34–46.

2. Von Rauch, *Russland*, p. 197.

3. Theodore H. von Laue, *Why Lenin? Why Stalin?* (Philadelphia: Lippincott, 1964), p. 108.

4. M. Polanyi, *The Contempt of Freedom* (London: Watts, 1940), p. 77.

5. In *What Is To Be Done*, in Samuel Hendel, ed., *The Soviet Crucible* (Princeton, N.J.: Van Nostrand, 1960), p. 130.

6. As Lenin wrote in February, 1916. *Sochineniia*, 4th ed. (1952), XXII, 35.

7. Antony C. Sutton, *Western Technology and Soviet Economic Development 1917–1930* (Stanford, Calif.: Hoover Institution Press, 1971), p. 311.

8. M. Florinsky, *World Revolution and the U.S.S.R.* (New York: Macmillan, 1933), p. 42.

9. Raymond Garthoff, *Soviet Military Policy* (New York: Praeger, 1966), p. 13.

10. *Pravda*, January 18, 1972.

11. Weeks, *The First Bolshevik*, p. 30.

12. Stalin, *Works*, XII (1955), 38.

13. *Pravda*, December 4, 1939; quoted by Bray, *Russian Frontiers*, p. 81.

14. Stuart R. Tompkins, *The Triumph of Bolshevism* (Norman: University of Oklahoma Press, 1967), p. 26.

15. Louis Fischer, *The Life of Lenin* (New York: Harper, 1964), p. 510.

16. Sutton, *Western Technology*, I, 346.

17. *Ibid.*, vols. I and II passim, esp. II, 346.

18. *New York Times*, February 3, 1972, p. 8.

19. *Kommunist sovetskoi Latvii*, no. 6 (1972), 40.

20. Wallace, *Russia*, p. 264.

21. *Ibid.*, p. 589.

5 SOVIET AMBIVALENCE

1. Gerald Freund, *Unholy Alliance: Russian-German Relations from the Treaty of Brest-Litovsk to the Treaty of Berlin* (New York: Harcourt, Brace, 1957), pp. 19, 28.

2. Sutton, *Western Technology*, p. 6.

3. Louis Fischer, *The Soviets in World Affairs* (Princeton, N.J.: Princeton University Press, 1951), p. 321.

4. Xenia J. Eudin and Harold H. Fisher, *Soviet Russia and the West, 1920–1927* (Stanford, Calif.: Stanford University Press, 1957), p. 165.

5. Alexander Werth, *Russia at War* (London: Barrie and Rockliff, 1964), p. 573.

6. Josef Korbel, *The Communist Subversion of Czechoslovakia* (Princeton, N.J.: Princeton University Press, 1959), p. 84.

7. *New York Times*, September 3, 1945.

8. *Ibid.*, April 22, 1958.

9. *Pravda*, September 11, 1968.

10. *Ibid.*, November 13, 1968.

11. *Ibid.*, September 26, 1968.

12. F. Barghoorn, in Jacob C. Hurewitz, ed., *Soviet-American Rivalry in the Middle East* (New York: Praeger, 1969), p. 157.

13. *Literaturnaia gazeta*, February 25, 1970, p. 9.

14. *Pravda*, June 28, 1972.

15. *Ibid.*, December 22, 1971.

16. *Ibid.*, January 8, 1971, p. 2.

17. *Sovetskaia Kultura*, June 15, 1971, p. 1.

18. S. Kaltakhchan, *Pravda*, November 26, 1968, p. 3.

19. Cf. Henry S. Bradsher, "The Sovietization of Mongolia," *Foreign Affairs*, L, 3 (April, 1972), 546.

20. *Pravda*, December 26, 1968, editorial.

21. I. A. Kirilin, ed., *Istoriia mezhdunarodnykh otnoshenii* (Moscow, 1967), III, 250.

22. Declaration of 1969 Conference of Communist Parties, quoted by *Pravda*, January 8, 1971, p. 3.

23. *Pravda*, January 3, 1972, p. 1.

24. *Ibid.*, June 1, 1969.

25. *Ibid.*, December 26, 1970, editorial.

26. Ts. P. Agaian, *Vekovaia druzhba narodov Zakavkasia* (Yerevan, 1970), pp. 6, 7.

27. Cf. Zhores A. Medvedev, *The Medvedev Papers* (London: Macmillan, 1971), for examples of illegal coercion carried out with respect for legal forms.

28. *Pravda*, August 11, 1970, p. 2.

29. Stalin is quoted by Ernest J. Simmons, ed., *Continuity and Change in Russian and Soviet Thought* (Cambridge, Mass.: Harvard University Press, 1955), p. 95.

30. *Die Zeit*, November 9, 1971, p. 2.

6 LENINISM DECADENT

1. Trotsky, quoted by Leopold Labedz, "The Destiny of Writers in Revolutionary Movements," *Survey*, XVIII, 1 (Winter, 1972), 8, 11.

2. Concerning some efforts to apply this principle, see Robert G. Wes-

son, *Soviet Communes* (New Brunswick, N.J.: Rutgers University Press, 1962), Chap. 6.

3. John Scott, *Behind the Urals* (Boston: Houghton Mifflin, 1942), pp. 5, 91, and passim.

4. Nadezhda Mandelshtam, *Hope Against Hope* (New York: Atheneum, 1970), p. 44.

5. *Pravda*, February 26, 1972, p. 3.

6. *Ibid.*, February 28, 1970, p. 4.

7. A. Z. Rubinstein, in *Current History*, LXII, 365 (January, 1972), 11–12.

8. *Pravda*, December 22, 1971, p. 3.

9. *Ibid.*, February 12, 1972, p. 2.

10. Zhores A. Medvedev, *The Medvedev Papers* (London: Macmillan, 1971), p. 64.

11. *Pravda*, September 11, 1971, p. 3; *Current Digest of the Soviet Press*, XXIII, 37, p. 23.

12. M. P. Shendrik, *Obshchenarodnoe gosudarstvo—novyi etap v razvitii sotsialisticheskoi gosudarstvennosti* (Lvov: Izd. Lvovskogo Universiteta, 1970), p. 116.

13. L. Finkelstein, in *Studies on the Soviet Union*, XI, 2 (1971), 62.

14. A. V. Shumakov, *Nagliadnia agitatsiia* (Moscow: Izdatelstvo politicheskoi literatury, 1970), p. 130.

15. *Literaturnaia Gazeta*, July 7, 1971, p. 11.

16. *Pravda*, January 26, 1972, p. 1.

17. *Ibid.*, August 12, 1971.

18. Anatole Shub, "From Russia with Chutzpah," *Harpers*, May, 1972, p. 72.

19. Zhores A. and Roy Medvedev, *A Question of Madness* (New York: Knopf, 1971), p. 219.

20. *Pravda*, October 12, 1970, p. 1.

21. *Ibid.*, February 5, 1973, editorial.

22. *Ibid.*, December 29, 1971, p. 3.

23. S. Zakariadze, in *Pravda*, December 13, 1970, p. 3.

24. Kovalevsky, *Russian Political Institutions*, p. 57.

25. Zbigniew Brzezinski, "The Soviet Political System: Transformation or Degeneration?", *Problems of Communism*, XV, 1 (January–February, 1966), 1–15.

26. Cf. Robert G. Wesson, "The USSR: Oligarchy or Dictatorship," *Slavic Review*, XXXI, 2 (June, 1972), 314–322.

27. *Pravda*, February 12, 1972, p. 2.

28. Nicholas S. Timasheff, *The Great Retreat* (New York: Dutton, 1946), p. 166.

29. *Literaturnaia gazeta*, August 28, 1968, p. 10.

30. *Pravda*, August 2, 1970, p. 3.

31. Boris Meissner, *Social Change in Bolshevik Russia* (Notre Dame, Ind.: University of Notre Dame Press, 1972), pp. 55–56.

32. *Science,* CLXXIII, 3999 (August 27, 1971), 798.

33. *Voprosy raboty sovetov deputatov trudiashchikhskh* (Moscow: Izdatelstvo Izvestia, 1968), p. 478.

34. *Pravda,* November 22, 1971, p. 4.

35. *Literaturnaia gazeta,* July 7, 1971, p. 11.

36. Harvey J. Pitcher, *Understanding the Russians* (London: George Allen and Unwin, 1964), p. 36.

37. *Pravda,* February 14, 1972, p. 2.

38. *Ibid.,* February 14, 1972, p. 2.

39. Wallace, *Russia,* p. 205.

40. Robert J. Osborn, *Soviet Social Policies* (Homewood, Ill.: Dorsey, 1970), pp. 82–83.

41. At least when meeting foreigners, as pictured in *Pravda,* November 14, 1971, p. 6.

42. *New York Times,* December 29, 1971.

43. *Vestsi. Akad. Navuk BSSR,* April, 1971, pp. 68–76; *ABSEES,* January, 1972, p. 42.

44. *Izvestia,* November 17, 1971, p. 3; *Current Digest,* XXIII, 46, p. 6.

45. *Pravda,* September 7, 1970, p. 2.

46. *Izvestia,* December 2, 1971, p. 5; *Current Digest,* XXIII, 48, p. 31.

47. *Pravda,* December 29, 1971, p. 3.

48. *Literaturnaia Gazeta,* May 26, 1971, pp. 10–11; *ABSEES,* October, 1971, p. 3.

49. Leon I. Twarog, in *Studies on the Soviet Union,* XI, 3 (1971), 90.

50. *Pravda,* November 25, 1972, p. 3; *Current Digest,* XXIV, 47, p. 3.

51. *Literaturnaia Rossiia,* October 22, 1971.

52. Cf. R. G. Wesson, "The Military in Soviet Society," *Russian Review,* XXX, 2 (April, 1971), 139–146.

53. *Pravda,* January 11, 1972, p. 3.

54. Sergei Smirnov, in *Pravda,* December 13, 1971, p. 4.

55. *Literaturnaia gazeta,* September 2, 1970, p. 1.

56. *Sovetskaia Rossiia,* November 1, 1970, p. 4.

57. *Selskaia zhizn,* May 11, 1971, p. 3, and June 20, 1971, p. 2; *ABSEES,* October, 1971, p. 25.

58. *Pravda,* November 16, 1971, p. 3.

59. Cf. Steven J. Staats, "Corruption in the Soviet System," *Problems of Communism,* XXI, 1 (January–February, 1972), 40–48.

60. *New York Times,* December 8, 1971, p. 10.

61. *Pravda,* January 29, 1971.

62. *Ibid.,* February 6, 1970, p. 2.

63. *Ibid.,* July 29, 1970, p. 3.

64. *Ibid.,* December 12, 1971, p. 6.

65. *Ibid.,* February 18, 1972, p. 6.

66. *New York Times,* March 7, 1972.

67. *Literaturnaia gazeta,* September 2, 1970, pp. 12–13.

68. *Sovetskaia Moldavia,* May 14, 1971, p. 2; *ABSEES,* October, 1971, p. 31.

69. *Pravda,* August 8, 1971, p. 4; *ABSEES,* January, 1972, p. 9.

70. *Komsomolskaia pravda,* July 25, 1971; *ABSEES,* October, 1971, p. 26.

71. *Sovety deputatov trudiashchikhskh,* no. 5 (1971), 18–27; *ABSEES,* October, 1971, pp. 37–38.

72. *Sovetskaia Rossiia,* November 14, 1970, p. 2.

73. Letter in *Pravda,* August 13, 1971, p. 3; *Current Digest,* XXIII, 32, p. 19.

74. *Pravda,* November 4, 1971, p. 1.

75. *Ibid.,* September 1, 1971, p. 3.

76. *Newsweek,* January 31, 1972, p. 30.

77. *New York Times,* November 10, 1971.

78. *Sovety deputatov trudiashchikhskh,* no. 5 (May, 1971), 97.

79. *Izvestia,* September 14, 1971, p. 4; *Current Digest,* XXIII, 37, p. 18.

80. *Komsomolskaia pravda,* July 2, 1971, p. 4; *ABSEES,* October, 1971, p. 103.

81. Cf. John Dornberg, *The New Tsars: Russia under Stalin's Heirs* (Garden City, N.Y.: Doubleday, 1972).

82. S. Cohn in V. G. Treml, ed., *The Development of the Soviet Economy* (New York: Praeger, 1969), p. 36.

83. *Voprosi ekonomiki,* cited by Keith Bush, *Studies on the Soviet Union,* XI, 3 (1971), 9.

84. *Selskaia zhizn,* August 28, 1971; cited by *Radio Liberty Dispatch,* November 15, 1971.

85. Cf. Sheila Ostrander and Lynn Schroeder, *Psychic Discoveries Behind the Iron Curtain* (New York: Bantam Books, 1971).

86. Wm. E. Griffith, "Communist Cadre Training," *Newsletter on Comparative Studies of Communism,* IV, 4 (August, 1971), 16–24.

87. Leroy-Beaulieu, *Empire of the Tsars,* II, 475.

88. *New York Times,* January 20, 1973.

89. *Ibid.,* January 13, 1972, p. 4.

90. Susan Jacoby, *Moscow Conversations* (New York: Coward, McCann and Geoghegan, 1972), p. 74.

91. L. Finkelstein, in *Studies on the Soviet Union,* XI, 2 (1971), 44.

92. *Literaturnaia gazeta,* June 17, 1970, p. 1.

93. Leroy-Beaulieu, *Empire of the Tsars,* II, 470–472.

94. *Novyi mir,* no. 3 (March, 1971), 5.

95. Cf. Zhores A. Medvedev, *Medvedev Papers.*

7 RUSSIA AND THE NEW WORLD ORDER

1. *Literaturnaia gazeta,* August 18, 1971, p. 13.

2. *Pravda,* January 26, 1972, p. 3.

3. *Ibid.,* February 26, 1972, p. 3.

4. *Komsomolskaia pravda,* May 25–27, 1971; *ABSEES,* October, 1971, p. 30.

5. *Pravda,* August 12, 1971.

6. Tony Longrigg, "Soviet Science and Foreign Policy," *Survey,* XVII, 4 (81) (Autumn, 1971), 43.

7. *Literaturnaia gazeta,* August 18, 1971, p. 13.

8. *Ibid.,* March 12, 1969, p. 13.

9. Zhores A. Medvedev, *Medvedev Papers,* p. 131.

10. Medvedevs, *A Question of Madness,* pp. 63, 85.

11. *New York Times,* September 28, 1972.

12. *Business Week,* May 13, 1972, p. 64.

13. Cf. "A Word to the Nation," *Survey,* XVII, 3 (Summer, 1971), 191–199, for a chauvinistic statement.

14. Article by S. Kaltakhchan, *Pravda,* November 26, 1968, p. 3.

15. *Pravda,* January 24, 1972, p. 4.

16. Edward Allworth, *Soviet Nationality Problems* (New York: Columbia University Press, 1971).

17. *Pravda,* March 20, 1971.

18. *Newsweek,* June 26, 1972, p. 38.

19. Cf. Michael Browne, ed., *Ferment in the Ukraine* (New York: Praeger, 1971).

20. *Pravda,* October 28, 1972; *Current Digest,* XXIV, 43, p. 23.

21. *Filosofskie nauki,* April, 1971, pp. 43–48; *ABSEES,* January, 1972, p. 37.

22. *Pravda,* July 16, 1971, p. 4.

23. *Ibid.,* January 8, 1971, p. 3.

24. As by V. S. Shevtsov, "Sovereignty in the Soviet Federal State," *Sovetskoe gosudarstvo i pravo,* no. 6 (June, 1972), 49–58.

25. *Pravda,* November 26, 1968, p. 3.

26. *Ibid.,* April 18, 1972, p. 5.

27. *Literaturnaia gazeta,* April 29, 1970, p. 9.

28. *Pravda,* May 30, 1972, p. 1.

29. *Ibid.,* January 8, 1971, p. 2.

30. *Ibid.,* September 29, 1971, p. 4.

31. *Ibid.,* February 8, 1973, beginning of editorial.

32. *Ibid.,* December 15, 1972, p. 4.

33. A. A. Topornin, in *S. Sh. A.,* no. 11 (November, 1971).

34. *Pravda,* February 7, 1972, editorial.

35. Robert G. Wesson, *The Soviet Russian State* (New York: Wiley, 1972), p. 272.

36. Walter D. Connor, *Deviance in Soviet Society: Crime, Delinquency, and Alcoholism* (New York: Columbia University Press, 1972).

37. *New York Times,* August 18, 1972, p. 29.

38. Nish Jamgotch, Jr., *Soviet-East European Dialogue: International Relations of a New Type?* (Stanford, Calif.: Hoover Institution Press, 1968).

39. Concerning travel between Eastern Europe and the Soviet Union, cf. *New York Times*, August 29, 1972, p. 2.

40. Edwin Weit, *Ostblock Intern* (Hamburg: Hoffmann u. Campe, 1970), p. 252.

41. Tompkins, *Russian Intelligentsia*, p. 249.

42. *New York Times*, August 18, 1972, p. 29.

Index

absolutism, *see* autocracy; dictatorship; tsardom

Achaemenid dynasty, 30

Afghanistan, 96

Africa, 4, 10, 11, 118; European colonies in, 109, 113. *See also specific countries*

agriculture, 11, 13, 28, 32, 64; communal tradition in, 27, 33, 48, 56–57, 65, 76, 79, 135, 145; Soviet control of, 74, 76, 77, 135, 140, 146, 157, 161, 163, 165, 192

aircraft, 174

Akademgorodok Integral Club, 170

Aksakov, Ivan, quoted, 57

Alaska, 11

Alba, Fernando Álvarez de Toledo, duke of, quoted, 37

Albania, 59

Albanian Communist party, 180

Alexander I, tsar of Russia, 23, 26, 33, 53, 152; quoted, 20; Holy Alliance and, 42; Westernization and, 46–47, 51, 60

Alexander II, tsar of Russia, 48, 53

Alexander III, tsar of Russia, 52, 53, 61

Alexandra Feodorovna, tsarina of Nicholas II, 69

Alexis, tsar of Russia, 24, 37, 42

Algeria, 12, 113, 175, 183

Allied Powers (World War II): formation of, 100–101, 102; German invasion of Russia and, 105–106; NATO and, 186; Soviet European territories and, 108

alphabet reform, 144, 157

Alsace-Lorraine, 12

Amanullah Khan, amir of Afghanistan, 96

Amazon River, 13

anarchism, 16, 73, 101–102

Anatolia, Turkey, 109

Andropov, Iurii, 151

Anna, tsarina of Russia, 23, 45

anti-Communism, 189; German, 99, 102, 103, 106

anti-Semitism, 122, 139, 178; German, 102; language and, 180; tsarist, 63, 66; revival (1920's), 100

Arab nations, 15, 114, 118. *See also specific countries*

Archangel, Russia, 7

aristocracy, 11, 48; absolute monarchy and, 25–26, 30, 31, 45, 46, 51,

aristocracy (Cont.)
142; European, 7, 38, 39, 42, 54–55, 60; Kerensky and, 72; local government and, 54; revolutionary sentiment and, 58, 70–71; Tatar government and, 6, 18, 19, 50
Armenia, 8, 15, 85, 122; World War II and, 106
Asia, 3, 4, 36, 74; autocracy and, 29, 39, 45; British interests in, 44, 65, 96, 182; Russian expansion and, 5, 7, 9, 10, 11, 15–16, 19, 40, 41, 43, 112–13, 181–82, 183, 185, 197–98. *See also specific countries*
Assyria, 40
Astrakhan, 7, 19
Ataturk, Mustapha Kemal, 96
Augustus, emperor of Rome, 17, 30, 31
Australia, 174
Austria, 9, 110, 140; the Ukraine and, 62, 68
Austro-Hungarian empire, 30, 43, 60, 182, 197
autocracy, 17–28, 29–30, 43–47, 133; the Duma and, 63–64; industrialization and, 27–28, 39, 51, 52–53; socialism and, 58, 72, 189; tsarist decline and, 53, 54, 55, 64, 65, 66, 67, 68–70, 73, 81, 142, 152, 154, 197–98. *See also* dictatorship; tsardom
automobiles, 163–64, 173
Axis Powers (World War II), 99–100, 107–108; Soviet invitation into, 102–104
Azerbaidzhan, U.S.S.R., 158, 180*n*

Baku, U.S.S.R., 161
Baku Congress (1920), 96, 112
Bakunin, Michael, quoted, 16
balance-of-power doctrine, 41, 61, 189
Balkan nations, 5, 8, 59, 60, 68, 104, 107. *See also specific countries*
Baltic Sea, 4, 6, 7; blockades, 37, 69, 95

Baltic states, 5, 11, 85, 95, 179; German inhabitants of, 38; Stalin-Hitler Pact (1939) and, 102, 104. *See also specific countries*
Bangladesh, 186
banking, 174
Baptists, 160
Bashkir, U.S.S.R., 21, 180
Basil III, tsar of Russia, 7
Bavaria, 83
Belgium, 174
Belgrade, Yugoslavia, 110
Belinsky, Vissarion, quoted, 21
Belorussia, 59, 66, 83, 104, 122; ritual in, 159; United Nations seat, 121
Ben Bella, Ahmed, 113
Berdiaev, Nicholas, 160
Beria, Lavrenti, 178
Berlin, Germany, 103–104, 109–10, 111; blockade, 109; Wall, 191
Bessarabia, 102
Black Sea, 4, 6, 69
Bohemia, 9
Bolsheviks, 9, 15, 54, 69, 90; assumption of power, 71, 72, 73, 74–75, 76–77, 78, 80–81, 84, 89, 122, 134, 142–43, 148, 149, 153, 155–56; the Duma and, 64, 70, 134, 177; world revolution and, 41, 82–87, 94–95, 112–13, 116, 118–19, 190. *See also* Soviet Communist party
Bosnia-Herzegovina, 68
Bosphorus, Straits of the, 8, 9, 68, 104, 109
Bourbon dynasty, 47
bourgeoisie, 33, 161; Lenin and, 73, 79, 93; liberalism and, 31–32; Stalin and, 101; trade and, 10, 27, 31; Western dominance of, 56, 57, 58, 82, 107, 108, 149
Brazil, 13–14, 164*n*, 165
Brest-Litovsk Treaty, 75, 94, 95
Brezhnev, Leonid, 91, 117, 118, 126, 130, 150, 176; quoted, 120, 132, 156, 158; political rise of, 152, 153, 154; U.S. détente and, 139–40, 187

Brezhnev doctrine of limited sovereignty, 118, 121, 122–23

Britain, 6, 9, 10, 24, 29; Asia and, 44, 65, 96, 182; capitalism of, 93, 119; colonial liberations, 12, 109; Crimea and, 47; League of Nations and, 97, 100; Peter the Great and, 38; Russian trade with, 37, 41–42, 69, 95–96, 174; schools, 194; Soviet alliance (1941), 105–106; Spanish Civil War and, 102; voluntarism in, 151

Bukharin, Nikolai, 75, 153

Bukovina, 9

Bukovsky, Vladimir, quoted, 167

Bulganin, Nikolai, 110

Bulgaria, 60, 122, 175

bureaucracy, 52, 64, 162; conservatism of, 32, 49, 157–61, 192, 196–97; revolutionaries and, 55, 152–53, 154, 156; Stalin and, 110, 136, 156; trade and, 115; tsardom and, 11, 26, 31, 53, 142

Buriats, 66

Burma, 110, 175

Byzantium, 4, 6–7, 14, 17, 24, 30, 35

Caesar, Julius, 30

Canada, 11, 175

capitalism, 43, 64, 73, 83, 90, 144; agriculture and, 28, 65; class structure and, 26, 93, 154; colonies and, 96, 182; computers and, 165; disarmament issue and, 97; fascism and, 107–108; foreign investment in, 27, 52, 57, 65, 66, 79, 80, 91, 95, 113, 119, 139, 173; Peaceful Coexistence doctrine and, 111–12, 119, 188; Polish, 86; profiteering in, 69; socialist "leap" over, 58, 62–63, 74, 79, 80–81, 82, 87; socialist modifications of, 91–92, 119, 158, 161–64, 174, 188, 192; Stalin and, 98, 101, 105–106; Vietnam War and, 146–47, 189

Caracalla, emperor of Rome, 31

Caspian Sea, 6

Castro, Fidel, 113, 120

Catherine II (the Great), tsarina of Russia, 11, 23, 30, 50, 60, 73, 133; quoted, 15, 22, 45; Diderot and, 90; France and, 38–39, 42, 45–46; Freemasonry and, 51; local government and, 24, 46; the Ukraine and, 11

Caucasus, The, 8, 179

censorship, 23, 29, 31, 47, 90, 131, 144; Catherine the Great and, 46, 51; Khrushchev and, 137, 138, 172–73; Lenin and, 74–75, 77, 88, 92, 177; post-Khrushchev, 150, 167–70; of satellite publications, 176, 181, 195; science and, 129, 168–70, 172–73; Soviet failure of, 192; tsarist failure of, 53, 63, 64, 65; in World War II, 107, 140

Central Asia, 4, 5, 9, 122; independence movements in, 85, 105, 184; Russian settlement of, 10, 11, 13, 14, 114

Chaadaev, Peter, 56n, 139; quoted, 16, 55

Charles I, king of England, 42

Chernyshevsky, Nicholas G., 58

Chiang Kai-shek, 112

Chicherin, Georgi V., 96–97

Ch'in state, China, 40

China, 9, 12, 183; communism and, 92, 104, 112, 115–16, 146n, 180, 184, 185–86, 196; imperialism of, 18, 29, 30, 32, 35–36, 40, 41, 95, 141; Mongolia and, 85; peasant revolts in, 33–34; Soviet split, 184–86, 187, 195

Chinese Civil War, 104, 112, 142, 146n

Chinese Communist party, 180

Chinese Nationalist party, 104, 112, 116

Christianity, 4–5, 14, 16, 17, 19; evangelical sects, 160; Roman Catholic, 8, 10, 59. *See also* Russian Orthodox Church

Christmas, 172

Churchill, Winston, 105

Cierna-nad-Tisou Conference (1968), 130

civil rights, 31–32; of political action, 63–64, 77, 92, 125, 127, 177; post-Khrushchev pressure for, 119, 139, 140, 166–70, 196, 198; in pre-Tatar Russia, 17–18; Revolutionary views of, 55, 56–57, 60, 74–75, 76–77, 82, 118, 136; Soviet constitutional guarantees of, 127, 129, 166; tsardom and, 19, 20, 21, 22, 23, 46–47, 51, 133. *See also specific civil concerns,* e.g., courts

class structure, 7, 17–18, 30, 93, 126, 142; liberalism and, 31–32, 49, 50–51; Marx on, 73, 78; Revolution of 1917 and, 70–71; serf emancipation and, 27, 51; socialist persistence of, 131, 157–59, 161, 166; "table of ranks," 25–26, 48, 64; United States, 107. *See also* aristocracy; bourgeoisie; élites; peasants

Cold War, 109, 113, 189

collectivism, 33–34, 190; post-Revolution, 151–52, 193; revolutionary, 55, 56, 58, 59, 76, 79, 135. *See also* communes

Comecon (Council for Mutual Economic Assistance), 115, 124

Comintern, 84, 96–97, 98, 99, 101, 112; dissolution of, 106

communes (peasant), 27, 33, 48, 76, 79, 135; revolutionary view of, 56–57, 58–59; withdrawal from, 65

computers, 91, 165

Condorcet, Marie Jean de Caritat, marquis de, quoted, 143

Conference of Communist Parties (1969), 147

Confucianism, 31, 33

Congress of Berlin (1878), 61

Congress of Soviets, 72, 74

conservatism, 32, 64, 72; decline of the autocracy and, 20, 54; Soviet,
133, 148–49, 155–61, 166, 178, 192, 196–97

Constantine I (the Great), Roman emperor, 141

Constantine Pavlovich, grand duke of Russia, 51

Constantinople, 7, 8, 68

constitutionalism, 29–30, 61, 133, 157, 182; bourgeoisie and, 31–32; reform movements under, 154, 155, 177; of Stalin, 128; tsarist, 20, 44–47, 48, 51, 54, 63–64, 66, 69, 74

corruption, 28, 32, 34, 161–63

Cossacks, 20, 21, 71, 85

courts: economic crimes and, 138; judicial hierarchy, 157; literary trials in, 167–68; Party control of, 130–31; Stalinist, 76, 99; tsarist, 24, 47, 48, 52, 64; war crimes and, 146

Crimea, 166, 179

Crimean War (1854), 8, 12, 39, 42, 47; postwar liberalization, 51, 52, 60, 196

Cuba, 111, 113, 114, 117, 138; status of, 123

Custine, Astolphe, marquis de, 20

Czechoslovakia, 60, 122, 195; Germany and, 102, 140; repression of 1968, 117–18, 123, 130, 132, 138, 191, 194, 196; tourist trade in, 175

Czechoslovakian Communist party, 130, 132

Daniel-Siniavsky case (1966), 167

Danilevsky, Nicholas, 93; quoted, 15, 59

Decembrists, 16, 47, 51, 55

democracy, 55, 60, 67, 73, 75, 99; Chinese adaptations of, 186; of Marxism, 80; Nazism and, 103; Russian understanding of, 26, 93, 131–32; Soviet adaptations of, 88, 89, 90–91, 93, 107, 126, 127, 128–29, 130–33, 155, 166, 177, 198; Soviet satellite nations and, 108, 130; Soviet-Western common front and, 100–101

Democratic Centralism, doctrine of, 88

Denmark, 42, 175

de-Stalinization policy, 110, 114, 137, 138, 154

dictatorship: ideology and, 76, 77, 78–87, 90–91, 92–93, 104–105, 108–109, 143, 187–88, 189, 195–98; party roles in, 88, 99, 121–22, 124–27, 128–33, 134, 196; personal roles in, 108, 109, 110, 114, 126, 135, 136–37, 152–61, 196; revolution and, 55, 72, 73–78, 141, 148, 196

Diderot, Denis, 51; quoted, 90

Diocletian, emperor of Rome, 141

disarmament issue, 97, 187, 197

dissent, 21, 23, 33, 51; Lenin and, 74–75, 77, 92; post-Khrushchev, 119, 127, 139, 166–70, 196. *See also* censorship

Dosaaf, 162

Dostoevsky, Fedor, 9, 13, 57, 60, 90, 160; quoted, 15, 16

Dubček, Alexander, 132

Dzerzhinsky, Feliks, 178

East Germany, 108, 109–10, 122, 176, 196

East Indies, 5

East Prussia, 9, 28

education, 47, 92, 190, 191, 194; bilingual, 66–67; classical studies, 48; cultural change and, 39, 43, 49, 50–51, 53, 54–55, 65, 70, 159, 166; equal access to, 26, 127, 157–58, 162–63; indoctrination and, 31, 53, 107, 148, 160, 167, 192; nationalism and, 60, 61, 179–80, 181; Peter the Great and, 38; Revolution of 1917 and, 77; state nurseries, 138, 156; technical, 137, 162; tsarist colonial systems of, 11, 20; zemstvo reforms in, 64

Egypt, 30, 109, 147, 183, 184

Eisenhower, Dwight D., 175

elections, 63–64, 66, 72, 75, 168; in China, 186; leadership and, 155; party systems and, 87–89, 126–27, 131, 156, 176, 177, 191; Soviet constitution on, 128

élites, 31, 32; in China, 186; education and, 48, 49, 50–51, 54–55, 70, 93, 179–80; professionals as, 52, 64, 166; revolutionary, 55, 76, 136, 152–53; Soviet, 92, 100, 131, 138, 148–49, 150–51, 152–61, 162, 163, 185, 191, 193, 196, 197, 198

Elizabeth I, queen of England, 41

Elizabeth, tsarina of Russia, 23

Encyclopedic Dictionary, Soviet (1963), on democracy, 131

England, 6, 24, 29. *See also* Britain

English Civil War, 42

Enlightenment, The, 39, 42, 45, 46, 93

environmental concern, 172, 173

equalitarianism, 26, 33, 125; Chinese, 186; revolutionary, 55, 78–79, 93; Stalin and, 99, 100

Estonia, 11, 66, 71

Ethiopia, 36, 176

Europe, 41, 57, 112; Asia and, 3, 4, 5, 9–10, 16, 36, 45, 182, 183; autocratic cultures in, 21, 29–30, 42; communist regimes in, 83, 108, 109–10, 114–15, 117, 122–24, 129–30, 171, 172, 176, 182, 184, 185, 187, 191, 192, 193–95; Dostoevsky on, 15; post-World War II recovery, 186–87. *See also specific countries*

European Common Market, 187

expansionism, 3–17, 50, 59, 65, 68; fascist, 99–100, 102, 103, 104, 182. *See also* imperialism; universalism

famines, 69, 72, 77

fascism: rise of, 97, 99–100, 101, 102, 104, 105, 107–108, 182; productivity and, 164n

Federal Republic of Germany (West Germany), 119, 174, 187

federalism, 71, 85, 89–90; limited sovereignty and, 118, 121, 122

Fiat Company, 164

Finland, 5, 8, 21, 66, 71; independence of, 85, 90; Porkkala base in, 110; Soviet attack (1940), 104, 145; Soviet trade, 174

firearms, 4, 37

Five-Year Plans, 76, 119, 135, 164, 173

Forsyte Saga, The (TV dramatization), 172

France, 6, 8, 10, 11–12, 119, 175; absolute monarchy in, 29, 42; aristocracy in, 26, 54–55; Brezhnev in, 176; Directory of, 147; fall of, 104; League of Nations and, 97, 100; oil refineries in, 174; Popular Front in, 101; Russian alliance, 61, 69, 100–101, 102; Russian influence from, 38–39, 43, 45–46, 47, 48, 49, 51, 60; Suslov in, 188

Freemasonry, 51

French Communist party, 188

French Revolution, 39, 42, 47, 60; Russian analogies, 143–44, 145, 147, 196

Fundamental Law (Nicholas II), 21–22, 48

fur trade, 7, 10

Galicia, 9, 68

General Electric Corporation, 95

Genghiz Khan, 19

Genoa Conference (1922), 95, 97

gentry, *see* aristocracy; bourgeoisie

geography, 35; expansionism and, 4, 5, 7, 9, 10, 11–12, 13–14; state power and, 19–20, 22, 29–30, 39

Georgia, 15, 60, 109, 121, 162, 195; Bolsheviks and, 85, 86; Russian annexation of, 8, 12; Stalin and, 122, 178

German Communist party, 96

German Democratic Republic, *see* East Germany

Germany, 8, 9, 11, 19n, 29, 61, 93, 186; Catherine the Great and, 23; fascist rise in, 97, 99–100, 102, 104, 105, 107–108, 164n, 182; Marxism and, 84, 96; Russian alliance (1922), 96; Russian influence from, 37, 38, 43, 45, 48, 70, 91; Soviet Pact (1939), 102–103, 104, 105; Soviet sphere in, 108 (*see also* East Germany); Soviet Union invasion by, 104, 105–107, 140, 145–46, 147; Western sphere in, 119 (*see also* West Germany); World War I and, 68–69, 83, 94–95, 135

Ghana, 113

Gierek, Edward, 130

Gogol, Nikolai, 60

Golden Horde, *see* Tatars

Gomulka, Wladyslaw, quoted, 196

grain, 28, 174, 187

Great Britain, *see* Britain

Greece, 4, 32, 40, 42, 59, 110; production rates in, 164n

Gromyko, Andrei, quoted, 188

Gulf of Finland, 38

Habsburg dynasty, 197

Hadrian, emperor of Rome, 32

Haile Selassie, emperor of Ethiopia, 176

Hegel, Georg Wilhelm Friedrich, 89

Henry VIII, king of England, 29

Herder, Johann Gottfried von, 59

Herzen, Alexander, 16, 57, 58, 168

Hitler, Adolf, 97, 100, 103, 105, 106, 140; Molotov and, 104; on Soviet army losses, 145

Holland, 5, 9, 10, 38, 42

Holy Alliance (1815), 42

Holy Russia concept, 14, 21. *See also* Russian Orthodox Church

Holy Synod, 24

housing, 150, 161, 163, 164

Humanité, l' (newspaper), 176

Hungarian Communist party, 115

Hungarian Revolution of 1848, 43

Hungary, 9, 37, 43, 176, 195; economic system of, 83, 194; revolt suppression in, 108, 115, 118, 122, 196; tourist trade of, 175

ideology, 12–17, 42–43, 180; of Bolshevik authoritarianism, 76, 77, 78–87, 90–91, 92–93, 104–105, 142–44, 148; economic performance and, 165, 166, 175, 179, 181, 183, 186, 192, 193, 194; of intellectual revolutionaries, 31–34, 55–59, 65; nuclear threat and, 111, 197; political tensions and, 47, 133–40, 171, 181, 191, 195–98; post-Khrushchev, 116–20, 144, 147–48, 149–52; science and, 129, 168–70, 172–73. *See also specific ideologies*
imperialism, 3–17; autocracy and, 19–20, 21–23, 29–30, 55, 67, 189; ideology and, 12–17, 31–34, 50, 56, 59, 104–105, 180, 182, 187–88, 189, 195, 197–98; of Lenin, 82–83, 84–87, 89–90, 93, 95, 98, 105, 112, 171, 182, 183, 189, 190; overseas qualification of, 10, 11–12; revolutions and, 141–42, 196; Stalin and, 100, 105, 109, 112; technology and, 4, 5, 9–10, 11, 36, 39–40, 43, 57, 114, 190; in Vietnam, 146–47
Incas, 30, 40
India, 5, 7, 9, 10, 30, 112, 118; China border dispute (1959), 116; independence of, 109, 183; Khrushchev visit, 110, 175; Pakistan War (1971) and, 120, 184, 186
industrialization, 3, 64, 121, 166, 190–91; anti-industrial attitudes and, 54, 58, 79, 160, 179; capitalist experience of, 154; of China, 186; Five-Year Plans for, 76, 119, 135, 164, 173; forced, 74, 89, 91–92, 129, 146, 149, 192; imperialism and, 4, 32, 39, 51, 91; of Japan, 186; Khrushchev and, 112, 113, 156, 157; Peter the Great and, 27, 28, 38, 52; social sci-

ences and, 169; Stalin and, 76, 91, 98–99, 110, 135, 140, 145, 164; trade development with, 52–53, 62, 65, 119, 164–65, 173–74; World War I level of, 69, 77, 81, 83
Industrial Revolution, 4, 27, 51
inflation, 69, 72
Instruction (Catherine II), 22, 45–46
intelligentsia, 12, 180; clandestine publications and, 167, 192; Lenin and, 73, 134, 153; religion and, 53; Russian empire and, 14–15, 16, 21, 28, 32, 55, 57, 140; Sakharov on, 193; socialism and, 58, 78, 89, 113; Stalin and, 76, 108, 136, 152–53; Western political modes and, 28, 43–44, 49, 51, 52, 54, 56, 58–59, 65, 119, 132–33, 166
internationalism, *see* universalism
Iran, 109, 110, 183. *See also* Persia
Iraq, 123
Israel, 114, 180
Italian Communist party, 123
Italy, 37, 40, 42, 103; colonies of, 109; Soviet recognition by, 95
Ivan I (Kalita), grand prince of Muscovy, 6, 37
Ivan III (the Great), tsar of Russia, 6–7, 17, 19, 25, 35, 37
Ivan IV (the Terrible), tsar of Russia, 22, 26, 29, 73, 136, 152; aristocracy and, 25, 42, 142; Baltic trade routes and, 7, 37; the Church and, 21, 24; counselors of, 154; England and, 41; parliamentary system and, 44; technology and, 36, 37, 50; tsarinas of, 23; Volga khanates and, 7, 19
Izvestia, 159

James I, king of England, 41
Japan, 36, 41, 103; economic growth of, 3, 112, 119, 183, 186; expansionism of, 5, 99, 104, 182, 195; Russo-Japanese War (1904), 9, 12, 39, 48, 63, 107, 198; Soviet trade, 173, 174

Jerusalem, 9
Jews, 63, 66, 79, 102, 122, 178; emigration of, 139, 163, 175, 176, 180,
193; Stalin and, 100, 106
Julian Calendar, 44, 144

Kadar, Janos, 122, 130
Kaganovich, Lazar, 136, 178
Kalmucks, 66
Kamenev, Lev, 75, 178
Karamzin, Nicholas, 14; quoted, 12–
13, 20
Kazan, 7, 19, 37
Kerensky, Alexander, 72
KGB, 119, 140, 151, 165
Khrushchev, Nikita, 126, 148, 152,
157, 171; Asia and, 112–13, 183; de-
Stalinization policy of, 110, 114,
137, 138, 154; European satellites
and, 114–15, 117, 194; imperialism
and, 112, 182–83; Jewish emigra-
tion and, 139; Party Program of,
15, 127, 150, 153, 156; science and,
172–73, 183; United States and,
111–12, 175
Kievan Rus, 4
Kokovtsov, Vladimir, quoted, 67
Kolokol (periodical), 168
Komsomol, 159
Korea, 9, 63, 92, 110, 174; Chinese
protectorate of, 36
Korean War, 110
Kornilov, Lavr, 72
Kosygin, Aleksei, 117, 150, 156–57,
176
Kremlin, The, 37
Krivoshein, Alexander, quoted, 20
Kronstadt Rebellion, 75

labor, 73, 116; assignment, 127, 163*n;*
productivity (1972), 164; rewards
of, 157, 161; Soviet unrest of, 172,
191, 193, 194; white-collar, 149;
workers' councils, 83; unions, 63,
64, 75, 77, 89, 129, 159
labor camps, 77

La Harpe, Frédéric de, 46
land, 33, 34, 58, 65; aristocratic estates, 25, 45, 46, 48; Church ownership of, 24; Crown ownership of,
22, 30; peasant seizures (1917), 70,
72; serf emancipation and, 27; Soviet policy, 90; Tatar administration of, 18. *See also* agriculture
languages, 20, 45, 49, 66–67, 129, 161;
Bashkiri, 180; English, 172; French,
38, 48, 60; German, 37, 48; Polish,
62; political misuse of, 88–89, 90,
131–33, 186; Slavic group, 59; spelling reform, 144, 157; Tatar, 18;
Ukrainian, 11, 62, 179
Latin America, 4, 5, 10, 13
Latvia, 63, 66, 71, 121, 179
League of Nations, 97–98, 100–101
"Leftist" opinion (Soviet), 75, 133,
134, 135, 136, 139
leisure, as a civil right, 127
Lenin (Vladimir Ilyich Ulyanov),
3, 17, 25, 58, 68–93, 100, 111, 175;
Bolshevik authority of, 73, 74, 75,
76–77, 81, 114, 134, 148, 152, 153,
155–56; Comintern and, 84, 96,
106; cult of, 139, 151, 166; Duma
and, 64, 134, 177; empire and, 13,
21, 34, 40, 54, 82–83, 90, 91, 92, 93,
98, 105, 112, 171, 182, 183, 184–85,
189, 190, 191; minority national-
isms and, 66, 86–87, 89, 105, 107,
118, 135, 177, 178, 179, 180–81;
moral values of, 143–44, 148, 149,
154; tomb of, 176; war industries
and, 83; Western investment and,
91, 94–95; Winter Palace attack by,
72; works of, 153
Leningrad, U.S.S.R., 174
Leontiev, Constantine, quoted, 9
Lermontov, Mikhail, 60
liberalism, 73, 133; absolutism and,
20, 31–32, 42, 45–46, 67; economic,
79; education and, 49, 50–51
Libya, 109

limited sovereignty doctrine, 118, 121, 122–23
Literaturnaia gazeta, 120, 157, 161, 168, 173
Lithuania, 5, 8, 36, 71, 179
Livonia, 11, 36
Livonian War (1558–1581), 37
London, England, 24
Louis XIV, king of France, 29

Macedonia, 40
Magnitogorsk, U.S.S.R., 145
Malenkov, Georgi, 110, 137
Manchuria, China, 9, 63
Mandelshtam, Nadezhda, cited, 145*n*
"Manifest Destiny" doctrine, 14
Mao Tse-tung, 156
Maoism, 116, 180, 184, 185–86; "Hundred Flowers" revolution, 196
"Marseillaise, La," 61
Marshall Plan (1947), 108, 115
Martov, Julius, 134
Marx, Karl, 58, 89; Trotsky on, 143; on tsarist Russia, 3, 189–90; on the withering of the state, 79, 82, 90, 150
Marxism, 14, 25, 33, 57, 58, 96, 120, 121; determinism of, 32, 131; Lenin's adaptation of, 3, 78–81, 82, 89, 90, 117, 134, 144, 166, 184–85, 189; minority unrest and, 63, 79, 180; proletariat rule in, 73, 79, 80, 131, 138, 149; Stalin's adaptation of, 100, 107, 117, 145; Third World appeal of, 113, 116, 191. *See also* socialism
Mazepa, Ivan, 11
medicine, 173
Mediterranean region, Stalin and, 109
Medvedev, Roy, 151
Medvedev, Zhores A., 151, 167, 173
Mensheviks, 71, 74, 90, 134
Mexico, 5
Michael Romanov, tsar of Russia, 44
middle class, *see* bourgeoisie
Miliukov, Paul, 71; quoted, 20
millenarianism, 34, 57–58, 142–43

mining, 173
minorities, 20–21, 144; cultural development of, 129, 179–80, 181, 193; disenfranchisement, 63, 66–67; favored groups, 15, 122, 178; federalism and, 89; Russian intermarriage with, 11; Russian nationalism and, 60, 61, 62, 100, 105, 106, 107, 119, 121, 166, 177–81; Russian Revolution of 1917 and, 71, 135; self-determination principle and, 84–86, 118, 177, 184, 198
Moghul dynasty, 30
Molotov, Viacheslav, 103–104, 106
monarchy, absolute, *see* tsardom
Mongolia, 9, 85, 116
Mongolian People's Republic, U.S.S.R., 122, 123
Mongols, *see* Tatars
Montesquieu, Charles de Secondat, baron de La Brède et de, 45; quoted, 30
Moors, 10
Moscow, U.S.S.R.: automobile traffic in, 164; capital status of, 5, 6, 24, 74, 120, 178, 181; Dubček in, 132; foreign culture and, 37, 60, 172, 174, 175; Nixon in, 139, 187; Patriarchate of, 6, 24; "Purges" of 1936–1938 in, 101, 128, 140. *See also* Muscovy
Munich Agreement (1938), 102
Muscovy, 5, 50; colonial administrations of, 10–11, 12, 17–18, 20–21; renaming of, 83; Tatar heritage of, 3, 6–8, 18–19; technology and, 9, 37
Muslims, 8, 9, 11, 62, 179

Nadezhdin, Nicholas I., quoted, 13
Napoleonic Wars, 8, 39, 42, 50, 117, 181
Narva, battle of (1700), 38
nationalism, 47, 49, 133, 193; anticapitalism and, 113, 120; empire and, 9–10, 12, 13–17, 21, 29–30, 39, 40, 43, 60, 105, 182; minority group,

nationalism (Cont.)
66–67, 71, 107, 119, 121, 166, 177–81, 184, 193, 194; post-Khrushchev, 117, 120, 179–80; revolutionary, 16, 21, 56, 58, 59–63; ritual and, 159, 160; Stalinist, 100, 101, 104–105, 106, 107, 108, 109, 135, 137, 177–78; universalism *versus*, 79, 82–83, 85, 89–90, 93, 100, 101, 105, 106, 113–14, 121, 150, 151, 178, 182, 184–85, 188–89, 193–98; World War I and, 68
Nazis, *see* fascism
Nazi-Soviet Pact (1939), 102–103, 104, 105
Netherlands, 9, 29. *See also* Belgium; Holland
Nicholas I, tsar of Russia, 22, 60; quoted, 20; accession of, 51; punishments under, 23, 139, 162; Westernization and, 47, 181, 197
Nicholas II, tsar of Russia, 9, 48, 128; abdication of, 20, 68–69, 70, 71; pogroms of, 66; the press and, 64
Nikon, Patriarch, 24
Nixon, Richard M., 139, 187
Nkrumah, Kwame, 113
nobility, *see* aristocracy
nomads, 4, 5, 7, 36, 56. *See also* specific peoples
North America, 4, 5, 9, 10, 14
North Atlantic Treaty Organization (NATO), 186
North Korea, 174
Norway, 175
Novgorod, 5, 10, 17, 19, 161
nuclear technology, 111, 184, 185, 187, 197
Nuclear Test Ban Treaty (1963), 116

October Manifesto (1905), 63, 64
Odoevsky, Vladimir, quoted, 57
oil, 174
Oprichnina, 23
Orwell, George, 90
Orthodox Church, *see* Russian Orthodox Church

Ottoman Empire, 30, 36, 42, 182
Owen, Robert, 58

Pacific Ocean, 7
Pakistan, 120, 184, 186
Pan-Russianism, 12–13, 16, 59; Orthodox Church and, 9, 10, 14, 15
Pan-Slavism, 43, 59, 107
Parthia, 35
Paul I, tsar of Russia, 7, 22, 23, 51
Peaceful Coexistence doctrine, 111, 112, 113, 117, 189; Brezhnev on, 120; China and, 195; *Pravda* on, 119, 147; Suslov on, 188
peasants, 45, 48, 49, 160; communes (*See* communes (peasant)); land ownership and, 27, 33–34, 46, 70; Polish refuge of, 8; revolts, 21, 63, 65, 70, 71–72, 73; settlement by, 7; Soviet collectives, 76, 135; Tatar administration and, 18, 26; as urban proletariat, 52, 116; Zemstvo reforms and, 64. *See also* agriculture
Pentecostal sects, 160
Persia, 7, 8, 9, 15, 30, 40. *See also* Iran
Persian Gulf, 174
Peru, 5
Pestel, Paul, 55
Peter I (the Great), tsar of Russia, 7, 8, 11, 17, 22, 23, 48, 53, 73; industrialization and, 27, 28, 38, 52; merit system of, 25–26, 48, 142; minority revolts and, 21; Muscovy renamed by, 83; parliamentarism and, 44–45; St. Petersburg and, 24; Western technology and, 37–38, 50, 56, 135, 181
Peter II, tsar of Russia, 23
Petrograd, Russia, 69, 74. *See also* Leningrad, U.S.S.R.
Petrograd Soviet of Workers' and Soldiers' Deputies, 72
Philotheus, quoted, 14
Pioneers organization, 130, 179
Plato, 34
plebiscites, 128, 138
Plekhanov, G. V., 93

Pobedonostsev, Constantine, 54
Podgorny, Nikolai, 154
Poland, 9, 12, 36, 59, 176, 178; Baltic blockade, 37; constitutionalism in, 7, 29, 42, 45, 61; independence, 71, 85, 86, 94, 96; Nazi Germany and, 102, 103, 104; partitions of, 8, 42, 46; post-World War II status of, 108, 114–15, 118, 122, 194–95; Russian Duma and, 66; tourist trade of, 175; uprising (1863) in, 11, 48, 61, 62, 196
police, 31, 127; post-Khrushchev, 119, 140, 160, 162, 163, 179, 181, 192; revolutionary, 55, 74, 75, 77, 92, 177, 178; tsarist, 23, 47, 48, 63, 77
Populism, 58, 73, 87, 93; autocracy and, 21, 22, 26
Porkkala, Finland, 110
Portugal, 5, 9, 12
Potemkin, Grigori A., "villages" of, 28, 46
Poznan, Poland, 114
Pravda (newspaper), 13, 64, 123, 146, 172; on dancing, 162; on electoral procedure, 128; on Finlnd, 90; on folk custom, 159, 160–61; on literary criticism, 150; on nationalism, 179, 180, 181; on Peaceful Coexistence, 119, 147
press, the, 131; Bolshevik party and, 83, 92, 116, 177; broadcasting and, 172; on China, 185–86; clandestine, 167; East European, 176; historical themes and, 160–61, 168; post-Khrushchev, 119, 120, 150, 151, 181; revolutionary, 55, 74–75, 93; scientific, 169, 173; Soviet constitution on, 127; tsarist, 23, 46, 49, 51, 64, 65; Ukrainian, 62; U.S.-Soviet détente and, 140, 175; on Vietnam, 147
printing, 4, 23, 37, 38
private enterprise, *see* capitalism
proletariat, 52, 72, 73, 79, 80, 131; factory seizures by, 81; Khrushchev

and, 138; Stalin and, 99. *See also* labor
property rights, 27, 33, 34, 45, 82, 142; in China, 186; revolutionary antimaterialism and, 143, 145. *See also* land
Prussia, 9, 29
Pskov, 10, 17, 19
psychiatric prisons, 127, 139, 151, 173
psychic research, 166
Pugachev, Emelyan, 21
Pushkin, Alexander, 15, 60, 119

Radek, Karl B., 178
Radio Free Europe, 172
Radio Liberty, 172
Radishchev, Alexander, 51
railroads, 29
Rapallo Pact (1922), 96
Rasputin, 64, 81
Razin, Stenka, 21
Red Army, *see* Soviet Union. Army
Red Guards, 72, 73
religion, 31. *See also* Christianity; Muslims; *and see specific sects*
revolutionary sentiment, 34, 47, 142–43; authoritarianism of, 55–56, 58–59, 118; decline of, 144, 147–48, 149–52, 155–61, 166, 191–92; the Duma and, 63, 64; education and, 39, 53, 55; foreign agitation of, 83–84, 94–95, 97, 98, 99, 111, 112, 113–14, 116, 150, 188; Holy Alliance *versus*, 42; moderate *versus* activist, 134; nationalism and, 16, 21, 56, 58, 59–63, 104–105, 109, 188; Nazi, 103
Riazan, 10
Ribbentrop, Joachim von, 103
Riga, Latvia, 162
"Rightist" opinion (Soviet), 75, 133, 139
ritual, 159, 160, 172
Roman Catholicism, 8, 59; Spain and, 10
Roman empire, 7, 15, 17, 30, 141; competition and, 35, 36; industry of, 32, 40

Romanov dynasty, 25, 26, 37, 51, 53; fall of, 21, 69; Zemsky Sobor and, 44

Rousseau, Jean-Jacques, 51

Rumania, 59, 60, 115, 122, 175; China and, 184

Rumanian Communist party, 180

Russia: Muscovite consolidation of, 6–12, 17–18, 19, 50; Soviet Federated Socialist Republic of, 122, 163, 178, 180. *See also* Soviet Union

Russian Academy of Sciences, 38, 129

Russian Army (Soviet), *see* Soviet Union. Army

Russian Army (tsarist), 8, 11, 15, 60, 63; conscription in, 7, 61; discipline of, 22, 70; French influences in, 47, 51; literacy rates in, 65; Tatar troops, 19; Western technology and, 37, 38, 43, 52; in World War I, 68–69, 70

Russian City Councils (dumas), 47, 52

Russian Civil War (1918–1920), 17, 77, 81, 85, 92, 95, 109, 142, 144, 164; Mongolia and, 122; political parties and, 75, 140; Russian Orthodox Church and, 76; Stalin and, 136; "whites" in, 83, 86, 87, 143, 147. *See also* Russian Revolution of 1917

Russian Constituent Assembly, 75

Russian Duma (national), 63–64, 65, 133; dissolution (1917), 70, 134, 177; elections, 88*n;* minority demands and, 66, 67

Russian Legislative Commission (tsarist), 45–46

Russian Navy (tsarist), 38

Russian Orthodox Church, 4–5, 7, 49, 58, 193; absolute monarchy and, 6, 21, 24–25, 33, 43, 47, 93, 125, 133; citizenship laws and, 19, 24–25; Holy Synod of, 24; pan-Russianism and, 9, 10, 14, 15, 16; secularism and, 53, 54; Soviet persecution of,

76, 82, 138, 143, 159; Soviet revival of, 160, 166, 178; Turkish subjects and, 42; the Ukraine and, 8; World War II and, 107

Russian Provisional Government (1917), 70–72

Russian Revolution of 1905, 63–64, 66, 68, 196

Russian Revolution of 1917, 21, 196; Menshevik moderation in, 134; the Orthodox Church and, 25; values of, 92–93, 127, 142–44, 146, 147–48, 151, 152, 155–61, 189, 190, 198; World War I and, 68–69, 74, 75, 94–95, 135, 142

Russian Senate (tsarist), 44–45

Russian Society for the Preservation of Ancient Landmarks, 159–60, 178

Russian Soviet Federated Socialist Republic, U.S.S.R., 163, 180; privileges of, 122, 178

Russian Workers' Social Democratic Party, 63, 82, 99, 134

Russification policy, 11, 67, 179, 181, 193; Poland and, 61, 62; Soviet resumption of, 100, 178

Russo-Japanese War (1904), 9, 12, 39, 48, 63, 198; Stalin on, 107

Russo-Turkish War (1877–1878), 59, 61, 109

Rykov, Aleksei, 75

St. Petersburg, Russia, 24, 38, 59, 64. *See also* Leningrad, U.S.S.R.; Petrograd, Russia

St. Simon, Claude Henri de Rouvroy, comte de, 58

Sakharov, Andrei, 167, 169, 173; quoted, 193, 198

Samizdat, 55, 167

science, *see* technology

Scott, John, 145

Second International, 84

self-determination principle, 84–86, 177, 180–81, 182, 198

Serbia, 68, 197

serfdom, 26, 49, 59, 192; Catherine the Great and, 46, 51; emancipation act, 27, 47, 48, 51; fugitives from, 5, 7

"Sesame Street" (TV program), 194

Shakespeare, William, 119

Shelepin, Alexander, 154

Shevchenko, Taras, 62, 71

Sholokov, Mikhail, 168

Siberia, 7, 10, 13, 69, 121; China and, 116, 184; Lenin in, 77; mining, 173

Sinkiang, China, 116

Slavophilism, 41, 57, 60, 93, 133–34; contemporary, 166, 178; socialism and, 58, 59, 79. *See also* Pan-Slavism

Slovakia, 9

Social Democratic party, 63, 82, 99, 134

socialism, 58, 74, 124, 174, 188; of China, 185; class structure in, 131, 157–59, 161, 166; corruption and, 161–62, 163; interventionism and, 118, 123; Khrushchev and, 113, 116; Lenin and, 78–79, 80–81, 82, 89, 91–92, 93, 94–95, 111, 144; minority nationalism and, 62–63, 71, 118, 121, 180; Orthodoxy and, 9, 59; Soviet achievements in, 190–91, 197; Stalin and, 98–99, 103, 135

Soloviev, Vladimir, 160

Solzhenitsyn, Alexander, cited, 188–89

Sophia Alekseevna, Regent of Russia, 37, 44

South America, 4, 5, 10, 13

Soviet Communist party: censorship and, 168, 169–70; class structure and, 93; electoral procedure and, 87–89, 126–27, 156; foreign party organization and, 84, 86–87, 96, 97, 98, 99, 101, 106, 109, 117, 123, 124, 135, 180, 193; government roles of, 40, 121–22, 124–27, 128–32, 140, 177, 196–97; graft and, 162, 163; language and, 90; membership requirements, 107, 125, 127, 138, 158–59, 178; Party Program (Khrushchev), 15, 127, 150, 153, 156; value conflicts in, 133–40, 166, 193. *See also* Bolsheviks

Soviet Communist party. Central Committee, 75, 121, 126, 127, 128, 132

Soviet Communist party. Politburo, 75, 126, 127, 128, 132, 150, 176; non-Slavs in, 178; succession in, 155

Soviet Communist party. Secretariat, 126, 127, 128, 132, 151, 178; succession in, 154–55

Soviet Scientists' Committee on Human Rights, 169

Soviet Union, 3, 12, 32; Autonomous Republic system of, 9, 121–24, 129, 177, 193, 194; European satellites (*See* Europe, communist regimes in); foreign policy shifts in, 82–87, 94–105, 108–10, 111, 113–14, 116, 123, 124–25, 130, 171–76, 181–89, 197–98; German invasion (1941) of, 104, 105–107, 140, 145, 147

Soviet Union. Army, 81, 92, 95, 148; in Georgia, 85; German invasion and, 106, 107, 145; ideology and, 193; Mongolian troops, 122; in Poland, 86, 104, 114; Red Guards and, 72, 73; satellite control and, 108, 109, 117–18, 138, 191, 194, 196; Stalin and, 100, 104

Soviet Union. Central Statistical Bureau, 164

Soviet Union. Commissariat of Foreign Affairs, 96–97

Soviet Union. Constitution, 83, 121, 124, 127–28; on civil liberties, 127, 129, 166

Soviet Union. Council of Ministers, 126

Soviet Union. Navy, 103, 117, 118

Soviet Union. Procuracy, 157

Soviet Union. Supreme Soviet, 44, 128

Soviet Writers' Union, 129, 158, 168
space science, 112
Spain, 5, 6, 9, 10, 12, 42; Popular
    Front in, 101–102; stability of, 165,
    177
Spanish Civil War, 101, 102
Stalin, Josef, 88, 90, 126, 146, 165, 173,
    175, 192; quoted, 15, 84, 107, 132;
    cult of, 75, 108, 109, 114, 154, 166;
    death of, 110; foreign policy and,
    96, 97–105, 106, 108–10, 112, 117,
    178, 182, 194, 196; industrialization
    and, 76, 91, 98–99, 110, 135, 140,
    145, 149, 164; Soviet constitution
    and, 128; terrorism of, 23, 101, 128,
    136–37, 138, 145, 152, 155, 156, 167;
    works of, 153
Stalingrad, U.S.S.R., 75
Stalin-Hitler Pact (1939), 102–103,
    104, 105
steel, 3
Stolypin, Peter, 67; quoted, 65
Straits, The (Bosphorus), 8, 9, 68,
    104, 109
Stuart dynasty, 29
Sudan, The, 184
Sudetenland, 102
Sukhomlinov, Vladimir Aleksandro-
    vich, 143
Suslov, Mikhail, quoted, 188
Suzdal, 19
Sweden, 7, 8, 11, 36, 42; Peter the
    Great and, 38, 45

Taiwan, 116
tariffs, 65
Tatars, 10, 36, 59, 85; Crimean groups,
    166, 179; imperialism of, 3, 4, 5, 12,
    18–19, 24, 27, 35, 40, 141, 198; Ivan
    IV and, 7; Russian aristocracy and,
    6, 17, 18, 19, 26, 50
taxation, 32, 33; Soviet, 76, 135, 157;
    Tatar, 5, 6, 18, 26, 59; tsarist, 28, 48,
    65
technology, 4, 5, 9–10, 11, 57, 65, 114;
    computers, 91, 165; Japan and, 186;

Nazi Germany and, 103; nuclear,
    111, 116, 184, 185, 187, 197; Russian
    importation of, 36–37, 38, 39–40,
    41, 43, 50, 52, 56, 79, 87, 91, 98, 125,
    135, 173, 182, 183, 188, 190, 192;
    Russian inventions, 32, 108–109;
    scientific freedom and, 129, 168–70,
    172–73; space studies, 112
television, 172, 176, 194
Teutonic Knights, 38
Third International, 83, 84
Third Rome concept, 14, 17, 30, 84
Third World, 113–14, 118, 176, 183–
    84, 191. *See also* Africa; Asia;
    South America
Tibet, 9
Time of Troubles (1605–1613), 17,
    20–21, 24, 50
Tito, Marshal (Josip Broz), 110, 130
Tiutchev, Fedor, quoted, 12, 14
Tkachev, Peter, quoted, 56
Togliatti, Palmiro, 138
Tolstoy, Count Leo, 60
tourism, 175, 194
trade, 10, 27, 41, 62, 65; autocracy
    and, 31, 32, 39, 45, 66; of Comecon
    countries, 115; consumer demand
    and, 163–64, 173–74, 192; illegal
    practices of, 161, 162, 163, 192;
    Japan and, 186; Marxist view of,
    57, 191; routes of, 4, 6, 7, 29, 37, 69,
    95; Soviet volume of, 52, 74, 77, 82,
    95, 96, 97, 98, 99, 103, 108, 110, 119,
    124–25, 137, 173–75, 187, 188; West
    European bloc, 187
trade unions, 63, 64, 159; functions
    of, 75, 77, 89, 129
Trajan, emperor of Rome, 32
Transcaucasia, 85
travel rights, 23–24, 52, 66, 90, 92,
    163, 180, 193; constitutional guar-
    antees of, 127–28; internal, 159, 162;
    Khrushchev and, 137, 139, 172–73;
    post-World War II restriction of,
    108; tourism and, 175–76, 194

Trotsky, Leon, 58, 75, 96, 153, 178; quoted, 143; labor and, 136; Spain and, 102

tsardom, 18–34, 93, 125, 152; class structure and, 25–27, 30, 31–32, 45, 51, 126, 142, 158; expansionist necessity in, 19–20, 22, 29–30, 35, 39, 67, 189, 197–98; overthrow of, 16, 21, 42, 68–69, 70, 71, 73, 78, 81, 160, 196; reform movements and, 44–48, 51, 54, 55, 63–64, 66, 67, 92, 154, 155, 192

Tsarytsin, Russia, 75

Turgenev, Alexander I., 56n

Turgenev, Ivan S., 60; quoted, 49

Turkestan, 12

Turkey, 8, 38, 39, 42, 110, 118; Catherine the Great and, 46; imperial decline of, 182; revolution of 1920 in, 96, 109. *See also* Ottoman Empire

Turkic peoples, 10, 15, 36, 105, 122

Tver, 6

Ukraine, 59, 104, 121; German occupation of, 107; nationalism in, 60, 62, 66, 68, 71, 85, 86–87, 166, 179, 184, 195; privileges of, 122, 178; Russian annexation of, 8, 10–11, 83

Union of Soviet Socialist Republics, *see* Soviet Union

United Nations, 109, 111, 188; China in, 184, 186; Soviet Autonomous Republics in, 121, 122, 123

United States of America, 3, 14, 41, 83, 117, 190; Chicherin and, 97; China and, 116, 186, 187; Cold War and, 109; Khrushchev and, 111–12, 175; Korea and, 110; Soviet détente, 139–40, 175, 187, 198; Soviet trade, 173–74, 175; technology and, 91, 119–20, 165, 169, 173; Vietnam withdrawal of, 140, 146–47, 187, 189; World War II and, 106, 107, 108, 186

universalism, 41, 79, 82–87, 90, 93, 94, 134, 151; as a multinational political structure, 121, 129–30, 177–81, 182, 184–85, 188, 189, 191, 193–98; peaceful means and, 111, 113–14, 117, 120, 188; Stalin and, 98–99, 100, 101, 103, 105, 109, 135, 178; World War II and, 106, 150, 189

Ural Mountains, 5, 7

Uvarov, Count Sergei, 47

Varga, E., 107

Versailles Treaty, 96, 100

Vietnam, 36, 92

Vietnam War, 117, 138, 140, 146–47, 187, 189

Vladimir, 6

Vladimir-Suzdal Principality, 19

Volga River region, 5, 41; German inhabitants of, 106, 179; Tatar khanates of, 7, 19

Voltaire, 51

Warsaw, Poland, 86

Warsaw Treaty Organization (WTO), 115, 117, 123, 124

West, The, 8, 9, 21, 48–49, 50, 51; Bolsheviks and, 73, 74, 87–93; collective security policy and, 100–101, 102; disarmament issue and, 97; nationalism in, 60, 87, 113, 182; Peaceful Coexistence doctrine and, 111, 112, 113, 117, 119, 120; post-World War II Soviet rupture with, 109–10; Russian mission in, 15, 16, 43, 57, 93, 113; secularism and, 54; socialism and, 58, 79, 83–84, 87, 89, 113, 190, 191; Soviet continuing Westernization, 132, 133–40, 151, 171–76, 177, 181, 182, 192, 194, 198; Soviet defense and, 105–107; technological advantage in, 3–5, 7, 27, 28, 36–37, 41, 56, 57, 65, 79, 87, 91, 98, 120, 165, 181, 182, 186, 190, 192, 197; World War I Russian rupture

West, The (Cont.)
  with, 69–70, 72, 74, 77. *See also specific countries*
Westernization policies, *see* industrialization; West, The
West Germany, 119, 174, 187
West Indies, 11
"Whites" (anti-Communists), 83, 86, 87, 143, 147
White Russia, *see* Belorussia
White Sea, 37, 41
Winter Palace, The, 72
wiretapping, 168
Witte, Count Sergei, 52, 63; quoted, 20
women, 44, 128, 144
World War I, 9, 30, 64, 72, 74, 77, 81, 108, 142; colonial empires and, 182; Russian separate peace in, 75, 82, 83, 94–95, 135; tsardom overthrow in, 68–69, 70

World War II, 76, 114, 158, 178; alliances preceding, 99–102; German invasion of Russia in, 104, 105–106, 140, 145–46, 147; industrialization levels in, 164; territorial settlements after, 108, 109–10, 137, 149–50, 182, 186, 190, 194

Yakut peoples, 66
Yevtushenko, Evgeni, 158; quoted, 150
Yezhov, N. I., 136
Yugoslavia, 108, 110, 111
Yugoslavian Communist party, 180

Zemsky Sobor, 44
zemstvos, 47, 48, 52, 54, 62, 64
Zhiguli automobiles, 164
Zhivkov, Todor, 130
Zinoviev, Gregori, 75, 178; quoted, 83